A BRIEF GUIDE TO WRITING FROM READINGS

Third Edition

A BRIEF GUIDE TO WRITING FROM READINGS

Stephen W. Wilhoit
The University of Dayton

PEARSON
Longman

New York San Francisco Boston
London Toronto Sydney Tokyo Singapore Madrid
Mexico City Munich Paris Cape Town Hong Kong Montreal

Vice President/Publisher: Eben W. Ludlow
Executive Marketing Manager: Ann Stypuloski
Production Manager: Eric Jorgensen
Project Coordination, Text Design, and Electronic Page Makeup: Electronic Publishing
Services Inc., NYC
Cover Design Manager: Nancy Danahy
Cover Designer: Keithley & Associates, Inc.
Cover Image: © Getty Images, Inc./PhotoDisc
Manufacturing Buyer: Roy Pickering
Printer and Binder: RR Donnelley & Sons Company
Cover Printer: Coral Graphic Services, Inc.

For permission to use copyrighted material, grateful acknowledgment is made to the copyright
holders on pp. 287–288, which are hereby made part of this copyright page.

Library of Congress Cataloging-in-Publication Data
Wilhoit, Stephen.
    A brief guide to writing from readings / Stephen W. Wilhoit.—3rd ed.
    p.   cm.
    Includes index.
    ISBN 0-321-19461-6 (pbk.)
    1. English language—Rhetoric—Handbooks, manuals, etc. 2. Academic
writing—Handbooks, manuals, etc. 3. Interdisciplinary approach in education. 4. College
readers. I. Title.
PE1408.W586 2003
808`.0427—dc21

                                                                    2003043393

Please visit our Web site at **http://www.ablongman.com**

ISBN 0-321-19461-6

1 2 3 4 5 6 7 8 9 10—DOH—06 05 04 03

CONTENTS

Chapter 3 QUOTATION *39*

Chapter 4 PARAPHRASE *57*

Chapter 5   SUMMARY *69*

Chapter 6   RESPONSE ESSAYS.. *83*

Chapter 7 CRITIQUE.. 95

Chapter 8 SYNTHESIS.. 127

Chapter 9 PLAGIARISM 191

PREFACE

From the first edition to the third, the goal of *A Brief Guide to Writing from Readings* has remained unchanged: to help students master one of the most common academic genres—writing from readings. Numerous studies—and my own experience as a teacher—confirm that, no matter what their major, students will be asked to write source-based papers throughout their academic careers. In classes across the curriculum, college students are repeatedly required to summarize, analyze, evaluate, and synthesize readings, especially during their first two years of course work. I still believe that helping students master these skills should be a primary goal of any introductory composition course.

Based on responses from students using this book and on suggestions from faculty reviewers, *A Brief Guide to Writing from Readings* has gone through some changes over the years. For example, the second edition included a chapter on timed writing assignments, which many students and instructors have found helpful, updated instruction on MLA documentation practices, and several new readings.

The third edition offers a few more changes. First, I have expanded the instruction on argumentation found in Chapter 8, Synthesis. Because several reviewers wanted more information on the elements of argument and persuasion, I now include material on Toulmin argumentation (claims, grounds, and warrants) and the classical appeals (logos, pathos, and ethos). While I hoped to keep this section of the text *brief,* I also wanted to point out to students how writers typically employ material from readings to bolster their arguments and make their work more persuasive.

The third edition of the textbook also includes six new readings: three on the issue of race-based admission policies and three on the issue of teenage suicide. Race-based admission policies are back in active public debate because of upcoming Supreme Court decisions on the matter. In my experience, this is a topic students find interesting and one that stirs classroom debate. Likewise, students seem interested in the topic of teenage suicide—its causes, its cure, and its effect on others. I have attempted to assemble readings from credible academic sources that represent a range of views on each subject, readings that vary not only in perspective but also in length and level of formality. These readings offer students additional opportunities to hone their skills at summary, analysis, critique, and synthesis.

Chapter 10, which covers documentation practices and conventions, reflects the most recent guidelines published by the American Psychological Association (5th ed., 2001), the Council of Biology Editors (recently renamed the Council of Science Editors) (6th ed., 1994), and the Modern Language

Association (6th ed., 2003). For each style, the text includes sample citations from a variety of sources as well as sample works cited lists or bibliographies.

Despite these changes, the third edition retains many of the readings and features that students and teachers have found helpful. Each chapter still ends with summary charts that students can consult to review the material, and most chapters contain checklists that students can use to revise their work. The book can still function as a primary course text or as a supplemental text that students can consult on their own as needed. In addition, an Instructor's Manual is available for teachers who would like even more suggestions on assignments and class activities.

As I stated in the preface to the first edition, I hope students find *A Brief Guide to Writing from Readings* helpful and accessible. Many students and instructors have commented that they find its step-by-step instructions clear and its tone collegial and inviting. My goal, as always, is to offer a textbook that helps students develop the skills they need to complete source-based college writing assignments successfully, to read texts honestly and critically, and to explore connections they find between the material they read and their own knowledge, experience, and beliefs.

ACKNOWLEDGMENTS

I would like to thank the following reviewers for their helpful suggestions: Jane Creighton, University of Houston–Downtown and Anne Pici, University of Dayton.

Stephen W. Wilhoit

Chapter 1

CRITICAL READING

DEFINITION AND PURPOSE

Most successful college writers are also sophisticated, critical readers. They assume a skeptical attitude toward texts: instead of believing whatever they read, they critically examine the author's ideas and their own responses to the reading. They are active, reflective readers who ask questions about the words on the page, mark passages, take notes, and draw connections between the author's ideas and their own experiences and knowledge. They are open to new ideas, but do not accept them without serious, reflective consideration. Unreflective readers, however, tend to accept unquestioningly what they see in print. In their view, if something has been published, it must be accurate. Instead of asking questions about what they read, they tend to accept the author's words at face value.

A major difference, then, between reflective and unreflective readers is the way they try to learn from what they read. Unreflective readers usually believe that the meaning of a text can be found in the words on the page: to understand a text, all a reader has to do is understand the meaning of the author's words. For them, reading is a rather simple, straightforward process: they read through a text, look up any words they do not know, isolate the author's main ideas, perhaps take some notes, then move on to the next reading. They also tend to believe that because the meaning of a text resides in the author's words, students reading the same material ought to come away with the same information; the text should mean roughly the same thing to any competent reader who studies it.

Reflective, critical readers, however, tend to adopt a different view of reading. They believe that the meaning of a text resides in the *interaction* between the reader and the words on the page: to understand a text, readers must be aware of how their own knowledge, feelings, and experience influence their *interpretation* of the words on the page. For them, reading is a rather dynamic, fluid process: they read through a text skeptically, assess the author's words and ideas in light of their own knowledge and experience, jot down some notes that capture their questions and responses, reread the text after they have had some time to consider what the author had to say, then move on.

Viewing reading as an interactive process can help you better understand the complex nature of writing from sources and the need to be an active, critical reader. For example, it helps you understand why a story you read your first year in high school means something different to you when you read it again your first year in college. The words on the page have not changed, you have, and because you have changed, the "meaning" of the story has changed for you as well. This interactive view of reading also helps explain how twenty students in an introductory philosophy class can read the same meditation by Descartes and come away with twenty slightly different interpretations of the piece. Active, critical readers understand that for any given person the meaning of a text results from the interaction between the words on the page and that reader's knowledge, feelings, and expertise; reading involves more than a simple transfer of information from the words on the page to the mind of the reader.

Does this mean that all interpretations of a reading are equally valid? No. While every person forms his or her own understanding of a reading, people can and often do misread texts: they may not read carefully, they may not understand certain terms or ideas, or they may lack the knowledge and experience they need to form an adequate interpretation of the text. As a safeguard against misinterpretation, critical readers discuss the material with others who have read it. Comparing their own reading of a text with a teacher's or a peer's reading can help clarify the material and prevent misunderstanding.

In addition, the author of the piece plays an important role in reading. Good writers try to influence their readers' understanding of and response to a text. When writing, authors manipulate the language, structure, and content of their prose to achieve a certain effect on their audience. Success is never guaranteed, but good writers know that they can at least influence how readers might respond to their work through the choices they make while composing. Critical readers take this into account when approaching a text—they try to be aware not only of what they bring to the reading, but also of the choices the writer has made to achieve a certain goal.

Learning to read material actively and critically can be difficult. However, critical readers tend to understand course material more fully, prepare for class more efficiently, and write from readings more effectively. Below you will find a number of suggestions aimed at helping you become a more active, critical reader. Central to this process is the ability and willingness to ask good questions about your reading of a text and to keep a written record of your responses. Critical readers refuse to sit back passively while they read; they actively question and respond to texts in light of their own knowledge, feelings, and experience.

ASKING QUESTIONS ABOUT WHAT YOU READ

Instead of passively accepting the ideas an author presents, a critical reader attempts to engage in a dialogue with the text, posing and working out answers to tough questions concerning the material's purpose, audience, language, and content.

The most productive critical questions center on the connections that exist between a text's author and his or her audience, subject, and language. Everything you read has been written by someone for someone about something using certain words on a page. Learning how to identify and question the relationship between these various aspects of a reading can help you understand the material more fully and determine its meaning and importance.

Typical questions you should ask of a reading include:

- Who is the author of the piece?
- What is her stand on the issue she's addressing?
- What are her interests, qualifications, or possible biases?
- What was her intent when writing this piece?
- Who is the intended audience?
- How does the author support her contentions?
- What language has she used to convey her ideas on this topic to this audience for this purpose?
- Based on my own knowledge and experience, what do I think about her ideas, intent, language, and support?
- How well does the author achieve her goal?

When you are confronted with conflicting sources of information on a topic (as is frequently the case in college), asking questions such as these is a particularly important way to sort out the authors' different positions, evaluate the worth of each source, and decide who presents the clearer, more convincing case.

Forming a full, critical understanding of a reading requires asking the right kinds of questions about the author, subject, audience, and language of the piece. Below you will find a series of questions to ask before, during, and after your reading. However, these questions are merely suggestive, not exhaustive; they indicate only starting points for your critical assessment of a text.

Your teacher and peers may suggest other questions to ask as well. Finally, it is a good idea to write out your answers to these questions. Do not rely on your memory alone to keep track of your responses.

QUESTIONS TO ASK BEFORE YOU BEGIN A CLOSE READING OF A TEXT

Whether you are assigned to read material in history or art, biology or sociology, before you begin you need to ask yourself a series of questions concerning the author and publication in which the piece appeared as well as your own knowledge of and attitude toward the topic. Answering these questions may help you determine any biases present in the reading and help ensure that you remain open to any new perspectives or information the author has to offer.

Questions Concerning the Author

- Who is the author?
- What are her credentials?
- What else has she written on the topic?
- What possible biases might have influenced her work?

Before you begin to read a text, try to assess the credibility and expertise of the person who wrote the piece. Who is the author, and what are his or her qualifications for writing on this topic? If, for instance, you are writing a paper about global warming for your English class and find an article you want to use in your essay, note whether you are reading a research report produced by a scientist who conducted her own studies on the topic, an informative article composed by a reporter who interviewed that scientist, or an opinion piece written by a television star who has no particular expertise in climatology. The first author is probably well qualified to offer expert opinion; the second author, while less qualified than the first, may still be a legitimate source of information. However, approach the third author skeptically: good actors are rarely good scientists. If you plan to use any of these readings to support a position of your own in an essay, understand that academic readers will tend to believe authors with solid, professional credentials and demonstrated expertise in the topic.

Also determine, as best you can, any biases operating in the authors' work. Note who the writers work for, who supported their research, who publishes their results. No writers are completely objective; all writers bring to their work certain biases or preferences—political, religious, methodological. These biases may influence the type of study authors conduct, the type of evidence they use to support their contentions, the language they employ, the conclusions they draw. When researching a paper on abortion, for instance, it would be important to note whether the author of a piece is a member of the National Abortion Rights Action League or Operation Life, even if the writer claims to be presenting the results of an objective study. In college you will often read expert testimony that presents conflicting views and interpretations of the same topic, data, or event. Often your job as a *writer* is to examine these different perspectives, compare their quality or worth, and use them to form and defend a position of your own. However, recognizing potential authorial bias in a reading does not disqualify it as a legitimate source of information: it simply puts you in a better position to read the work skeptically and to ask better, more critical questions.

Most academic journals include brief biographical entries on the authors at the beginning or end of each article or in a separate section of the journal typically labeled "Contributor Notes" or "Contributors." Many popular magazines also include some information on the author of each article they publish. (If you cannot find this information, see a reference librarian for help locating biographical dictionaries. Later, including in your essay the credentials of the authors whose work you are quoting or paraphrasing can help increase the credibility of your assertions.)

Questions about the Publication

- In what regard is the publication held by professionals in the field?
- Toward what type of readership is the publication aimed?
- How long ago was the piece published?
- What, generally, is the editorial stance of the publication?

When assessing the quality of a publication, your first questions ought to address its credibility and audience. Do members of the profession or the academy consider this a reputable journal? Does it publish scholarly work or general interest features? What type of reader is this publication trying to reach: scholars or the general public? Answering these questions can help you determine whether work published in this journal or magazine is appropriate for inclusion in an essay of your own.

To answer these questions about the publication, first consult your teacher. He or she can probably tell you in what regard a particular journal is held by professionals in the field. Also, if you want to consult only scholarly sources of information, you may want to limit your research to scholarly indexes and databases—drawing information from *The Applied Science and Technology Index* or ABI/Inform rather than from *The Readers' Guide to Periodical Literature* and InfoTrac. Again, your teacher or a reference librarian can help you identify scholarly reference works.

Just as individual authors have certain biases or preferences that may influence their writing, publications have certain editorial slants that may influence what they print. Some publications will have definite political or ideological agendas. For example, *The New Republic* and *The National Review* are not likely to publish the same article on gun control. Other publications may exhibit certain methodological biases: they prefer to publish only historical studies or empirical studies or marxist studies of a topic. Determining the editorial or methodological slant of a publication can be difficult: if you have not read widely in a field, you may not know a great deal about its principal publications. Often, your best recourse in gathering this type of information is to scan the titles and abstracts of other articles in the journal to determine its political or methodological preferences or, if you are reading newspaper or magazine articles, to read the editorials.

However, a particular periodical's political or methodological slant does not necessarily make it any more or less valid a source of information. Recognizing these preferences, though, should help you read material more skeptically. A publication's biases may affect the content of the articles it publishes, its authors' interpretations of statistics, even the nature of the graphics and illustrations accompanying the text. When you are thoroughly researching a topic, gathering information from several different sources is one way to guard against one-sided, unbalanced treatments of a topic.

Questions Concerning Your Own Views of the Topic

- What are my beliefs about the issue addressed in the reading?
- How open am I to new ideas on this topic?

Just as every author and publication presents material from a particular perspective, readers, too, bring their own prejudices and preferences to a text. Though absolute objectivity may be impossible for readers and writers to attain, knowing your own predispositions toward the topic an author addresses can help you guard against unfairly judging someone else's arguments or shutting yourself off from potentially helpful ideas.

Author Peter Elbow suggests two frames of mind students ought to assume when reading material. First, he advises students to play the "believing game"—that is, to assume that what the writer has to say is correct. If the author of the piece is right in what he says, how do his ideas influence your current views on the topic? What are the implications of the author's ideas? Can you draw any connections between what the author has to say and what you already know? Next, Elbow suggests that students play the "doubting game"—that is, assume a more critical stance toward the author's ideas. What are the weaknesses in the writer's arguments? What are the limitations of his ideas? In what ways are the author's ideas incompatible with what you already know about the topic?

Being aware of your own stance on an issue *before* you begin to read something for the first time can help you play the believing and doubting games more effectively. First, reading with your own beliefs firmly in mind can help you recognize which ideas are hard for you to accept or even to consider fairly. We all resist ideas that run counter to our beliefs: giving them legitimacy forces us to question our own positions. However, being a critical reader means you are willing to do just that, to consider ideas that you might otherwise ignore or reject. When you dismiss an idea in a source text, consider why: if it is only because that idea runs counter to your views, try playing the believing game before moving on.

Second, reading with your beliefs firmly in mind can help you recognize which ideas are hard for you to question and criticize. We all like to read material that confirms our present positions, because such reinforcement is comforting and reassuring. However, as a critical reader you must be willing to question authors who voice opinions you endorse, to criticize fairly and thoroughly ideas you are predisposed to accept unquestioningly. If you accept information without question, consider why: if it is only because you agree with the author, try playing the doubting game before moving on.

QUESTIONS TO ASK WHILE YOU READ AND REREAD MATERIAL

After you have read material with these questions in mind, reread it. If necessary, read it a third or fourth time—very few of us truly understand a text the first time we read it. When rereading material, though, you should consider another set of questions that focus your attention on the audience, purpose, content, and organization of the piece, along with your response to the author's ideas.

Questions Concerning the Audience of the Piece

- What audience does the author seem to be trying to reach?
- What type of reader would be attracted to the author's writing, and what type would be alienated by it?
- How does your sense of the text's audience influence your reading of the piece?

Audience is one of the most important concepts in writing: an author's sense of audience will greatly affect, among other things, the language she uses, the material she includes, and the organizational strategy she employs. However, *audience* can be a difficult term to define. In one sense, it refers to actual people a writer may know. When composing a letter to a friend, for instance, a writer can make fairly accurate predictions about the way her reader will react to what she says or the language she uses.

In another sense, though, *audience* can have very little to do with specific people the author has in mind as he writes a text. Much of what you read in college, for example, was written by people who possessed a much more nebulous sense of audience as they wrote. They knew the *type* of reader they were trying to address (for example, a first-year student taking an introductory geology course) or perhaps the *type* of reader they wanted to interest (for example, people curious about feminist interpretations of literature). When writing, they did not have in mind as their audience a specific, individual reader. Instead, they were trying to produce prose that would attract or interest a particular type of reader.

Therefore, as you read and reread material, try to determine the audience the author is trying to address: how is she attempting to interest or appeal to that type of reader? How successful is she in achieving that goal? Pay attention to the language, content, and organization of the piece, as you try to answer questions such as these:

- Was the author trying to reach a general reader, an educated reader, or a specialist?
- What language does the author use to try to reach this audience? What examples? What graphics?
- What type of reader would actually find the work helpful, informative, valuable, or difficult?
- Would any readers be alienated by the material in the piece? Why?

Answering these questions will help you better understand how the text you are reading came to assume its present form. When writing, authors choose language, examples, and a structure they believe will help them achieve their desired effect on an audience. Part of reading a text critically is determining in your mind how successful each writer has been in making these choices.

Realize, too, that when you read something, you become a member of that writer's audience. *Your* response to what you read is extremely important to note as you try to understand what the author has to say. Is the writer communicating his ideas effectively to you? Do you find the material in the piece interesting or boring, helpful or irrelevant, engaging or alienating? What choices has the writer made that led to these responses? What knowledge or experience do you bring to the text that contributes to your reaction? Understanding the complex relationship between the audience and the writer of a piece can help you become a more sensitive, critical reader.

Questions about Purpose

- What was the author's purpose in writing the piece?
- What is the author's thesis?
- Does the author successfully achieve his or her goals?

 Generally, when writing a text, an author will have one of three aims: to entertain, to inform, or to persuade his readers. Many times a work will serve multiple purposes—it will both entertain and inform, inform and persuade. However, as a critical reader, you ought to identify the primary purpose of the piece you are reading. To criticize an article for failing to present an effective argument on a topic would be unproductive and unfair if all the author intended was to write an informative essay.

However, determining an author's purpose or goal can be difficult. In social science and natural science journals, look for the author's stated purpose in his abstract or thesis ("The purpose of this article is…" and "The authors

seek to prove that…"). The conventions of most humanities journals, however, require authors to be less straightforward or declaratory in stating their
purpose, but again thesis statements and abstracts are good places to start your
search. Even if the author states his or her goal somewhere in the paper or
abstract, be wary. When you finish rereading the piece, ask yourself, "Given
the content, language, and structure of this piece, what do *I* believe to be the
writer's primary goal or purpose?"

Questions about Content

- What are the author's major assertions or findings?
- How does the author support these assertions or findings?

When examining the content of any reading, try first to locate the author's
thesis and paraphrase it. A thesis statement will be either stated or implied. If
it is stated, you will be able to point to a sentence or two in the reading that
serves as the thesis. If it is implied, a general idea or argument unites and
guides the writing, but the author never explicitly puts it into words. When
you paraphrase this general idea or argument, you have identified the thesis. In
either case, as a first step in analyzing a reading's content, restate the author's
thesis in your own words to form a clear idea of what the author is trying to
accomplish in the piece.

Next, note how the author supports her thesis—identify her primary
ideas, arguments, or findings and the evidence, reasons, or examples she offers
to support them. As you reread the piece, ask yourself what empirical, philosophical, theoretical, or other type of evidence or reasoning the author has
provided to support her thesis and achieve her goal.

Finally, be sure to examine what you already know about the topic—what
you have learned in the past, what you are learning now by reading *this* piece.
Has the author left out any important information or arguments; has she
neglected certain interpretations of evidence others have offered? If so, why
do you think that is? How can the reading's content be explained by its author,
audience, or purpose?

Questions about Organization

- How is the material organized?
- What headings and subheadings does the author provide?
- What does the organization of the essay tell you about the author's view
  of the material?
- What gets stressed as a result of the organization?

As a writer composes his piece, he has to make a series of decisions about organization: he needs to determine the order in which he will present his findings,
ideas, or arguments. Good writers organize their material purposefully—to
make their article clear, to make their book more persuasive, to make their

findings more accessible. Through the order in which they present their material and through their use of paragraph breaks, headings, and subheadings, they try to help the reader understand or accept their views.

As you read a source text, think critically about its organization. First, form at least a rough idea of how the writer has organized his ideas. What are the major sections of the text? In what order are the ideas, arguments, or findings presented? You might want to produce a scratch outline or list that captures the reading's organization. Also, use the headings and subheadings the author provides to get a better understanding of how he views his material and how he sets priorities among his findings. For example, what ideas, arguments, or findings get emphasized through the author's selection of headings? How do the headings and subheadings guide you through the piece? Are there any instances in which you think a heading or subheading is misleading or poorly stated? Why?

Questions about the Author's Sources

- How does the author use other people's ideas or findings?
- How credible are the sources the author uses to support his ideas or findings?

As you analyze the content of a reading, examine the sources the author relied on when writing. What is documented? Flip back to the works cited list or bibliography at the end of the piece. Where does the author's information come from? Is the paper based on library research, primary research, interviews? If much of the text's material comes from previously published work, how credible are the sources the author used to support her claims? For example, is the author relying on scholarly sources of information? Is there any apparent bias in the author's use of source material: is most of his material taken from journals that share similar editorial stances, or has the writer tried to draw information from sources representing a variety of political, theoretical, or methodological perspectives? Answering questions such as these can help you determine the credibility and utility of the author's ideas, arguments, or findings.

Questions about Graphics

- How clear are the charts, graphs, tables, or illustrations the author provides?
- How well does the author explain the graphics?
- How well do the graphics support or explain what the author has to say?

Graphics include charts, tables, graphs, drawings, and pictures. While authors may add graphics to entertain readers, most include them to support arguments, summarize findings, or illustrate ideas. As you read a text, try to determine how the author is using graphics in her work and how clear, helpful, or informative you find them.

Questions about Your Reactions and Responses

- How do I feel about the topic, issues, or findings addressed in the reading?
- What is convincing? What is unclear?
- What ideas in the piece contradict my understanding of the topic?
- What ideas in the piece are new to me—which ones do I accept and which ones do I reject?

People's beliefs and knowledge influence how they read material—what they take note of, what they understand the author to be saying, what they remember after they read the piece. Understanding your response to the material you read can help you become a more critical reader and a more effective writer in several ways. First, honestly assessing your response can help you be balanced and fair. As a skeptical reader you need to be both critical of ideas you at first enthusiastically support and open to ideas you at first strongly reject.

Second, examining your response to what you read can help you decide on and develop effective paper topics—your responses may help you identify an interest or question you can later pursue more thoroughly in an essay. Especially consider what you learn from a reading: what information is new? How do the author's ideas or findings confirm or contradict what you have come to think? Examining your answers to questions such as these can result in some interesting essays.

MARKING TEXTS

Look at the books of active, critical readers and you will see pages filled with underlined passages, marginal comments, questions, and reactions. Because they have recognized the close link between reading and writing, they rarely read without a pencil in hand. They underline the reading's thesis statement and any important passages they find. As they question the material they are reading, they annotate the text and write down the answers to the questions they ask so that when they return to the material later they can recall the author's purpose and findings, remember how they responded to the author's ideas, and locate the information they want to use in their papers.

The two most common ways of marking texts are highlighting and annotating. Highlighting typically involves underlining, circling, bracketing, or color coding passages, while annotating involves writing comments or questions in the margin or at the end of the text.

HIGHLIGHTING TEXTS

Highlighting involves underlining, color coding, or in some other way marking important passages in a reading. Most students tend to highlight too little or too much. Some never make a mark in their books. Perhaps in high school they were trained not to mark up readings, or maybe they are concerned about the resale value of their books. For some reason, these students rarely, if ever, highlight material they read. Other students highlight too many passages in a reading—practically every sentence is underlined, almost every paragraph is shaded yellow or pink. You have to be selective in what you highlight: you mark up a reading in order to understand it more clearly and to identify important passages you may return to later when you write your paper.

In order to highlight a reading effectively, you need to develop your own marking system, a kind of code that helps you locate certain types of information in a text. Good writers usually develop unique ways of highlighting readings: they underline certain kinds of passages, place brackets around certain types of information, circle other parts of the text. Later, when they return to the reading to write their paper, they can easily find the information they need. Below are some suggestions about what to mark in a text:

1. Mark an author's thesis, primary assertions, and supporting evidence.
2. Mark the names of authors, dates of studies, locations of research projects, and other important facts mentioned in the reading.
3. Mark key passages you might want to reread, quote, or paraphrase later as you write your paper.
4. Mark words or terms you do not know so you can look up their definitions.

Establish your own way of highlighting a text: circle authors' names; bracket dates; use a yellow highlighting pen to mark any passages you may want to quote, blue ink to indicate questionable statements, whatever. Once you establish your own highlighting system, writing from readings will become much easier for you.

ANNOTATING TEXTS

While you are highlighting a reading, you should also annotate it—that is, *write out* your responses, questions, observations, or conclusions. Generally, there are two types of annotations you will use—marginal and end comments. Marginal annotations are notes that you make to yourself in the top, bottom, or side margins of the page; end annotations are notes that you make at the end of the text.

Marginal Annotations

Marginal annotations are typically short and in many cases may make sense only to the person who wrote them. Generally, they can be divided into content notes, organization notes, connection notes, questions, and responses.

Content notes typically identify the meaning or purpose of the marked passage. For example, after bracketing an author's first argument—that eliminating a particular government program may have negative consequences on the poor, for instance—you may write in the margin, "Argument 1—consequences for poor." When you review a reading to find material you want to use in your paper, content notes help you easily locate what you need, which is particularly important if you are completing a research project involving multiple readings.

Organization notes identify the major sections of a source text. After underlining an article's thesis, you may write _thesis_ in the margin in order to find it more easily later, then bracket the first few paragraphs and write _introduction_ in the margin. You might draw a line down the margin beside the next few paragraphs and write _first argument_ in the margin, then highlight the next section and write _refutation of first argument_. Organization notes help you understand how the author has structured the piece and may help you locate particular sections of the text you would like to review.

Connection notes identify the links you see between an author's ideas and those offered by other writers or between ideas an author develops in different sections of a reading: "this idea echoes Weber's argument," "illustrates first point," or "contradicts teacher's position." As you read an article, you should note how the author's ideas confirm or refute ideas developed by other writers. Note the connections in the margin of the essay you are reading in case you want to examine the link more closely later: do not rely on your memory. If you are reading multiple sources on the same topic, distinctions between the texts can quickly blur; you may have a difficult time remembering who wrote what if you do not write good connection notes. Also, use connection notes to trace the development of each writer's thesis. Note in the margin of the reading the link between the various ideas, arguments, or findings the writer offers and his or her thesis.

Questions can serve several purposes. First, they can identify passages you find confusing: in a question try to capture _precisely_ what you find confusing in a passage, especially if you will have a chance to discuss the reading in class. Second, questions can help you identify in a reading the material you want to dispute. Try to capture in a critical question or two why you disagree with what the author has written. Finally, questions can identify where the author has failed to consider important information or arguments. These are typically "what about" questions: "What about the theory proposed by Smith?" "What about people who can't afford day care?" Your goal is to indicate with a question possible limitations to an author's ideas or arguments.

Response notes record your reactions to what you read. These notes may indicate which ideas you accept, which ones you reject, which ones you doubt. They can range from a simple "yes!" or "huh?" to more elaborate and detailed reactions that allow you to explore your response in some detail.

Remember to keep your marginal notes brief. Their purpose is to help you read the text more critically and recall your responses and questions when you reread the material.

End Annotations

End annotations typically make some type of comment on the source as a whole and can assume different forms, including summaries, responses, and questions.

Summaries offer brief, objective overviews of a reading. You may want to write a one- or two-sentence summary at the end of a reading, especially if you are reading several source texts for your paper. The purpose of these summaries is to jog your memory about the reading's content or thesis so you don't have to reread the entire text. These summaries are especially helpful if you have to read several texts with similar titles: it is easy to confuse these readings, and the summaries can often help you find the particular text you need.

Responses capture your reaction to the work as a whole. Try to capture in your note your response to the author's ideas, argument, writing style, or any other aspect of the reading that strikes you as important. These responses can help you form comments to offer in class when you discuss the piece, and often they serve as a good starting point for developing a topic for a paper: you may want to investigate and develop your response more thoroughly and formally in an essay.

Questions written at the end of a reading typically address the source's clarity, purpose, or effectiveness. Your questions might address the reading's claims, evidence, or reasoning, its syntax, tone, or structure. Other questions might address the reading's relationship to what you already know about the topic or what you have already read. These questions help you draw connections between the readings and your own knowledge and experience. Still other questions might indicate specific aspects of a topic you still need to investigate ("I wonder how his ideas might have an impact on part two of my paper—need to reconsider?") or links between two or more authors' claims that need further consideration ("Do her arguments refute the textbook's claims?").

You will usually jot down several different types of endnotes when you finish reading a text. You may write out a brief one- or two-sentence summary, a few questions, and a response. These endnotes can prove very helpful when you return to the material later: they indicate your assessment of the source text's content, strengths, weaknesses, and worth.

Together, highlighting and annotating can help you fully understand a reading and determine the best way to use it in your own writing. A word of warning, though: do not be blinded by your own annotations and highlights. When you review a source text you have already marked and annotated and are now planning to use in your paper, be critical of your *own* highlighting and annotations. Be sure to question whether your highlighting and annotations *really* capture the source's key points. As you review your comments and marked passages, ask yourself whether you feel the same way now about the reading. If you have been engaged in researching a topic, are you now in a better position to assess the value and meaning of the reading before you? Have your views changed? Also, try to answer the questions you asked in the margins or at the end of the article. Reassess your original reactions.

SAMPLE ANNOTATED READING

Below is a sample annotated reading. Your system for marking a reading will likely be different from the system used here. Note, though, how the reader used highlighting and annotations to gain a better understanding of the author's content, structure, language, and purpose.

Hard Choices

Check bio. notes—who is this person.?

Patrick Moore, Ph.D.

founded Greenpeace

More than 20 years ago, I was one of a dozen or so activists who founded Greenpeace in the basement of the Unitarian Church in Vancouver, British Columbia. The Vietnam War was raging and nuclear holocaust seemed closer every day. We linked peace, ecology and a talent for media communications and went on to build the world's largest environmental activist organization. By 1986, Greenpeace was established in 26 countries and had an annual income of more than $100 million.

open w/ personal information

In its early years, the environmental movement specialized in confronting polluters and others who were damaging public lands and resources. Groups such as Greenpeace played a valuable role by ringing an ecological fire alarm, wakening mass consciousness to the true dimensions of our global predicament.

Brief history of environ movement

ecological movement wins?

By the 1980s, the battle for public opinion had been won. Virtually everyone inside and outside politics and industry expressed a commitment to environmental protection and good stewardship. Environmentalists were invited to the table in boardrooms and caucuses around the world to help design solutions to pressing ecological problems.

Are companies environ. friendly now?

Rather than accept this invitation to be part of the solution, many environmentalists chose instead to radicalize their message. They demanded restrictions on human activity and the uses of natural resources that

Thesis?

too "radical"

anti-science?

not build on earlier successes

far exceed any scientific justification. That tactical decision created an atmosphere in which many environmentalists today must rely on sensational rhetoric and misinformation rather than good science. Programs have gone forward without input from more knowledgeable environmentalists and other experts; the public debate has been needlessly polarized as a result of the movement's unwillingness to collaborate with others less radical.

environ not work w/others?

In addition to choosing a dubious tactic, the environmental movement also changed its philosophy along the way. It once prided itself on subscribing to a philosophy that was "transpolitical, transideological, and transnational" in character. Non-violent direct action and peaceful disobedience were the hallmarks of the movement. Truth mattered and science was respected for the knowledge it brought to the debate.

says current movement rejects truth & science

Thesis →

That tradition was abandoned by many environmental groups during the 1990s. A new brand of environmental extremism has emerged that rejects science, diversity of opinion, and even democracy. These eco-extremists tend to be:

note headings

*Anti-technology and anti-science. Eco-extremists entirely reject machinery and industry; they invoke science as a means of justifying the adoption of beliefs that have no basis in science to begin with.

anti-science

*Anti-free enterprise. Although communism and state socialism have failed to protect the environment, eco-extremists are basically anti-business. They have not put forward an alternative system of organization that would meet the material needs of society.

anti-business

point not developed well

*Anti-democratic. Eco-extremists do not tolerate dissent and do not respect the opinions and beliefs of the general public. In the name of "speaking for the trees and other species," we are faced with a movement that would usher in an era of eco-fascism.

anti-democratic

The international debate over clearcutting offers a case study of eco-extremism in action. Groups such as Greenpeace and the Sierra Club have mounted major

example of clearcutting

need clearcutting

campaigns against clearcutting, claiming that it is responsible for "deforestation" on a massive scale in Canada and elsewhere. In fact, no such deforestation is taking place in Canada or the United States, and a ban on clearcutting could do more harm than good.

It is an ecological fact that many types of forest ecosystems thrive most successfully when they are periodically cleared and allowed to regenerate. Fire, volcanic eruptions, windstorms, insect attacks, disease and climate change (ice ages) destroy massive areas of forests, part of a natural cycle of forest destruction and renewal that has existed since long before modern humans arrived on the scene.

ignores diversity— usually replanted w/only one type of tree

hype and myths of Green & Sierra

The use of hype and myths by Greenpeace and the Sierra Club is symptomatic of the larger problems facing the modern environmental movement. Confrontation too often is preferred over collaboration, and eco-extremism has shoved aside the earlier spirit of tolerance and concern for the fate of humanity. The results have been harmful to the movement as well as to the environment we seek to protect.

he is in political center how defined?

founder now an enemy?

As an environmentalist in the political center, I now find myself branded a traitor and a sellout by this new breed of saviors. My name appears in Greenpeace's "Guide to Anti-Environmental Organizations." But surely the shoe belongs on the other foot: The eco-extremists who have taken control of the nation's leading environmental organizations must shoulder the blame for the anti-environmental backlash now taking place in the United States and elsewhere. Unless they change their philosophy and tactics, the prospects for a protected environment will remain dim.

why a backlash?

Patrick Moore earned a Ph.D. in ecology from the University of British Columbia in 1972. He was a founding member of Greenpeace and for seven years served as director of Greenpeace International.

credentials but who does he work for?

Summary— "Eco-extremists" reject science, truth, alternative views →why lose pop. support?

NOTE TAKING

Especially when working on an extended writing project, you may want to take notes on a source text after carefully reading and annotating it. If you are working on a research paper for a class, check with your instructor about any requirements he or she might have concerning your notes. Some teachers, for example, require their students to take notes on index cards following rather specific guidelines. Other teachers set no guidelines concerning notes. It is always a good idea to check with your instructor concerning his or her requirements.

If you take notes on index cards, be sure you indicate somewhere on each card the title and/or author of the work you are reading. If your cards get out of order, you need some way of identifying the source of the information on each card. If you are more comfortable taking notes on paper, try to use only one side of each sheet. Using your notes to write your essay is easier if you are not constantly flipping over sheets of paper to find the information you need.

Some writers like their notes to consist only of quotes; others mix quoted, paraphrased, and summarized material. Some write notes in complete sentences; some use a combination of sentences, sentence fragments, and even single words or diagrams. As with annotations, you will need to work out your own system for taking notes, one that helps you sort out and organize the useful material you find in the sources you read.

Below are some guidelines to keep in mind as you take your notes. Following them can help you avoid problems later as you use your notes to write your paper.

Before Jotting Down Any Notes, Always Write Down the Source Text's Full Bibliographic Information

Whenever you take notes on a reading, be sure to write down the author's full name, the exact title of the piece, the full title of the publication, all the publication information, and the inclusive page numbers. Often students will be completing a paper the night before it is due and realize they used material that needs to be documented. Without having the full bibliographic information with their notes, they have to make a frantic last-minute dash back to the library. If you are careful to write down this information before you take your notes, you can avoid some problems later.

In Your Notes, Carefully Distinguish between Material You Quote and Material You Paraphrase

One of the major sources of unintentional plagiarism is faulty note taking. This problem occurs when, in taking your notes, you copy down a passage word-for-word from a source text but fail to enclose that passage in quotation marks. If you then copy that material directly from your notes into your paper—thinking you originally paraphrased the passage—and fail to quote it in your essay, you will be guilty of plagiarism. You can avoid this problem if you carefully indicate with quotation marks in your notes which passages are exact quotations and which are paraphrases of an author's ideas.

Carefully List Page Numbers

In your notes, be sure to indicate the exact page number of the source text that contains the material you are quoting, paraphrasing, or summarizing. You will need this information later for proper documentation.

Pay Attention to the Punctuation in the Source Text

If you are quoting material in your notes, reproduce the original punctuation exactly as it appears on the page. Many times students misquote material because they incorrectly copied in their notes the original punctuation.

In Your Notes, Clearly Differentiate between the Author's Ideas and Your Own

Again, failing to differentiate between what an author says about a topic and what you have to say is a major source of unintentional plagiarism. As you take your notes, you may want to jot down some observations or ideas of your own—reading other people's ideas will often lead you to new insights of your own. However, if you do not make the distinction clear in your notes—if, when reviewing your notes, you cannot tell which ideas were yours and which were the other writer's—you might attribute ideas to authors who never suggested them or take credit for ideas that were originally developed by someone else. To make this distinction clear in your notes, perhaps you could place your ideas and reflections in brackets.

Be Consistent with Your Note-Taking System

Whether you use a notebook, looseleaf paper, index cards, or a personal computer for taking notes, be consistent in how and where you note bibliographic information, page numbers, and your responses to the material. Adhering to a system will make it easier for you to find material in your notes and will help you avoid making mistakes.

ADDITIONAL READING

Getting Serious about Eradicating Binge Drinking

Henry Wechsler

Henry Wechsler *directs the College Alcohol Studies program at Harvard's School of Public Health.*

Most of us are aware that binge drinking is a major problem on many college campuses. Since the Harvard School of Public Health's first College Alcohol Study used that term, in 1994, to describe the drinking pattern of significant numbers of American college students, the problem has drawn media attention across the nation. Despite this, the problem has not declined over the past four years. In fact, our latest research findings, released in September, showed little change in the proportion of college students who binge. Among more than 14,500 students surveyed at 116 institutions, 43 per cent reported that they had binged at least once in the preceding two weeks, compared with 44 per cent in the earlier study.

Although the number of students who abstain from alcohol grew to 19 per cent this year from 15.6 per cent in the first study, among students who drink we found an increase in drunkenness, in drinking deliberately to get drunk, and in alcohol-related problems—including injuries, drunk driving, violence, and academic difficulties. For example, among students who drink, 52 per cent said a major motivation was "to get drunk," compared with 39 per cent in the first study. Thus, despite a spate of widely publicized student deaths in alcohol-related incidents, the binge goes on.

Why isn't this behavior decreasing? For one thing, binge drinking has been so deeply entrenched for so long at colleges that it can't be expected to disappear overnight. However, the more important reason that change eludes us is that some colleges have relied too much on one approach to solve the problem—trying to get the binge drinkers themselves to stop, rather than focusing equal attention on factors that make it easy for students to drink too much.

Of course, some campuses use multiple approaches to attack the problem, but many focus most of their energies on educational efforts directed at drinkers, particularly during events such as the recent Alcohol Awareness Week. Such educational efforts are an important way to teach some students the facts about alcohol abuse. But those efforts overlook the environment around binge drinkers that condones and supports and often even encourages their behavior.

So what are the factors that promote binge drinking at colleges? One is that students who binge tend to think they represent the norm; they argue that they're just doing what most of their peers do. Most binge drinkers don't think they have a problem. They think they are only having fun, and most consider themselves to be moderate drinkers. Doing research into actual behavior and then informing students about how many students actually binge—generally fewer than binge drinkers believe—can help to reduce the behavior.

Another approach to changing student norms is to focus on the disruptive behavior of binge drinkers. Colleges are civic communities, and all too frequently they are disrupted by the behavior of students who drink excessively. Rather than search for contraband alcohol, a college would be wise to engage student leaders in helping administrators work out a clearly worded code of conduct that penalizes drunken behavior—and then to enforce it consistently.

Students who become drunk and disorderly should be made to take responsibility for the messes that they have created: They should have to clean up vomit in the bathrooms made unusable on weekends, help care for drunken students at the college health center, repair damage from vandalism, and pick up litter. The punishment should fit the crime.

But with repeat offenders, colleges need to consider enforcing a "three strikes and you're out" policy for alcohol-related violations of the student conduct code.

At the center of binge drinking on many campuses are fraternities and sororities. While they attract only a small percentage of students nationally, they continue to play a prominent role in campus life at many institutions. Our data shows that in fraternity houses, four of five residents binge, and more than half are frequent binge drinkers. And fraternity parties are attended by many more students than just members. They attract even some high-school seniors—future college students who are introduced to binge drinking as a social norm. Not surprisingly, most of the alcohol-related deaths of college students recently reported in the media involved fraternity parties.

While some colleges have begun to address the drinking culture created by fraternities, many administrators are still hesitant to move strongly against fraternities, for fear of angering alumni donors who fondly remember their own college years of partying. But administrators have a responsibility to protect all of their students against alcohol-related disruptions and injuries, and should not wait for tragedy to strike before they revoke official recognition of fraternities that consistently cause problems. College also can require all first-year students who live on campus to reside in dormitories, and not in fraternity or sorority houses. Of course, then those colleges must work to create interesting alcohol-free activities centered in the residence halls, to show students that out-of-control drinking need not be the focus of social life.

A third impetus for binge drinking on college campuses—one rarely mentioned publicly—involves alumni at tailgate parties during homecoming activities and sporting events. Any alcohol-control measures adopted for students must also apply to visiting alumni. Banning alcohol at home sporting events for everyone except alumni who contribute more than $50, as one college did recently, is not a good way to win students' support for new alcohol-control policies. I would hope that most alumni, if informed that an institution is trying to cope with a serious problem, would cooperate. Colleges that base their decision making on fund-raising concerns must ask themselves: What will cost the college more money—alumni who might decrease their contributions if they're cut off from alcohol at sporting events, or a few large jury awards of damages to families of injured or deceased students?

Another center of college binge drinking is found in athletics programs. Athletes binge more than other students, according to our data. In fact, involvement in athletics—compared with time spent in other activities— increases rather than decreases a student's propensity for binge drinking. Students involved in athletics are one and a half times as likely to be binge drinkers as are other students. This tradition is kept alive through the beer-advertising blitz that surrounds sports. After all, Mark McGwire's 70th home run was hit at Busch Stadium.

As a first step, college athletics officials should stay clear of alcohol-industry promotions and advertising. Further, although coaches at some colleges require team members to abstain from alcohol during the competitive season, relatively few coaches are involved in campus-wide programs to reduce alcohol abuse. Colleges should make it a priority to enlist their coaches and athletics directors in programs designed to reach all students with the message that binge drinking interferes with performance in every area of their lives. The National Collegiate Athletic Association should encourage this. Colleges also should press coaches to stress the institution's commitment to preventing alcohol abuse when they recruit high-school athletes.

Another important point of intervention is at the high-school level. Half of college binge drinkers start in high school. Colleges should begin to address this problem at high schools that send a large number of freshmen to their campuses, by sending college students from those high schools back to talk to the younger students about alcohol and other substance abuse. The volunteers should stress that one in five college students nationally abstains from alcohol, and that another two in five drink, but not to excess.

High-school students are more likely to believe the messages of college students than those of teachers and other adults. Let future freshmen get their first view of college life from these volunteers, rather than from attending fraternity parties or tailgate events. Once freshmen have unpacked and settled in, it may be too late to tell them about college rules on alcohol use. That message should be sent before they even apply.

Colleges also need to focus more attention a block or two away from the campus—on the ring of bars and liquor stores that encircles many institutions. Colleges need to map the density of those establishments; many institutions have more than 50 such alcohol outlets surrounding them. These are formidable competitors for students' attention, and cannot be coped with by the college alone; community leaders must be enlisted to help, particularly in barring the low-price specials that the outlets use to compete with each other: two-for-one offers, cut-rate drinks and free food during happy hours, and free drinks for women on certain nights. Some states and communities already have laws that ban those types of sales. Remember, the problem is not alcohol itself; it is the availability of a large volume of alcohol at a low price, usually to be consumed in a short period of time.

All of the problem areas that I've cited cannot be attacked by every college at once. Some issues may be more pressing than others on particular campuses, and the solutions must be fashioned to fit local circumstances.

Some important actions are being taken by colleges and universities across the country. Many are trying to sever the connection between alcohol and sports by banning advertising in the programs for sporting events and prohibiting alcohol at college stadiums. Some colleges are discontinuing the practice of not holding classes or exams on Fridays, and are no longer allowing local bars to advertise drink specials in campus publications. And some colleges are experimenting with new student-housing arrangements, such as living–learning centers that take faculty members and classes into the dorms, to try to completely change the environments there.

Institutions also are trying to give students more alcohol-free entertainment options. Some are working with neighborhood groups, as well as community and state officials, to find legal and other means of controlling students' behavior off campus. Other colleges are imposing stricter sanctions on students who break the rules—notifying parents after a certain number of infractions, and suspending or expelling repeat offenders.

What institutions need to avoid are one-dimensional programs that focus on particular students but ignore the ways in which colleges help enable some students to continue binging for four years. Not holding classes or exams on Fridays, for example, enables students to binge from Thursday to Sunday without interruption. Making new rules, but not enforcing even the old ones—for example, banning alcohol in the dormitories, but allowing it to be carried in unmarked cups—tells students that the college is not serious about eradicating the problem.

   To anyone who thinks that binge drinking is behavior that cannot be changed, I offer the following challenge. At the next meeting you attend, look around and count how many people are smoking. Not many years ago, the room would have been filled with smoke. Today, because of the wide recognition that smoking hurts both the smoker and people nearby, through secondhand effects, the air is clear. Binge drinking can become equally unacceptable on college campuses.

Summary Chart

CRITICAL READING: ASKING QUESTIONS

1. **Questions to Ask Before You Begin a Close Reading of a Text**

   Questions concerning the author

   - *Who is the author?*
   - *What are her credentials?*
   - *What else has she written on the topic?*
   - *What possible biases might have influenced her work?*

   Questions concerning the publication

   - *In what regard is the publication held by professionals in the field?*
   - *Toward what type of readership is the publication aimed?*
   - *How long ago was the piece published?*
   - *What, generally, is the editorial stance of the publication?*

   Questions concerning your own views of the topic

   - *What are my beliefs about the issue addressed in the reading?*
   - *How open am I to new ideas on this topic?*

2. **Questions to Ask While You Read and Reread Material**

   Questions concerning the audience of the piece

   - *What audience does the author seem to be trying to reach?*
   - *What type of reader would be attracted to the author's writing, and what type would be alienated by it?*
   - *How does your sense of the text's audience influence your reading of the piece?*

   Questions concerning the purpose of the piece

   - *What was the author's purpose in writing the piece?*
   - *What is the author's thesis?*
   - *Does the author successfully achieve his or her goals?*

Questions concerning the content of the piece

- *What are the author's major assertions or findings?*
- *How does the author support these assertions or findings?*

Questions concerning the organization of the piece

- *How is the material organized?*
- *What headings and subheadings does the author provide?*
- *What does the organization of the essay tell you about the author's view of the material?*
- *What gets stressed as a result of the organization?*

Questions concerning the author's sources

- *How does the author use other people's ideas or findings?*
- *How credible are the sources the author uses to support his ideas or findings?*

Questions concerning graphics in the piece

- *How clear are the charts, graphs, tables, or illustrations the author provides?*
- *How well does the author explain the graphics?*
- *How well do the graphics support or explain what the author has to say?*

Questions concerning your reactions and responses to the piece

- *How do I feel about the topic, issues, or findings addressed in the reading?*
- *What is convincing? What is unclear?*
- *What ideas in the piece contradict my understanding of the topic?*
- *What ideas in the piece are new to me—which ones do I accept and which ones do I reject?*

Summary Chart

CRITICAL READING: MARKING TEXTS

1. **Highlighting Texts**

   Highlight the text's thesis, primary assertions, and supporting evidence.

   Highlight the names of authors, specific dates mentioned, and principal sources cited.

   Highlight key passages you may want to reread, quote, or paraphrase later.

   Highlight terms you do not understand or want to discuss in class.

2. **Annotating Texts**

   Marginal annotations

   - *Content notes: identify the meaning or purpose of the marked passages.*
   - *Organization notes: identify the major sections of the text.*
   - *Connection notes: identify links between readings and within a reading.*
   - *Questions: identify confusing, controversial, or questionable passages.*
   - *Response notes: identify your reactions to the reading.*

   End annotations

   - *Summaries: convey a brief overview of the reading.*
   - *Responses: convey your overall reaction to the piece.*
   - *Questions: convey your assessment of the reading's clarity, purpose, or effectiveness.*

Summary Chart

CRITICAL READING: NOTE TAKING

1. Before jotting down any notes, always write down the source text's full bibliographic information.

2. In your notes, carefully distinguish between material you quote and material you paraphrase.

3. Carefully list page numbers in your notes.

4. Pay attention to the punctuation in the source text.

5. In your notes, clearly differentiate between the author's ideas and your own.

6. Be consistent with your note-taking system.

Chapter 2

JOURNALS

DEFINITION

Keeping a journal can be very helpful in a course that requires you to write from readings; you can use your entries to summarize and respond to the material you study and to develop ideas and plans for your own writing. Journal entries are usually informal and personal. Though individual teachers may have their own grading standards, in most cases they do not mark spelling or grammar errors when they read and evaluate journals. Instead, most instructors evaluate entries in terms of the student's dedication and engagement. Students receive high marks for their journals when they have the required number of entries and when those entries demonstrate a sincere effort to address the course material.

Journals have much in common with other types of notebooks or logs you may also be assigned to keep in various college courses. For example, in some science classes you might be asked to keep a lab notebook or log in which you record the procedures you follow when you set up an experiment, the observations you make while conducting the study, and the conclusions you draw. Keeping a journal likewise gives you the opportunity to record your thoughts and observations concerning a course you are taking or a project you are completing. However, the entries you make in a journal are typically much less structured than the types of entries you make in a lab notebook. With journals you will likely have much more freedom in choosing the topic, language, and form of your entries.

In other classes you might be asked to keep a field notebook. For instance, in a biology class you might be asked to study the interaction between humans and animals in a local park, record your observations in a notebook, then use those notes later to write up a report on what you saw and learned. Such assignments are also common in education classes in which you might be asked to watch a group of students at an elementary or high school, record your observations in a log, and later use these notes to write up a response or evaluative report. Some journal entries may well resemble the types of entries you make in field notebooks, but others will not. Some journal entries might be based on your observations and experience; however, others might be based on your course readings, your teacher's or peers' comments in class, or even your dreams, fantasies, and imagination.

In a journal you typically record your reactions and responses to course lectures, discussions, and readings as well as any personal experiences, reflections, and observations that are relevant to the class. You may find yourself writing about other courses you are taking, television shows, movies, music, almost anything so long as your comments relate to the material you are studying in that course. Your journal can be the place you compare what various authors have to say about a topic, examine your own experiences and feelings, raise questions, develop ideas, or plan your papers. The forms journal entries can assume are usually as varied as the topics: you can include freewriting, formal or informal essays, lists, maps, charts, pictures, whatever serves your interests or stimulates your thinking.

Do not, however, think of your journal as a diary in which you record the daily events of your life. Your entries should be related to the course you are taking, the readings you are studying, or the paper you are writing. Your teacher will be reading and perhaps responding to your journal—do not include in it material you do not want your teacher to read. Finally, your journal should not be used as a course notebook in which you simply record information covered in class. Keep your class notes in a separate location.

PURPOSE

Journal entries can serve many different purposes. First, your journal can function as a kind of reading-response notebook, a place for you to record information as well as your responses to that material. In entries you can summarize and respond to readings, course lectures, class discussions, films, television shows, speeches, interviews, or any other source of information. Keeping such a journal allows you to collect in one place all the material you gather while taking a course or working on a particular writing project.

Second, rather than just recording and responding to information you gather from others, in your journal you can also analyze, critique, or synthesize this material and reflect on your own ideas and experience as you work out a position on a topic. Writing about ideas often leads to insight, and informal journal entries can be particularly productive. Instead of worrying about grammar, spelling, or structure, when you write informally in your journal you can concentrate on the content of your entries, the ideas you are considering and articulating. When you reread these entries, you may often be surprised by what you have written: you will discover ideas or conclusions you sensed only vaguely until you wrote them down. You can then write about these ideas or findings more formally in an essay or report.

With other entries you might begin to organize a paper that is due in a course. In this case, your journal serves the same purpose that a sketchbook may serve an art student. Before painting a picture, an artist may complete a series of preliminary drawings or plans in a sketchbook, gaining from this work a better sense of how the completed piece might appear. Your journal can serve a similar purpose; in it, you outline larger writing projects, practice composing various sections of an essay (such as the thesis statement or opening paragraph), or consider how you might articulate or arrange the various arguments you want to put forward in a piece.

Finally, writing journal entries gives you the opportunity to experiment with language. In journal entries you can try writing in a variety of styles, from formal to informal, academic to conversational. Through this experimentation, you may discover new ways of communicating your ideas clearly and forcefully. However, experimenting with language offers another advantage, as well. Changing the language we use to explain an idea often leads us to understand that idea in new, powerful ways. For example, suppose you are working on a paper advocating changes in our government's welfare policy. In your journal you might want to compose three entries, explaining your ideas to three different types of readers: someone who agrees with your ideas, someone who disagrees with them, and someone who knows little about the topic and needs all the issues carefully and thoroughly explained. Communicating your ideas successfully to these different audiences will likely require you to use different types of language, which could well lead you to some new insights about your topic.

Noting and responding to information from readings encourages you to reflect on its meaning, to explore your own ideas in light of this information, and to find language and structures that best communicate your understanding. Because your grade on entries is not determined by their adherence to the standards of formal written English, journals often offer the best opportunity for you to take risks as a writer and to learn from what you have studied. Writing in your journal gives you the opportunity to develop material you will use in a more formal essay, achieve a better personal understanding of the topic you are studying, or simply gain more practice writing and using language.

TYPES OF ENTRIES

In your college courses you will encounter two different types of journal assignments: required and open. With required entries, the teacher specifies a topic you are to address or task you are to undertake: a reading you need to discuss, questions you need to answer, exercises you need to complete. With open assignments, though, you are free to develop your own entries, so long as they are relevant to the course and follow any general guidelines the teacher establishes concerning length, form, and deadlines. (Always check with your instructor if you have any questions about the appropriate subject or form of open entries in a journal.)

Below is a partial list of the types of entries you can make in a journal. If your teacher allows you to compose open entries, experiment with them to determine which kind of entries you find most comfortable, helpful, and productive.

SUMMARIES

Here your goal is to restate in your own words someone else's primary assertions, arguments, or findings. You can summarize articles, chapters, lectures, films, speeches—any source of information. In writing these summaries, attempt to be fair, objective, and thorough. Writing summaries is a very effective way to study and learn material: successfully summarizing a reading indicates you understand its meaning.

ANALYSES

In these entries you identify the primary elements of a reading. If you concentrate on the text's content, you are likely to write about its assertions, evidence, warrants, and assumptions. If you concentrate on its structure, you are likely to write about its thesis, organization, introduction and conclusion, and transitions. If you concentrate on its style, you are likely to write about its word choice, syntax, tone, and voice.

RESPONSES

Here you give your personal reaction to someone's work. You can write about its content, style, or structure, identifying what you found interesting or boring, effective or ineffective, informing or confusing, whatever your response might be. To be most helpful though, responses should go a step further. Once you have stated your response, identify what aspects of the reading gave rise to that reaction (which word or words, which image, which sentence, which argument, which graphic), and try to explain why you think it had that particular effect on you.

REFLECTIONS

In reflections you record your thoughts and feelings on a topic. Instead of summarizing, analyzing, or responding to someone else's ideas, you use those ideas as a starting point for your own reflections on the topic. In this type of entry, you are free to follow and develop trains of thought as they occur to you; your goal is to write your way to new or better understandings and insights.

QUESTIONS

A journal entry can serve as a place for you to record and explore any questions you have about a reading, discussion, or topic. These questions, for example, might concern a source's content or style, your reaction to the piece, your teacher's or peers' response to the material, or the relationship between the author's ideas and your experience. You can articulate questions you would like to have answered, answers to questions you find interesting, or both. These questions and answers should serve to spur your thinking on the topic.

CRITIQUES

A critique involves the formal analysis of a reading's strengths and weaknesses. Rather than record your own response to the piece, you evaluate it according to a set of more formal, established criteria. These criteria will be either general (those that can be used to assess material in many different disciplines) or specific (specialized criteria used to assess material in a particular course or discipline). Your goal in critiquing material is to establish its worth according to commonly agreed-on standards. Since other scholars will recognize these criteria, they will be in a position to understand and discuss your judgments using the same standards you employed.

SYNTHESES

In a synthesis, you combine in one entry information from two or more sources or from a reading and your own knowledge and experience. These entries will often examine what the sources have in common or how they differ. In a synthesis, you can demonstrate how one reading is correct in its assertions and others are wrong, that the readings are more alike than they are different, that ideas expressed in one can help people understand ideas contained in the other, that material in the reading confirms or counters your own experience. The range of possible entries is quite wide when you synthesize information.

APPLICATIONS

With this type of entry you assume a person is correct in what he or she has written or said, and then you speculate on the meaning or utility of that information.

Assuming that the author or speaker is correct, what are the consequences of his or her arguments, ideas, or findings? What do they mean to your life or your understanding of the topic under study? To what use can his or her ideas be put? Try to work out reasonable, logical applications of the material.

REFUTATIONS

With this type of entry you consider ways of disputing what an author or speaker has to say. You try to find weaknesses in the person's ideas or positions, consider the limitations of his or her assertions, or develop examples countering what he or she assumes to be the case. You can question or reject someone else's ideas for a number of reasons—for example, because the position is factually incorrect, illogical, contradictory, unsupported, unclear, or unethical. In this type of entry, you try to work out reasonable, logical objections to the material.

OUTLINES

In your journal you can outline a paper on which you are working. In developing your outline, you will consider what material to include in your essay and how it might best be organized. You can write a very formal outline with Roman numerals, capital letters, correct indention, and the rest, or a scratch outline, an informal list of what you might cover and the order in which you might cover it. Consider, too, the possibility of outlining a paper after you have written the rough draft. Besides helping you plan a paper before you write it, outlining your work can also help you revise: an accurate outline can help you visualize the structure of your rough draft and notice structural weaknesses you can address on subsequent drafts. Remember, though, that outlines are just planning or revising tools. As you actually draft and rewrite the piece, you have to be willing to modify or even abandon your outline if your paper is assuming a better, more effective structure.

DRAFTS

You might write in your journal a preliminary draft of a project on which you are working. You may want to write out the entire piece or perhaps some part of it—a thesis you are considering, a conclusion you think might work, an argument you want to make. As you draft the piece in your journal, you can experiment with ideas, arguments, language, structure. What works, you can incorporate into the final draft; what does not, stays in the journal.

PERSONAL EXPERIENCE

You might want to devote a journal entry to more personal kinds of writing, if your teacher allows you to include this type of entry. Remember that your journal is not a diary; any personal entries should somehow relate to the material you are studying in class. You might write about experiences that confirm or contradict ideas you have studied in class or that illustrate principles you have discussed in a course. If you include such entries in your journal, be sure to also explain their significance, how they relate to the course; otherwise your teacher might not understand the significance or point of the material.

SELF-REFLECTION

You might want to turn a critical eye on yourself in a journal entry, analyzing your own thinking and experience. As you analyze your own reasoning process, you try to determine why you have reached a particular position, responded to material in a particular way, or rejected arguments for a particular reason. You can also use such entries to analyze your experiences, trying to determine their meaning and significance. Through your writing you will try to determine why you acted in a certain way or why you made particular decisions. Finally, you can use self-reflection entries to think about the way you write papers. You can examine the steps you follow when writing an essay, identifying practices that help you compose effective papers or make your writing less effective, deciding on changes you might make in the way you compose papers.

CREATIVE WRITING

If your teacher allows such entries, you might want to experiment with some creative writing in your journal. You can try writing a story or poem that touches on issues or themes raised in class. Sometimes creative writing assignments can lead to important insights, especially if in the piece you try to assume a perspective different from your own.

DRAWINGS

Again, if your teacher allows it, you might want to include drawings in your journal. You can try to capture in these drawings ideas or themes you study in class or your responses to class material.

LANGUAGE AND FORMAT

When a teacher asks you to keep a journal for a class, he or she will usually give you a set of guidelines to follow when writing entries. These guidelines may specify what the teacher will accept in terms of language and content and may even specify a particular format your entries must follow. If, however, your teacher provides no specific requirements concerning language and format, you might want to follow the general guidelines provided below.

LANGUAGE

Since journals entries are not graded on the basis of formal correctness, you will write most of them in an informal style exhibiting much less regard for spelling, grammar, and sentence structure than you will when writing a formal paper. Does that mean that any language is acceptable? The answer to this question may well depend on your teacher's expectations. Many teachers will allow you to use any type of language you choose in your journal; they believe that the journal is the student's place to write what and how he or she chooses to write. Many other teachers will not accept entries that employ profanity or noninclusive language (language, for example, that is racist, sexist, or homophobic). Even if an instructor does not offer any guidelines on language use in journal entries, he or she may find writing that employs such language to be unacceptable. Though you are encouraged to employ informal writing in your journal, remember that you are producing a public document, not a diary. Because others will be reading your journal, you should consider avoiding offensive language that may alienate your audience.

FORMAT

If your teacher does not specify a particular format to follow when writing journal entries, you might consider these general guidelines:

1. Begin each new entry on a separate page in your journal.
2. At the top of the page, date each entry.
3. If you are completing a required assignment, at the top of the page list the assignment number or title.
4. If your entry concerns a specific reading, begin your entry with the bibliographic citation of the source text.
5. Leave a healthy margin, either on the right- or left-hand side of the page, for your teacher's comments.
6. Try to make each entry at least a page long: writing will often spur thinking, so give yourself the chance to discover new ideas.

Some teachers will ask you to purchase a spiral notebook or three-ring binder to serve as your journal; others prefer students to use a "composition" book, which is usually smaller than a spiral notebook and has a hard, cardboard cover. Because computers have become increasingly common on campuses, more and more teachers are encouraging students to type their journal entries, either printing them out, turning them in on diskette, or sending them to the teacher as e-mail. If you type your journal entries, follow the same general guidelines described above, leaving a margin of an inch and a half to two inches on the right or left in case your teacher wants to respond to your ideas.

Dual Entry Format

Some teachers may ask you to employ a "dual entry" format in your journal, especially if you will be responding to a number of readings. With this format, you open your journal so that you have a lined sheet on both your right and left. On the right-hand sheet of paper you keep the notes you take while reading a source—you summarize information, copy relevant quotations, paraphrase material, and so on. On the left-hand sheet of paper you record your responses to the reading—what you agree with, what you disagree with, any questions you have. If you type out your journal entries, place a line down the length of the page, leaving two thirds of the sheet on the right, one third on the left. Type your notes to the right of the line, your reactions to the left. Together, these dual entries help you gain a solid understanding of a reading and your response to it.

Research Log Format

A research log is a special type of journal you keep as you work on an extended research project. In it you include all the material you gather for the paper, document the steps you undertake to complete the project, and reflect on the process you follow. In early entries you typically clarify the assignment, set out a series of steps you will need to follow to complete the project, and map out a plan for meeting your goals. As you work on the project, you keep in the journal the notes you take while researching the project, the plans you develop for organizing your paper, and any early drafts of the essay you compose. In later entries you analyze the research process itself: what research and writing strategies proved to be effective, which did not, what you will do differently the next time you work on a similar project.

FINAL CONSIDERATIONS

A journal can be a powerful learning tool, especially if you keep in mind a few simple principles. First, you should write in your journal on a regular basis. Unless your teacher specifies otherwise, you ought to write two or three journal entries a week. Second, your entries ought to be at least a page long. As you write about a topic, your mind will generate material to fill the page—that is one way writing stimulates thinking. Give yourself the opportunity for insight by making each journal entry at least a page long. Third, use your journal entries as an opportunity to delve deeply into a topic. Do not be satisfied with superficial thinking or easy answers. As you work on your entries, question your own thinking and positions, experiment with new language and new perspectives, see each entry as an opportunity to learn and grow.

Chapter 3

QUOTATION

DEFINITION AND PURPOSE

When you use someone else's words in your paper, you have to place them in quotation marks and supply proper documentation. Quoting and documenting material tells your readers where they can find that *exact* language in the source text. If you make any significant changes in a passage you are quoting, you need to indicate the alterations in your text with ellipses, brackets, or an explanation.

Generally, if you take more than three words in a row from a source text and incorporate them word-for-word in your essay, you need to place quotation marks around the passage. However, there are several exceptions to this general guideline. For example, if you repeat in your paper someone's official title as it appears in the source text (e.g., president of the school board), you do not need to quote the title, even if it is longer than three words. Also, if you use in your paper a *single* word or term from a source text that is significant or unusual, you *may* need to quote it. Learning what to quote and when to quote takes some time, practice, and thought. Making good decisions about quoting can be easier, though, if you keep in mind one of the main reasons for quoting material: you want to acknowledge an author's distinctive language.

When employed properly and judiciously, quotations can add color and credibility to your writing; they can help make your papers clearer, more entertaining, and more persuasive. If used improperly, quotations can give the

impression that you cannot think through a topic for yourself or cannot articulate ideas in your own words. Therefore, knowing how to quote material
properly is an extremely important part of writing from readings.

GUIDELINES ON WHEN TO QUOTE MATERIAL

You ought to have a good reason for quoting material in your paper. Do not
quote material just to fill up space or to avoid thinking about your topic.
Instead, you ought to consider how quoting material will help you support
your thesis or explain important ideas to your reader. Below are some guidelines to help you decide when to quote a word or passage and some suggestions
on how to use that material in your paper. As you plan and draft a source-based
paper, consider ways to integrate *a few* carefully selected quotations with your
own writing to present your ideas as clearly and effectively as possible.

QUOTE PASSAGES WHEN THE AUTHOR HAS WRITTEN SOMETHING IN A DISTINCTIVE OR ESPECIALLY INSIGHTFUL OR INTERESTING WAY

Often an author will express an idea so well it is difficult or impossible for you
to express it better by paraphrasing it. The author may have expressed the idea
succinctly, employed especially effective adjectives or metaphors, or supplied
an especially interesting example. In such cases, quote the word or passage—
it may help make your paper more entertaining or persuasive.

QUOTE MATERIAL THAT LENDS SUPPORT TO A POSITION YOU ARE TRYING TO MAKE IN YOUR PAPER

Letting your readers see for themselves that an expert agrees with a position
you are advocating can help persuade them to accept your argument or can
help them better understand your position. You must be sure, though, that in
your effort to find support for your position, you do not misrepresent an
author's thoughts or findings. By leaving words out of a quotation or by
adding language to it, you should not misrepresent what the author actually
had to say. For example, a few years ago a student of mine quoted an editorial
writer as saying, "President Reagan's proposed budget cuts will . . . double
the number of people living in poverty." I checked the original editorial; the
actual sentence read, "President Reagan's proposed budget cuts will not double the number of people living in poverty." By leaving out the word *not*, this
student clearly misrepresented the author's intended meaning. Such changes
to a quotation are unethical.

Also, in an effort to find support for your thesis, do not limit your research
to those authors who agree with the position you are advancing. For several

reasons, this strategy is a mistake. First, in doing research, you should learn about a topic by studying many different views. Quite often writers change their position as they write and rewrite their papers; shifting through the material they have read frequently leads them to rethink and restate their thesis. Second, as you will see below, you may want to quote authors who present ideas that challenge your thesis: doing so can increase your credibility in the eyes of many readers. Finally, by seeking out alternative perspectives and learning more about the topic, you place yourself in a better position to defend your assertions, improving the likelihood that your readers will value what you have to say on the topic because of your expertise. Therefore, do not neglect opposing viewpoints when searching for material to quote in your paper.

When you use expert testimony to support a position in your paper, it is a good idea to mention the person's credentials in your paper:

> According to Helen Carter, former president of the First National Bank, ". . ."

> Milton Friedman, noted economist and winner of the Nobel Prize, contends that ". . ."

Citing the credentials of the experts you quote may help convince your readers to accept or at least seriously consider what they have to say. Again, you do not need to cite the credentials of every author every time you quote from his or her work. You also do not want to cite so many credentials that the sentence is hard to read. Variety is the key to using quotations well—cite the credentials when you think they are significant, and do so in a way that fits the overall tone of your paper.

QUOTE AUTHORITIES WHO DISAGREE WITH A POSITION YOU ARE ADVOCATING OR WHO OFFER ALTERNATIVE EXPLANATIONS OR CONTRADICTORY DATA

Often it is a good idea to quote authors who offer views or data that call into question the position you are advocating in your paper. Many beginning authors balk at this idea. They believe that introducing opposing views will only weaken the impact of their thesis. However, when you include in your paper a variety of perspectives, your readers are more likely to perceive you to be fair and thorough in your treatment of the subject: these quotations demonstrate that you recognize and understand alternative points of view. Second, such quotations allow you the opportunity to examine critically the other person's position, acknowledging its worth or value when needed, criticizing it when appropriate.

If you decide to quote authors who challenge your thesis, you must somehow address their ideas or findings, usually in one of four ways. You need to explain in your own words:

a. how that author's ideas do not seriously damage your thesis;
b. how that author's ideas or findings may actually support your contentions;

    c. how your thesis may be altered slightly to accommodate the author's ideas; or

    d. how that author's ideas are incorrect or at least questionable.

If you do not somehow address the opposing ideas you quote in your paper, your reader will likely be confused, wondering how that material fits your paper's thesis.

GUIDELINES ON WHEN NOT TO QUOTE MATERIAL

When writing from sources, students often rely too heavily on quoted material: their essays are a string of quotations. These papers more accurately represent the ideas and language of the source texts than they do the ideas and language of the student. To avoid producing a paper like this, consider these guidelines outlining when you should *not* quote material. Use quotations *selectively;* they should never make up the bulk of your paper.

DO NOT QUOTE PASSAGES MERELY TO FILL SPACE

Too often when writing from sources, students try to pad their essays with extensive quotations, and their final papers end up being a patchwork of quoted material. This is especially true when students are writing to meet a length requirement. If a teacher wants a paper eight to ten pages long, some students think the easiest way to reach that length is to keep piling on quotations. However, in college your readers will usually want to know what *you* think about your subject, what conclusions *you* have reached through your research, how *you* understand material. Do not substitute other people's views and voices for your own; use theirs to *support* your own.

DO NOT QUOTE PASSAGES AS A SUBSTITUTE FOR THINKING

In addition to using quotations to fill space, too often students rely on quotations alone to clarify, defend, or substantiate a finding or position. They may introduce an idea in a topic sentence, then string together two or three quotations to substantiate the point they want to make. Instead of presenting their own ideas in their own language, they rely on quoted material to present and defend their case.

    The better course to follow is to integrate selected quotations into your essay carefully: their purpose is to advance your argument or support your conclusions or findings. Do not expect a quotation alone to convince your readers to accept some contention you want to make. As you work through a writing assignment, find language that reflects and communicates the conclusions you have drawn and the assertions you want to make. When appropriate, support or illustrate your position with quoted material. Also remember that when you do quote material, in most cases you will need to comment on it, explaining in your own words the quotation's meaning, relevance, or importance.

Do Not Quote Passages Because You Do Not Understand the Author's Ideas Well Enough to Paraphrase Them

As you read material in college, you will often run into words you do not know, ideas that seem strange, arguments that are hard to follow, research methodologies and discussions of findings that seem to be written in a language of their own. If you have to write papers based on these readings, do not rely on quotations as a way to avoid thought. You need to understand the material you quote. As a general guideline, if you cannot paraphrase the material, do not quote it. That is, if you cannot convey that information in your own words, quoting it is probably a bad idea.

INTEGRATING QUOTATIONS INTO YOUR WRITING

There are several ways to place quoted material in your papers. You should study and practice several of these techniques since varying the way you integrate quotations into your writing can make your papers more interesting.

One of the real difficulties in learning to write from readings in college is the fact that different disciplines follow different rules concerning the proper way to document and punctuate quotations. The three primary style manuals used in your college courses are those published by the Modern Language Association (MLA), primarily used in humanities classes such as English and history; by the American Psychological Association (APA), primarily used in social science classes such as psychology and sociology; and by the Council of Biology Editors (CBE), primarily used in the natural sciences such as biology and chemistry. (The organization's name changed in 2000 to Council of Science Editors, but the style is still commonly referred to as "CBE.") Because each of these manuals offers its own set of rules concerning the proper punctuation and documentation of quotations, when you receive an assignment, always ask your instructor which style manual he or she expects you to follow. (See Chapters 10 and 11 for a complete discussion of the documentation guidelines suggested by each.)

Two Basic Types of Quotations

When you quote material, you will either set it off in a block quotation or integrate it into the body of your essay. Your choice depends on length: longer passages must be block quoted, shorter quotations should be integrated.

Properly punctuating quotations can be tricky: again, the rules you follow depend on the academic stylebook your teacher wants you to follow. While the three major style manuals generally agree on how to punctuate integrated quotations, the three offer different guidelines for formatting, punctuating, and documenting block quotations. Pay close attention to how the following sample quotations are punctuated. All of the sample quotations will draw on passages from the following editorial published in *The New Republic*, October 5, 1992.

Missing Link

"U.S. government wants to sedate Black youth." This headline, in a black-oriented Washington weekly called *New Dimensions,* is part of the publicity that recently led the National Institutes of Health to withdraw funding for a conference on heredity and criminal behavior. As a result, the conference, scheduled for mid-October at the University of Maryland, has been canceled. It's a sad and disgraceful descent into craven racial politics. The episode exhibits several troubling themes: paranoia among many blacks; the surprising cowardice of the NIH; and time-honored confusion about biology and behavior.

Part of the muddle is the conflation of "genetic" and "biological." If the government really does want to identify and "sedate" crime-prone youths—black or white—it can do so without the help of conferences like this one. Such youths are easy to spot (they're the ones in handcuffs), and sedatives are available. But this has no special connection with genetics. The fact that some kids have a disposition toward wrongdoing says nothing about whether genes or early environment did the disposing. Neither does any responsiveness to chemical therapy. All behavioral influences, environmental and genetic, are biologically mediated, and thus all behavior tendencies are in principle subject to chemical intervention. As pharmacology advances, society will increasingly face questions about the chemical treatment of criminals, and of playground troublemakers—but it will face them regardless of whether criminals and troublemakers are born or made.

A second confusion involves genes and race. (Actually, nothing in the conference's literature implied anyone would talk about race. But charges of bigotry are routinely leveled at people who dare use the words "gene" and "behavior" in the same breath.) Young black men in America are more prone to crime than young white men. And individuals probably do differ in their genetic inclination toward aggression, impulsiveness, and other traits correlated with crime. Do these facts together suggest that the high black crime rate lies partly in "black genes"? The answer should be obvious—no, genetic differences among individuals don't imply aggregate differences between groups—but it's worth elaboration.

A five-minute visit to your local underclass neighborhood will leave you with no shortage of non-genetic explanations for the black crime rate. Indeed, given the family structures, the menu of role models, the state of inner-city schools, the bleak economic options and perverse incentives, and so on, it would be weird if black ghettos *weren't* fountains of crime. The American "black gene pool" (if so simple a term can be applied to something that is in fact quite variegated) didn't change appreciably between the 1950's, when black crime wasn't a mammoth problem, and today, when it is. What changed was the environment.

Assume, for a moment, the worst-case scenario—the most depressing and politically uncomfortable news about race that could emerge from the study of genes and crime: suppose scientists found a non-trivial statistical difference in the genetic underpinnings of crime between black and white populations. What would happen?

Certainly nothing *should* happen. Equal treatment before the law is an ideal whose logic transcends both the fact that people are different and the source of those differences. Whatever your color, whatever your genes, you're not a criminal until you've committed a crime. (The idea that we could ever give infants "gene tests" and say that they will or won't become criminals *regardless* of their upbringing betrays an unspeakably crude idea of how genes and environment interact.)

What of the distant, Huxleyan fears of eugenics? In the worst-case scenario, mightn't the government limit the reproductive options of blacks? Obviously, the government should stay out of the business of coercive eugenics. But biotechnology is rendering centralized eugenics obsolete anyway. Parents will one day be able to check embryos (or eggs fertilized in vitro) for behaviorally relevant genes and then decide about abortion (or reimplantation). Eventually, direct manipulation of sex cells—genetic engineering—may give parents much finer tailoring tools. Which manipulations are moral, which legal, and which of the legal ones are covered by government health insurance are massively dicey issues. But in any event, the most likely complaint of blacks will not be that they're subjected to eugenics, but that they're excluded from it—that, being disproportionately poor, black parents often lack the options richer parents exercise.

The truth about genes and human behavior, whatever it may be, is coming. The cancellation of a conference to investigate the subject was a cowardly denial of this reality. We suggest that aspiring defenders of black and any other interests muster the sobriety and moral courage to discern the real issues as they arise.

THE BLOCK QUOTATION

The APA, CBE, and MLA style manuals all agree that longer quotations must be set off from the rest of the text, but they differ in how they define "longer":

- APA states that quotations of 40 words or more must be block quoted.
- CBE advises the use of special typography to set off "longer" quotations but offers no length guidelines.
- MLA says to block quote passages that would be more than four typed lines in your paper.

Regardless of the style manual you follow, you should introduce a block quotation with a colon. You do not add quotation marks at the beginning or end of the passage, and all the punctuation in the source text stays the same in the block quotation.

APA Guidelines

According to the APA style manual, you should start a block quotation on a new line in your paper, setting the left margin of the quotation five spaces or one-half inch in from the original left margin. Subsequent lines of the quotation align on that indent. (If you are quoting additional paragraphs in the source text, indent the first line of each an additional five spaces.) The right margin stays the same, and the whole passage is double-spaced.

Example I

> In "Missing Link" (1992) the editors of *The New Republic* argue that the environment is much more responsible than genes for inner-city crime:

> A five-minute visit to your local underclass neighborhood will leave you with no shortage of non-genetic explanations for the black crime rate. Indeed, given the family structures, the menu of role models, the state of inner-city schools, the bleak economic options and perverse incentives, and so on, it would be weird if black ghettos *weren't* fountains of crime. The American "black gene pool" (if so simple a term can be applied to something that is in fact quite variegated) didn't change appreciably between the 1950's, when black crime wasn't a mammoth problem, and today, when it is. What changed was the environment. (p. 45)

> Changes in society, not in biology, are primarily responsible for the sharp rise in the black crime rate over the past few decades.

Analysis

Notice that the period at the end of the quotation precedes the parenthetical citation. (If the quotation runs longer than one page in the source text, use "pp." to introduce the inclusive page numbers.) There are no quotation marks added at the beginning or end of the block quote. The words "black gene pool" are quoted because they have quotation marks around them in the source text. Note also that the word "weren't" is italicized in the block quote because it is italicized in the source text (if you cannot print italics, underline words in your paper that are italicized in the reading). The left-hand margin of the block quotation is indented five spaces.

CBE Guidelines

According to the CBE style manual, block quotations should be printed in a smaller type face and/or with wider margins. The quotation may be single- or double-spaced. CBE suggests writers follow the format used in the journal they hope will publish their work. In Example 2, the "1" enclosed in parentheses after the article title is a part of the CBE's documentation system, explained in Chapter 10.

Example 2

In "Missing Link" (1) the editors of *The New Republic* argue that the environment is much more responsible than genes for inner-city crime:

> A five-minute visit to your local underclass neighborhood will leave you with no shortage of non-genetic explanations for the black crime rate. Indeed, given the family structures, the menu of role models, the state of inner-city schools, the bleak economic options and perverse incentives, and so on, it would be weird if black ghettos *weren't* fountains of crime. The American "black gene pool" (if so simple a term can be applied to something that is in fact quite variegated) didn't change appreciably between the 1950's, when black crime wasn't a mammoth problem, and today, when it is. What changed was the environment. (p 45)

Changes in society, not in biology, are primarily responsible for the sharp rise in the black crime rate over the past few decades.

Analysis

Note the change in type size and the punctuation at the end of the quotation. As with the APA guidelines, the parenthetical documentation follows the period at the end of the quotation. (Use "p" to introduce the page number of the material, whether that material is located on one or more pages in the source text.) No quotation marks are added to the block quote, but the words quoted in the source retain their original punctuation, as do the words originally in italics. Note the new left margin for the quotation and how the first sentence of the quotation is indented an extra five spaces because it was indented in the reading. If you were to quote material from the middle of a paragraph in the source text, the first line of the block quotation would *not* be indented an additional five spaces (see Example 3).

Example 3

> Genetic engineering raises some troubling questions, especially as parents are increasingly able to predict the biological makeup of their future children:
>
> > Parents will one day be able to check embryos (or eggs fertilized in vitro) for behaviorally relevant genes and then decide about abortion (or reimplantation). Eventually, direct manipulation of sex cells—genetic engineering—may give parents much finer tailoring tools. Which manipulations are moral, which legal, and which of the legal ones are covered by government health insurance are massively dicey issues. (1, p 45)
>
> Clearly, advances in technology will continue to pose new moral and legal questions: just because a procedure is possible to do, is it right to do?

MLA Guidelines

MLA says to begin a block quotation on a new line, indent the left margin ten spaces on the left (and five more spaces for new paragraphs within the block quote), leave the right margin unchanged, and double-space the block quotation.

Example 4

> In "Missing Link" the editors of *The New Republic* argue that the environment is much more responsible than genes for inner-city crime:
>
> > A five-minute visit to your local underclass neighborhood will leave you with no shortage of non-genetic explanations for the black crime rate. Indeed, given the family structures, the menu of role models, the state of inner-city schools, the bleak economic options and perverse incentives, and so on, it would be weird if black ghettos *weren't* fountains of crime. The American "black gene pool" (if so simple a term can be applied to something that is in fact quite variegated) didn't change appreciably between the 1950's, when black crime wasn't a mammoth problem, and today, when it is. What changed was the environment. (45)
>
> Changes in society, not in biology, are primarily responsible for the sharp rise in the black crime rate over the past few decades.

Analysis

Note how the parenthetical documentation follows the period at the end of the quotation. No quotation marks are added to the block quote. The words quoted from the original passage retain their punctuation, and words in italics in the original are italicized in the quotation. There is a new left margin, but the right margin remains unchanged.

THE INTEGRATED QUOTATION

Short quotations should be integrated in the body of your essay rather than set off in a block quotation. As you will see, you have several ways to integrate quoted material into your paper. Try to use several of these techniques when writing an essay—such variety can help make your paper more interesting to read.

The APA, CBE, and MLA style manuals generally agree on where to place quotation marks, how to use single and double quotation marks, and how to otherwise punctuate integrated quotations. Remember that all quotations must be documented. Again, see Chapter 10 for a detailed discussion on how to document quotations. In the following samples, I alternate among APA, CBE, and MLA documentation conventions.

Introduce a Quotation with a Verb

Probably the most common way of introducing a quotation is to give the author's name, perhaps his or her credentials, maybe even the title of the work, followed by an appropriate verb—*says, notes, comments, contends, asserts,* and so on. Place a comma after the verb of saying.

Example 5 (MLA Documentation)

> Parenthetically, the authors assert, "The idea that we could ever give infants 'gene tests' and say that they will or won't become criminals *regardless* of their upbringing betrays an unspeakably crude idea of how genes and environment interact" ("Missing" 45).

When you integrate material from a source text that already contains quotation marks (as the words "gene tests" are quoted in the original passage), the regular quotation marks in the original (" ") are changed to single quotation marks (' ') in your paper. Also, the word "regardless" is italicized in the quotation because it is in italics in the original. If your typewriter or computer does not have italic script, underline italicized words in your paper.

Note the punctuation at the end of the sentence; the final period follows the parenthetical citation. If the last sentence of the quotation ends with an exclamation point or a question mark, include it before the closing quotation mark and place a period after the parenthetical citation. This punctuation guideline holds true for the APA, CBE, and MLA style manuals.

Introduce a Quotation without a Verb

A more formal way of integrating a quotation into your paper is to introduce it with a colon. Commonly, quotations used as illustrations or elaborations of a point you have just made are introduced this way. Make sure that the colon comes at the end of a complete sentence; leave one space between the colon and the opening quotation mark.

Example 6 (CBE Documentation)

In "Missing Link"[1], the editors of *The New Republic* claim that social, not biological factors are primarily responsible for the rise of crime in some urban African-American communities: "Indeed, given the family structures, the menu of role models, the state of inner-city schools, the bleak economic options and perverse incentives, and so on, it would be weird if black ghettos *weren't* fountains of crime" (p 45).

Run Your Sentence and the Quotation Together

This particular technique can be hard to master. Instead of separating your words from the quoted passage with a comma or colon, you run the two together seamlessly, relying on the quotation marks to let your reader know when you begin using someone else's language. Integrating quotations in this way, while sophisticated stylistically, can also lead you to misquote material if you are not careful. As students first learn to run their sentence and the quotation together, they tend to alter the quotation to fit the sentence they are writing rather than to alter their sentence so it fits the quotation. As you practice this method of quoting material, try to craft your sentence so it runs smoothly into the quotation. If you have to change the quoted passage in any substantive way, you must indicate the changes (see the section on "Altering Quoted Material and Avoiding Misquotations," which follows).

When you employ this technique properly and read your essay aloud, a listener would not be able to tell where the quotation started and ended. Note that you do not need to place a comma before the quoted material or insert an ellipsis if you are picking up the quotation in midsentence.

Example 7 (APA Documentation)

In "Missing Link" (1992) the editors of *The New Republic* claim that "the truth about genes and human behavior, whatever it may be, is coming" (p. 45).

In this example, note that the capital *T* in *The* can be changed to lowercase without the addition of brackets. Also, when using this approach, you do not need to include an ellipsis if you begin a quotation in midsentence.

Example 8 (CBE Documentation)

> In "Missing Link," the editors of *The New Republic* make the point that in the future, African-American citizens may not be able to take advantage of advances in genetics because "being disproportionately poor, black parents often lack the options richer parents exercise" (1, p 45).

Pick Out Only Certain Words to Quote in Your Sentence

You do not always have to quote entire passages or sentences in your paper. Often you want to quote only a few key words or phrases. Be sure, though, to include proper documentation even if you quote only one word.

Example 9 (MLA Documentation)

> While certain people may have a "disposition" to break the law, in no way does that indicate whether "genes or early environment" are responsible ("Missing" 44).

This particular example needs only one parenthetical citation because all the quoted material comes from the same page in the source text. If it came from different pages in the source text, parenthetical citations would follow each quoted word or phrase.

ALTERING QUOTED MATERIAL AND AVOIDING MISQUOTATIONS

When you place quotation marks around material in your essay and document that passage, you are telling your readers that if they turn to that page of that source text they will find that passage as it appears in your paper: the words and punctuation have not been changed. If that is not the case—if you have made any substantive changes to material you are quoting—then you need to acknowledge those alterations.

APA, CBE, and MLA all agree that you do not need to acknowledge changing a capital letter at the beginning of a sentence to a lowercase letter if lowercasing makes it easier for you to integrate the quoted passage with your own writing; however, other changes must be acknowledged. Especially important is learning how to indicate that you left words out of a quotation, added words to a quotation, or changed the emphasis given words in a quotation.

Leaving Words Out of a Quotation

Use an ellipsis (…) to indicate that you left material out of a quotation. Add a fourth dot to act as a period if you omit the end of a sentence or leave out an entire sentence when block quoting. When you introduce a quotation with a colon, include an ellipsis if you pick up a quotation in the middle of a sentence in the source text.

Example 10 (APA Documentation)

> As the editors of *The New Republic* point out, "The American 'black gene pool'… didn't change appreciably between the 1950's, when black crime wasn't a mammoth problem, and today, when it is" (1992, p. 45).

Example 11 (APA Documentation)

> The conference on heredity and crime unfairly faced charges of bigotry and racism: "… nothing in the conference's literature implied anyone would talk about race" ("Missing," 1992, p. 44).

Adding Words to a Quotation

When you add words to a quotation, use square brackets, not parentheses, around the words. (If your typewriter does not have keys for square brackets, do not use parentheses as a substitute. Instead, when you type your paper, leave blank spaces where the brackets will go and add them later in black ink.) Add material to quotations sparingly. Do it only when absolutely necessary to avoid confusing your readers.

Example 12 (CBE Documentation)

> According to the editors of *The New Republic*, "The episode exhibits several troubling themes: paranoia among many blacks; the surprising cowardice of the NIH [National Institutes of Health]; and time-honored confusion about biology and behavior" (1, p 44).

Noting Emphasis Added to a Quotation

If you want to emphasize a word or passage in a quotation, put it in italics (if your typewriter or computer does not have italic script, underline the word or passage). The three major stylebooks offer different guidelines on how to indicate the addition of emphasis to a quotation:

* APA style: immediately after the emphasized words, place in square brackets the words "italics added."
* CBE style: immediately after the emphasized words, note in square brackets "italics mine."

- MLA style: after the quotation itself, place in parentheses the words "emphasis added," after the page number (if any). Or place "emphasis added" in square brackets immediately after the emphasized words.

If you do not indicate otherwise, readers will assume any words italicized in a quotation appear in italics in the source text.

Example 13 (APA Documentation)

According to the editors of *The New Republic*, "The fact that some kids have a *disposition* [italics added] toward wrongdoing says nothing about whether genes or early environment did the disposing" ("Missing," 1992, p. 44).

Example 14 (CBE Documentation)

According to the editors of *The New Republic*, "The fact that some kids have a *disposition* [italics mine] toward wrongdoing says nothing about whether genes or early environment did the disposing" (1, p 44).

Example 15 (MLA Documentation)

According to the editors of *The New Republic*, "The fact that some kids have a *disposition* toward wrongdoing says nothing about whether genes or early environment did the disposing" ("Missing" 44, emphasis added).

Summary Chart

GUIDELINES ON QUOTATIONS

1. **When to Quote Material**

   Quote passages when the author has said something in a distinctive or especially insightful or interesting way.

   Quote material that supports the assertions you make in your paper.

   Quote authorities who disagree with a position you are advocating or who offer alternative explanations or contradictory data.

2. **When Not to Quote Material**

   Do not quote passages merely to fill in space.

   Do not quote passages as a substitute for thinking.

   Do not quote passages because you do not understand the author's ideas well enough to paraphrase them.

Summary Chart

INTEGRATING QUOTATIONS INTO YOUR WRITING

1. **Block Quotations**

   Employ this method with longer quotations.

   Follow guidelines established by the style manual your instructor requires.

2. **Integrated Quotations**

   Introduce the quotation with an appropriate verb.

   - *precede with a comma*
   - *employ a verb of saying that fits the overall tone of your essay, such as:*

says	holds
states	maintains
asserts	contends
claims	explains

   Introduce the quotation without a verb.

   - *a more formal way of introducing the quotation*
   - *precede with a colon*

   Run your sentence and the quotation together.

   - *edit your sentence so it fits the tone and syntax of the quoted passage*

   Pick out only certain words to quote.

   - *quote interesting uses of language such as coined or controversial terms*
   - *quote terms to draw attention to them*

Chapter 4

PARAPHRASE

DEFINITION AND PURPOSE

When you paraphrase a passage, you express an author's arguments, findings, or ideas in your own words. Much of the writing you do in college will require you to paraphrase material. Some of these assignments will simply ask you to gather and convey information. To write this type of paper, you study the work of various authors, then paraphrase what they have written, trying to convey to your readers as clearly and accurately as possible what each has to say about the topic.

In other assignments you will rely on paraphrased material to help you develop and defend an argument. Paraphrasing the work of experts who agree with your position in a paper can be quite persuasive. Even paraphrasing the work of authors who *disagree* with a position you have assumed in your essay can be helpful: after you objectively present that opposing view, you can examine its strengths and weaknesses and adjust your position to accommodate ideas you can neither discredit nor dismiss. However, when paraphrasing information as a part of an argument you are advancing, you must fairly represent an author's views. It is always tempting to misrepresent what people say, especially when you disagree with them, either by oversimplifying their position or by employing misleading language. Try to resist these temptations; always try to be fair to an author when you paraphrase his or her work.

Finally, paraphrasing allows you to convey your unique understanding of a reading. Paraphrases of the same material written by different students are not likely to be exactly the same because writing a paraphrase involves a series of choices: each writer decides what information to include, what language to use, what organization to employ. Though you should attempt to be objective in your paraphrase of a reading, the details you choose to include and the language you choose to substitute for the author's will be communicating your unique view of the passage.

QUALITIES OF A GOOD PARAPHRASE

Generally, a good paraphrase of a passage exhibits four characteristics. It is thorough, accurate, fair, and objective:

- *Thorough*—it will include all of the author's primary ideas or findings.
- *Accurate*—it will reflect what the author actually wrote.
- *Fair*—your choice of language will be as even-handed as possible.
- *Objective*—you will avoid voicing your own opinion on the topic or on the quality of the source text.

THOROUGH

A paraphrase of a passage differs from a summary of a passage in its comprehensiveness: in a summary, you try to reduce the source material to its most essential message; in a paraphrase, you try to capture the entire content of the passage. Because you change words and sentence structure when paraphrasing material, your paraphrase of a passage may actually be longer than the original text. Summaries, however, will always be shorter than the original passage. Even though your goal is to be thorough, writing a paraphrase involves making some choices concerning content: you may leave out what you believe to be insignificant details, examples, or explanations found in the source text. Guiding these decisions, though, should be your desire to produce as complete a paraphrase as possible.

ACCURATE

Because you are not quoting authors when you paraphrase their work—because you are substituting your words for theirs—you must take care to be accurate in what you write. Your paraphrase should offer your reader a precise restatement of what the author wrote: though the language is different, your paraphrase should convey the same information or arguments found in the source text. However, accuracy can be hard to achieve. Even slight changes in language can drastically alter the meaning of a passage. Therefore, when writing and revising a paraphrase, check your work against your understanding of the source text. Have you at all misrepresented the *content* of the other writer's piece? Would the author read your paraphrase and agree that you have, indeed, captured what he or she wrote?

FAIR

Being fair in your paraphrase is related to being accurate. Writing a paraphrase involves putting into your own words someone else's ideas, arguments, or findings. When doing so, first you want to be fair to the author whose work you are paraphrasing. In exchanging your words for his or hers, you want to be as even-handed as possible. Avoid language, for example, that implies a judgment on your part or makes an author's work appear more sophisticated or more simplistic than it actually is. Second, you want to be fair to your readers. When people read your paraphrase of an author's work, they expect you to give them a fair and accurate understanding of that material. They do not expect you to censure or praise the source text—that's the function of a critique, not a paraphrase.

For a number of reasons, paraphrases are often inaccurate or unfair. First, students often *misread source texts* and make flatly incorrect assertions about the author's work. This type of problem can be avoided through a careful, critical reading of the source text before you try to paraphrase it and by discussing the reading with others. Second, students often *paraphrase material out of context.* Their paraphrase of a passage is misleading because in the larger context of the work the passage has an entirely different meaning from the one reflected in the student's essay. This type of error frequently occurs if the author of the source text is summarizing opposing views in his work. Students who paraphrase this material out of context will frequently misrepresent the author's views, making it appear the author actually agrees with his critics. When you paraphrase someone else's ideas, be sensitive to the relationship between the passage you are working with and the meaning of source text as a whole. Finally, students often produce unfair paraphrases of a source text by *relying on emotionally charged or heavily connotative language.* If an article talks about "presidential aides" and you substitute "presidential cronies," "presidential lackeys," or "presidential co-conspirators," you probably are not being entirely fair in your paraphrase.

OBJECTIVE

A good paraphrase does not take sides. Students often fail to be objective in one of three ways. First, as discussed above, they may employ language that clearly editorializes. In writing a paraphrase, try to use language that fairly and accurately captures the meaning and intent of the source text, not language that reflects your views of the topic or the quality of the source text itself.

Second, in writing a paraphrase, sometimes students want to comment directly on the topic the author is addressing—when paraphrasing an author's views on abortion rights, for instance, they may want to articulate their stand on the issue. That material does not belong in a paraphrase, where your goal is to communicate someone else's views. Finally, students sometimes want to include in their paraphrase comments on the quality of the author's work—that they found the argument convincing or faulty, that the author's style was cumbersome or flowing, that the article was "good" or "bad." These types of comments are appropriate for a critique, not for a paraphrase. Your goal in a paraphrase is to be as objective in your content and language as possible.

Before you try to paraphrase someone else's ideas, though, be sure you understand what he or she has written. Again, one of the most common causes of inadequate paraphrasing is failing to grasp the meaning of the source text. Therefore, whether you are paraphrasing a sentence, paragraph, chapter, or essay, you need to understand fully what the author has written before you attempt to put that person's ideas into your own words. Your paraphrase of that person's ideas or findings must be complete, accurate, fair, and objective. It cannot meet these standards if you are confused or at all uncertain about what the author has written.

However, paraphrasing a passage can also be an effective way of determining its meaning. If you are not sure what a passage means, try paraphrasing it. Putting someone else's ideas into your own words is often the best way for you to understand what the author has written. Always be sure to then reread your paraphrase and the source text to be sure you have been thorough and fair, especially if the paraphrased material is going to be a part of a paper you are turning in.

HOW TO PARAPHRASE MATERIAL

Generally, you paraphrase material by changing words, changing sentence structures, or changing the order of ideas in a passage. More often than not, you will make all three types of changes each time you paraphrase someone's ideas.

CHANGING WORDS

One way to paraphrase a passage is to substitute your words for the author's. However, finding appropriate synonyms for words in the source text can often be challenging. Many students are tempted to turn immediately to a thesaurus for a list of possible replacement words. However, it is usually better to try to come up with appropriate synonyms on your own. Remember, writing a paraphrase involves putting someone else's ideas into *your* own words. If you can come up with replacement words that are fair, accurate, and appropriate for the tone of your paper, use them. If you cannot come up with a new word on your own, then turn to a thesaurus. However, after you look up a possible substitute word in the thesaurus, check its definition in a dictionary to see if the word accurately reflects the meaning you want to convey. The words you find in a thesaurus are not always interchangeable; there are often subtle differences in meaning you can determine by checking the definition of each term in a good dictionary.

Whether you rely on your own resources or on a thesaurus, using synonyms in a paraphrase raises similar concerns:

a. Does the new word convey the author's original idea accurately and objectively?
b. Does the new word fit the overall tone of the rest of your essay? Is it too formal or informal? Too technical or too general?

Often, it may be impossible to find an adequate substitute for a word or phrase in a passage: perhaps the author coined a phrase or used an unusual or shocking term. In such cases, it is appropriate for you to quote the language found in the source text (see Chapter 3 for guidelines on quoting material). When paraphrasing material, though, try to keep the number of quotations to a minimum. Also, remember that *all* paraphrased passages you include in your papers must be documented—even though you change the language of the source text when you paraphrase, you need to acknowledge through your documentation the source of the *ideas* you are discussing.

Below are examples of passages paraphrased primarily through word substitution. You will find the original passage, a rough-draft paraphrase, and a final paraphrase. The original passages in all of the following examples are drawn from the readings included in Chapters 1 and 3.

Example 1

A. Original

"Whatever your color, whatever your genes, you're not a criminal until you've committed a crime."

B. Rough-Draft Paraphrase

No matter what your race or genetic background, you're not considered a criminal until you've committed a crime.

C. Final Paraphrase (CBE Documentation)

Whatever your race or genetic background, you're a criminal only if you break the law (1).

Discussion: In my rough draft, I began trying to change a few words: "whatever" became "no matter what" and "genes" became "genetic background."

I also tried to rephrase the second half of the sentence, adding the word "considered," but my first attempt was still too close to the wording of the original. In my final draft, I changed "no matter what" back to "whatever" because I thought the wording in my rough draft was too clumsy. I was satisfied with the words "race and genetic background" so I worked on the second half of the sentence. I changed the negative statement "you're not a criminal" to the positive claim "you're only a criminal" and altered "until you've committed a crime" to "if you break the law." The basic sentence structure has remained the same; I've only tried to change some of the words.

Example 2

A. Original

> "Indeed, given the family structures, the menu of role models, the state of inner-city schools, the bleak economic options and perverse incentives, and so on, it would be weird if black ghettos *weren't* fountains of crime."

B. Rough-Draft Paraphrase

> Given the problems with family structure, role models, education, and real economic opportunities, it would be strange if black ghettos didn't generate a lot of criminal activity.

C. Final Paraphrase (APA Documentation)

> Given all their problems—fractured family structures, negative role models, poor education, and depressed economic opportunities—black ghettos, not surprisingly, generate crime ("Missing," 1992, p. 45).

Discussion: This was a difficult passage to paraphrase because so many ideas had to be reworded. In the rough draft, I began by trying to find another way to restate the problems the author enumerated, choosing, first, just to list them: "family structure, role models, education, and real economic opportunities." In the second half of the sentence I changed "it would be weird" to "it would be strange" and "fountains of crime" to "generate a lot of criminal activity." However, I was not happy with my wording, especially at the beginning of the sentence. I did not capture the negative tone of the original passage. In my revision, I added language to reflect the author's tone—"fractured family structures, negative role models." In the second half of the passage, I changed "it would be strange" to the shorter "not surprisingly" and changed the wordy "criminal activity" back to "crime."

CHANGING SENTENCE STRUCTURE

Besides changing words, when composing a good paraphrase of material, you may also need to alter the sentence structure employed in the source text.

Often such changes involve rearranging the order of ideas in a sentence or altering the order of dependent and independent clauses.

Example 3

A.   Original

"Although communism and state socialism have failed to protect the environment, eco-extremists are basically anti-business."

B.   Rough-Draft Paraphrase

"Eco-extremists" oppose business interests even though communism and state socialism have failed to protect the environment.

C.   Final Paraphrase (MLA Documentation)

"Eco-extremists" oppose business even though communist and socialist governments have permitted environmental degradation (Moore 16).

Discussion: In my rough draft, I first changed the order of the ideas in the sentence. I could not think of an appropriate substitution for "eco-extremist" so I quoted it and changed "anti-business" to "oppose business." In my final draft, I had to find a better way of addressing the second half of my paraphrase. I started by changing "communism and state socialism" to "communist and socialist governments" and reworded the idea about failing to protect the environment to "have permitted environmental degradation." Looking at it now, I think "degradation" might not be the best word—some additional changes might be needed.

COMBINING SENTENCES

When you paraphrase longer passages, you will often have to "combine" sentences in the source text to paraphrase the material adequately. After you read the entire passage, you may feel that you can condense the information into fewer sentences while still being thorough and fair in your paraphrase. By changing words, altering sentence structures, and combining in your sentences information found in two or more source sentences, you can often achieve a smooth, effective paraphrase of material.

Example 4

A.   Original

"In addition to choosing a dubious tactic, the environmental movement also changed its philosophy along the way. It once prided itself on subscribing to a philosophy that was 'transpolitical, transideological, and transnational' in character. Non-violent direct action and peaceful disobedience were the hallmarks of the movement. Truth mattered and science was respected for the knowledge it brought to the debate.''

B. Rough-Draft Paraphrase

In recent years the environmental movement has adopted a new philosophy. It once believed its philosophy cut across political, ideological, and national lines. While its adherents believed in direct action and peaceful disobedience, truth also mattered, as did science, which brought knowledge to the debate.

C. Final Paraphrase (APA Documentation)

According to Patrick Moore (1995), the environmental movement has changed its guiding philosophy. They used to believe their ideas cut across political, ideological, and national lines. They also believed in peaceful protests, respected the truth, and valued science for the information it brought them.

Discussion: In my rough draft, I condensed the four sentences found in the source text into three sentences in my paraphrase. I was especially interested in combining the last two sentences. At the same time, I was trying to change some of the words. For example, I altered "transpolitical, transideological, and transnational" but let stand much of the language in those last two sentences. To begin my final draft, I added the author's name and dropped "in recent years," which I had added in the rough draft. In the next two sentences I tried to echo the term "philosophy" with the word "believed" and achieve parallel structure by using "They" twice. I continued to change some of the terms, substituting "peaceful" for "non-violent" and again tried to achieve some sense of parallel structure in my last sentence (which combines two sentences in the source text).

"UNPACKING" SENTENCES

Sometimes a sentence in a reading may be so densely written, so full of ideas, that in your paraphrase you may need two or three sentences to convey the same information. When "unpacking" a sentence like this, your goal remains to convey the author's ideas fairly and thoroughly in your own language. Be sure first, though, that you fully understand the source passage—densely written material is often hard to read.

Example 5

A. Original

"All behavioral influences, environmental and genetic, are biologically mediated, and thus all behavior tendencies are in principle, subject to chemical intervention."

B. *Rough-Draft Paraphrase*

Everything that influences our behavior, whether arising from the environment or from our genetic makeup, does so biologically: our behavior is biologically determined. Thus, in theory, all behavior can be altered chemically, since chemical intervention can alter the way our bodies respond biologically.

C. *Final Paraphrase (CBE Documentation)*

Everything that influences our behavior, whether arising from our environment or our genes, does so biologically—it influences our behavior by altering our biology. It holds, therefore, that behavior can be altered chemically, since chemicals can alter our biology, the ultimate source of our behavior (1).

Discussion: I found this a hard passage to paraphrase. First, I had to read the original sentence several times to understand what the author wrote. I decided I could paraphrase the passage in two sentences. As I worked to rewrite the passage, I knew my paraphrase would be longer than the original. It seemed to me the author was making, essentially, a cause-effect argument in the form of a syllogism: since all behavior is biologically based and since chemicals affect biology, chemicals can affect behavior. In my two sentences, I tried to capture this line of thought.

DOCUMENTATION

Remember that any material you paraphrase from a source must be properly documented. Failing to document paraphrased material is a form of plagiarism. While the various forms of documentation you will encounter in college are discussed in Chapter 10, remember that every discipline expects writers to document all paraphrased material properly.

Summary Chart

HOW TO WRITE A PARAPHRASE

1. Read, reread, and annotate the material.

   • *Use a dictionary to find the meaning of any words you do not know.*

   • *Form your own opinion about the meaning of the passage.*

2. Change words in the passage.

   • *Substitute synonyms for key terms in the passage.*

   • *Substitute pronouns for nouns when appropriate.*

   • *Change the verbs.*

3. Change the sentence structure in the passage.

   • *Rearrange the order of ideas presented in the source text.*

4. Combine sentences found in the source text.

   • *Combine into single sentences ideas presented in two or more sentences in the source text.*

5. Unpack sentences found in the source text.

   • *Convey in two or more sentences ideas presented in one sentence in the source text.*

Summary Chart

QUALITIES OF A GOOD PARAPHRASE

1. A good paraphrase is *thorough*.

   - *It attempts to include all of the author's primary ideas or findings.*

2. A good paraphrase is *accurate*.

   - *It attempts to reflect what the author actually wrote.*

3. A good paraphrase is *fair*.

   - *It attempts to employ even-handed language and content.*

4. A good paraphrase is *objective*.

   - *It attempts to avoid voicing the writer's opinion on the topic or the quality of the source text.*

Chapter 5

SUMMARY

DEFINITION AND PURPOSE

Summarizing a reading involves two separate processes: (1) identifying the important material in the text and (2) restating the material in your own words. Because part of your job when writing a summary is deciding what to include from the reading and what to leave out, summaries are always shorter than the source text. Like paraphrases, summaries are always written in your own words (you can use quotations in a summary, but only sparingly), and they should be as objective as possible (you do not include in a summary your own opinions, beliefs, or judgments, and you try to use neutral language).

The ability to summarize readings is fundamental to academic, source-based writing. You will likely be summarizing information when you prepare a lab report, review a movie, write a research paper, or take an essay test. Instructors will often ask you to summarize articles or book chapters to be sure you can read carefully and critically, identify key ideas and important supporting evidence or arguments, and express that information clearly in your own words.

Sometimes summaries are part of a longer work. In a history research paper, for example, you may summarize the work of several different theorists while presenting an argument of your own. Other times, though, summaries will be "freestanding," graded as independent formal essays. These free-standing, informative summaries are often called "reports." Your goal in writing them is to convey in your own words only the most important ideas, arguments, or findings in a reading. To write these types of assignments, you need to form a clear understanding of the source text, decide what to include in your summary and what to leave out, and choose language that clearly and objectively conveys the author's ideas.

Other times, though, you will use summaries to support a larger argument you are advancing in an essay. First, you may summarize the arguments or findings of experts who agree with the position you have assumed in your thesis: readers may accept your position if they see that other authorities support it as well. Second, you may summarize the work of experts who call into question your thesis. Doing so will help your work appear informed and balanced, again improving your credibility in the eyes of many academic readers. Be sure, though, that if you do summarize opposing views in your essay you then somehow address them. For example, following your summary, you can critique that information—pointing out its strengths and weaknesses—and explain how the opposing ideas affect the validity of your thesis.

Whether your summary is part of a longer work or stands on its own, it must make sense to someone who has not read the source text. If, for example, you are working as a loan officer in a bank and your boss hands you a financial report to summarize, she wants to be able to understand your summary without having to read the report herself. She wants *you* to read the report carefully and distill from it the information she needs to know.

TYPES OF SUMMARIES

In college you will probably write two different types of summaries: informative and explanatory. An informative summary simply conveys the author's main ideas, data, arguments, and supporting material; an explanatory summary conveys this information as well, but also indicates the overall structure of the source text, explaining how the author developed his or her assertions. Informative summaries are often shorter than explanatory summaries and are usually incorporated into longer works; explanatory summaries frequently mention the author's name, usually follow the organizational scheme of the source text, and are frequently independent, freestanding essays.

Below are two different summaries of the opening lines of the Gettysburg Address, one informative and one explanatory. As you read them, note the differences in content, structure, and word choice.

Example 1

Source Text

> Four score and seven years ago our fathers brought forth on this continent, a new nation, conceived in Liberty and dedicated to the proposition that all men are created equal. Now we are engaged in a great civil war, testing whether that

nation, or any nation so conceived and so dedicated, can long endure. We are met on a great battlefield of that war. We have come to dedicate a portion of that field, as a final resting place for those who here gave their lives that that nation might live.

Informative Summary

Eighty-seven years ago the United States was founded on the idea that all people are created equal. Currently a civil war is testing whether such a nation can survive. A portion of this battlefield is to be designated as a cemetery for those who fought in the war.

Explanatory Summary

Lincoln opens the Gettysburg Address by remarking that eighty-seven years ago the United States was founded on the idea that all people are created equal. He next points out how the country is engaged in a civil war that will determine whether such a nation can survive, then acknowledges the occasion of the speech: to dedicate part of a great battlefield as a cemetery for the combatants.

Notice that the point of the informative summary is simply to capture in your own words the important ideas found in the source text. In an explanatory summary, though, you repeatedly refer to the author of the work and indicate how the piece was organized through your choice of verbs ("opens," "points out") and transition words ("next," "then").

QUALITIES OF A GOOD SUMMARY

Informative and explanatory summaries need to be comprehensive, brief, accurate, neutral, and independent.

- *Comprehensive*—it conveys all the important information in the reading.
- *Brief*—it conveys this information concisely.
- *Accurate*—it correctly conveys the author's ideas, findings, or arguments.
- *Neutral*—it avoids judgments concerning the reading's topic or style.
- *Independent*—it makes sense to someone who has not read the source text.

COMPREHENSIVE

Your summary needs to include all of the important ideas, assertions, or findings contained in the source text as well as the most significant information or arguments the author provides to support them. When you paraphrase a passage, you try to capture in your own language everything the author has written. However, when you summarize that same passage, you have to be more selective in choosing material to include. You need to identify what you believe to be the most important material in the passage and include only that in your summary. In this way your summary is comprehensive—you have not left any important information out of your summary.

Does that mean that if a number of people were summarizing the same article, all of their essays would be identical, at least in content? No. Determining what to include in a summary requires judgment. Each individual writer must decide what is most important in the source text. Some writers will make good choices; some will make poor choices. Even those making good choices may decide to include different information. Consequently, students assigned to summarize the same reading will likely produce slightly different essays. You will probably produce a comprehensive summary if you carefully and critically read the source text before you begin to write your summary and if you check your work against the source text before you turn it in to be sure you have included all of the important information.

BRIEF

In writing a summary, you have to balance two concerns: you want your summary to be comprehensive, but you also want it to be brief. The point of writing a summary is to *reduce* a text to its most essential information. In a summary, brevity is usually achieved through carefully selecting your content and words. First, when writing your summary you need to include (1) the reading's primary ideas, arguments, or findings, and (2) the primary means of support the author offers for his or her contentions. Second, in writing and rewriting your summary, you must always be concerned about word count: if you can say something gracefully in four words rather than five, say it in four; if you can condense material by cutting unnecessary prepositions or adjectives, cut them. Composing a good summary requires disciplined writing.

ACCURATE

Your readers depend on you to be accurate in your summary. You have to be careful not to misrepresent—purposefully or accidentally—what the author wrote. Instead of reading the source text, your readers are depending on you to provide them a thorough, accurate, and fair overview of the piece. Misrepresenting an author in your summary is unfair to both your reader and the writer. However, accuracy can be hard to maintain. Because in a summary you are substituting your language for the author's, even slight changes in words can drastically alter the meaning of a passage. Therefore, when you review your summary, check it against the source to be sure you have accurately represented what the author wrote. Make sure you have not misrepresented the author's ideas or findings either by omitting some important information or by using inaccurate, slanted, or vague language.

NEUTRAL

Summaries should be objective. No matter how much you would like to praise or criticize an author's argument, interpretation of data, or style of writing, such comments do not belong in a summary. In a summary you do not present your views on the topic the author is addressing, you do not comment on the quality of the author's argument or writing, and you do not voice any of your opinions at all. Instead, you try to present what the author has written accurately and objectively. When reviewing your summary, make sure you have not included your own opinions and that you have used objective language. By avoiding highly charged or judgmental terms, you can help ensure that your summary is neutral, balanced, and fair.

When there are problems with objectivity in a summary, more often than not they appear in one of three places: at the beginnings of paragraphs, in the middle of long paragraphs, and at the very end of the piece. At the beginnings of paragraphs, students sometimes react to the material contained in the previous paragraph: instead of moving on to summarize the author's next point, they respond to the previous one. In the middle of paragraphs, students sometimes begin to debate the author. They may notice that the author has presented a weak argument, for example, and feel compelled to point that out. Such criticisms are appropriate for a critique, not for a summary. Finally, at the end of summaries, students sometimes add the kind of concluding line commonly found in high school book reports, "Overall, I really liked this book because…" or "Though I found the author convincing, sometimes I had a hard time…" Such statements do not belong in an objective, neutral summary.

INDEPENDENT

Your summary ought to make sense to someone who has not read the source text. Keep in mind the purpose of a summary. If, for instance, your employer asks you to summarize a report, she wants to learn from your summary the main points of the report without having to read the original text. Your summary must be able to stand on its own; read independently, it has to make sense. To achieve this goal, you need to pay special attention to word choice when drafting your summary. For example, are there any terms that, taken from the context of the source text, will need to be defined in your summary? Have you included in your summary any pronouns that refer to an antecedent in the source, not to an antecedent in your summary? Have you referred to people who were identified in the source but are not identified in your summary?

To make sure your summary is independent, before you turn it in for a grade let someone read it who has not read the source text. Ask that person to mark any words or passages he or she finds confusing.

HOW TO SUMMARIZE A TEXT

READ, REREAD, AND ANNOTATE THE SOURCE TEXT

Obviously, the first step in writing a summary is to read the material you are summarizing. As you read through it for the first time, try to get a sense of the passage's main ideas and structure—a sense of what the author covers and the order in which the ideas are presented. Next, read the material again, only more slowly this time. As you reread, carefully mark the passage, highlighting important material and in the margin taking notes that identify the main points and key supporting information as well as the structure of the piece.

If you are summarizing a paragraph, locate and mark the topic sentence. If there is no topic sentence, paraphrase the main point of the paragraph in the margin. If you are summarizing an entire essay or article, locate the thesis. If the author states the thesis, underline it and make a note in the margin. If the thesis is implied rather than stated, paraphrase the main point of the piece at the end of the passage. If the source text has headings and subheadings, note how they help structure the piece.

SUMMARIZE EACH SECTION OF THE SOURCE TEXT

Identify the major sections of the piece—where the author discusses one idea or develops one argument or explores one finding. These sections may consist of a single paragraph or a group of paragraphs. In the margin of the passage or on a separate sheet of paper, briefly summarize each section of the text. Using your own words, note the primary idea, assertion, or finding being developed in each section along with the primary supporting material the author provides—the most effective example, the most telling statistic, the most important authority cited.

WRITE YOUR FIRST DRAFT

As you write the first draft of your summary, keep in mind the following suggestions.

- In the **opening section** of your summary—usually the first paragraph or two—introduce the topic of the source text, give the title of the piece you are summarizing, give the name and credentials of the person who wrote the piece, and give your thesis. In a summary, your *thesis* will likely be a paraphrase of the source text's thesis. (Do not quote the source text's thesis to serve as your thesis—restate the reading's thesis in your own words.)
- In the **body** of your summary, present in your own words the author's primary assertions, conclusions, or findings, as well as the supporting examples or statistics you believe your readers will need to know to under-

stand and appreciate the author's contentions. Use as a guide the brief summaries of each section of the text you wrote earlier.

- Generally, summaries do not need a **conclusion:** simply end your essay with a summary of the author's last point. If you want or need a formal conclusion, make it a brief restatement of the author's thesis.

CHECK THE DRAFT AGAINST THE SOURCE TEXT

Once you finish your rough draft, reread the source text. Check to see if your summary is comprehensive, brief, accurate, neutral, and independent. This would be a good time to have someone else read your summary, preferably someone familiar with the source text who can offer constructive comments on your essay.

REWRITE THE SUMMARY

When you rewrite your summary, concentrate on correcting any problems with the content or tone you discovered when checking your first draft against the source text. Remember that your summary must stand on its own—it must read smoothly and make sense to someone who has not read the source text. Also, pay particular attention to the transitions you use to help guide your reader through your essay. If you are writing an explanatory summary, be sure to use narrative transitions (i.e., "first," "next," "then,"), especially at the beginning of your paragraphs, to help your reader follow the development of your summary. Next, check your paragraph breaks: while summaries of short readings may well be only one paragraph long, summaries of longer pieces will require multiple paragraphs. Finally, check to be sure your language is as objective and clear as possible. Inappropriate word choice can easily cause your essay to lose the appearance of objectivity. Also, see that you do not fall into the jargon of the source text. If you are summarizing highly technical or jargon-laden material, try to simplify the language without distorting the author's message.

DOCUMENTATION

Summarized material should be documented. Many students do not feel they need to document summaries because they are using their own language to convey the author's ideas. However, when you write a summary, you still need to give the author credit for those ideas, arguments, or findings. Documentation also tells your readers where they can locate the source text if they want to read the whole piece themselves.

SAMPLE SUMMARIES

Below are two summaries—one informative and one explanatory—of the following article, "AIDS and Population 'Control,'" by Gerard Piel, published in the February 1994 issue of *Scientific American*.

AIDS and Population "Control"

Gerard Piel

_____

Gerard Piel *is chairman emeritus of* Scientific American.

The now worldwide AIDS pandemic finds its ugliest manifestation in the proposition that AIDS has arrived in time to stop the population explosion. One hears it voiced by otherwise blameless people. Some see AIDS as the solution, in particular, for the "problem" of Africa. There the rate of population growth is highest and poverty deepest. Epidemiologists of the World Health Organization estimate that Africans constitute about 10 million of the 15 million people infected worldwide with the human immunodeficiency virus (HIV) and so fated to die of AIDS.

The AIDS proposition scants history and grossly underestimates the durability of the human species, Africans included. At its present rate of transmission, HIV will infect some 200 million people by 2010. The African share of the casualties might then approach 100 million. That, as a disciple of Thomas Malthus observed of the million Irish who perished in the 1845–50 potato famine, would scarcely be enough.

The Black Death, to which proponents of this cure for population growth hopefully compare the AIDS pandemic, carried off more than half the people of 14th-century Europe. By the middle of the 17th century, the European population had arrived at the point on the growth curve to which it would have increased by that time without deflection by the Black Death.

The paroxysm of violence that seized the industrial world through the three decades from the start of World War I to the end of World War II killed 200 million people. That was more than 10 percent of all the people who lived in those years. Their absence was not remarked in 1970, when the rate of world population growth reached its all-time peak, at around 2 percent.

It was Malthus who made economics the dismal science, but he also made this branch of moral philosophy a science. He rooted economics in what had been the unrelieved experience of humankind from the time of the agricultural revolution and the opening of the first village markets. "Apart from short exceptional periods," Alfred North Whitehead observed, "the normal structure of society was that of a comparatively affluent minority subsisting on the labors of a teeming population checked by starvation and other discomforts."

At the very time Malthus set out his baleful equation, however, industrial revolution had begun to make the growth of production outrun population. Within 20 years of Malthus's death, moreover, John Stuart Mill discovered from inspection of baptismal records that the birth rate of England had begun to decline. This discovery did not shake the conviction, which Mill shared with Malthus, that population growth was the "dynamics of political economy," for the population of prospering England was exploding.

The population of all the European countries undergoing industrial revolution was exploding during this period. Now, after this gigantic increase, which multiplied the number of Europeans 20 times over that in 1600 and avalanched them onto all continents, the populations of all the industrial countries are at or approaching zero growth. These lucky 1.25 billion people—counting the Japanese, the first non-European, in their number—are completing the so-called demographic transition. From near-zero growth in 1600 at high death rates and high birth rates with life expectancy at 25 years, they are arriving at near-zero growth again but at low death rates and low birth rates with life expectancy at 75 years.

Recent history gives every reason to expect that the other three quarters of the world population will make the demographic transition. The leading edge of industrial revolution—mass education, sanitation and primary medicine, and the green revolution—has brought down death rates and lengthened life expectancy throughout the preindustrial world. The rest of humankind has entered the first phase of the demographic transition. Hence the ongoing swelling of the population.

Entrance into the second phase is marked for some few developing countries by decline in their birth rates. These are countries where industrial revolution has proceeded furthest and where its increasing product is most widely shared—small countries like Costa Rica and Sri Lanka and also the biggest countries, India and China.

Whitehead cited India and China as "instances of civilized societies which for a very long period in their later histories maintained themselves with arrested technology.... They provided the exact conditions for the importance of the Malthusian Law." By the turn of the 19th century, when Malthus published his *Essay on Population,* they were the world's most populous countries.

Since the end of World War II, India and China have been engaged in industrial revolution, China leading. With life expectancy lengthening to 60 years in India and to 70 years in China, their huge populations have more than doubled. In both countries, calories per capita now meet the daily requirement, and potable water is available to three quarters of their citizens. India has reduced its child death rate to 142 per 1,000 live births, and China to 42. In India, 27 percent of the population lives in cities, in China, 33 percent. Literacy among the female population is 34 percent in India and 62 percent in China. Contraceptives are in use in 43 and 71 percent of their households, respectively. As these statistics suggest, both nations have entered the second phase of the demographic transition. The fertility rate in India has declined from more than six (infants per female reproductive lifetime) to four; in China it is 2.3, close to the zero growth rate of 2.1.

How to hasten the passage of the preindustrial world through the demographic transition was the principal topic before the United Nations Conference on Environment and Development, the Earth Summit, held in Rio de Janeiro in the summer of 1992. The major product of the conference, Agenda 21, is now the agenda of the United Nations. It sets out a program of "sustainable development" to bring human numbers and appetites into accord with the finite resources of the earth before the end of the next century. The AIDS pandemic can only divert physical resources and human energy from this hopeful and urgent enterprise. Delay portends a larger ultimate world population. Industrial revolution has set the terms of a morality different from that implied by the Malthusian equation. It is people living, not dying, who bring population growth to a stop.

SAMPLE INFORMATIVE SUMMARY

In "AIDS and Population 'Control,'" author Gerard Piel rejects the idea that AIDS will serve to control population growth, especially in Africa and other underdeveloped areas of the world. Piel suggests, instead, that industrialization leads countries through a "demographic transition" that results in zero population growth and greater longevity.

In the past, epidemics, wars, and natural disasters have had no long-term effect on population growth. Thomas Malthus had theorized that because the world's population would grow faster than our capacity to develop resources, such calamities were needed to curb overpopulation. However, the Industrial Revolution fundamentally changed the conditions on which Malthus based his theories. The experiences of Western Europe and Japan show that industrialization leads, at first, to a rapid rise in population as nutrition and health care improve (the "first phase" of the demographic transition) then to near-zero population growth as birth rates fall and life expectancy rises.

Today, India and China are going through such a shift. Both countries are becoming more industrialized, and their population is beginning to stabilize. Since the 1940s life expectancy has increased in both countries, child death rates have fallen, and fertility rates have declined.

The participants at the 1992 Earth Summit in Rio de Janeiro agreed that the United Nations needs to develop a plan to help newly industrial nations balance population growth and the demands on natural resources. AIDS is not a factor in controlling population growth—industrialization is (76–78).

SAMPLE EXPLANATORY SUMMARY

In "AIDS and Population 'Control,'" author Gerard Piel attacks the idea voiced by some that AIDS will serve to control rapid population growth, especially in less industrialized areas of the world such as Africa. Piel suggests, instead, that the preindustrialized world is now entering a period of "demographic transition," which the West experienced years ago, a change that will lead to zero population growth and a better quality of life for all.

Piel opens his essay by pointing out how previous epidemics, wars, and natural disasters have had no long-term effect on population growth. This fact counters the theories of Thomas Malthus, who had suggested that such calamities are needed to check population growth. Piel notes that at the time Malthus was writing, the Industrial Revolution was moving Europe into the "first phase" of a demographic transition—a period of rapid population growth generated by an equally rapid increase in the nation's ability to feed and care for its people. Following this period in Europe and Japan, birth rates fell, life expectancy rose, and near-zero population growth was achieved as these areas entered the final phase of the transition.

Piel next offers evidence that industrializing countries today are experiencing similar changes, focusing primarily on recent changes in India and China—countries Malthus used to support his earlier theories on population growth and epidemics. Since the 1940s both China and India have followed a course of steady industrialization. In both nations, life expectancy has increased (to 60 years in India, 70 years in China), child death rates have fallen, female literacy rates have increased, and fertility rates—due to more widespread use of contraceptives—have declined (from around 6 children per woman in India to about 4, and in China to 2.3). As each country has industrialized, it has also become better able to provide adequate food and water for its people, improving their quality of life.

Piel closes his essay by noting that those attending the 1992 Earth Summit in Rio de Janeiro urged the United Nations to develop programs to help developing nations reconcile their population growth and their use of natural resources. AIDS is not the key to controlling population growth, as some have suggested. Instead, Piel contends, industrialization, which leads to longer, better lives, will eventually solve the world's population problems (76–78).

Summary Chart

HOW TO WRITE A SUMMARY

1. **Read, reread, and annotate the material.**

   Carefully read the material, paying particular attention to the content and structure of the piece.

   Reread and annotate the material, being sure to note:

   - *the thesis;*
   - *the primary assertions, arguments, or findings; and*
   - *the primary means of support for each point.*

2. **Write one-sentence summaries of each section of the text.**

   Identify the major sections of the reading, in which the writer develops one idea before moving on to the next.

   In your own words, restate the main point developed in each section of the text and primary means of support the author provides.

3. **Write the first draft of your summary.**

   Introduce the topic of the reading.

   Include, early in your essay, the author's full name and the full title of the piece.

   In the body of your summary, elaborate on the one-sentence summaries, clearly explaining the important content of the reading.

4. **Check the rough draft of your summary against the source text. As you review your work, make sure your summary is:**

   Comprehensive—you have included in your summary all of the author's important ideas, assertions, or findings.

   Accurate—in choosing words and selecting material for your summary, you have not misrepresented the author's positions or findings.

   Neutral—in choosing words and selecting material for your summary, you have attempted to be objective and fair.

   Independent—your summary will make sense to someone who has not read the source text.

5. Rewrite your summary.

Based on your evaluation of your rough draft, make any needed changes in the content, organization, or language of your summary.

If you are writing an explanatory summary, include any transition words you need to guide your reader through your work.

Chapter 6

RESPONSE ESSAYS

DEFINITION AND PURPOSE

Response essays ask you to examine, explain, and often defend your personal reaction to a reading. In this type of essay you explore why you liked the reading, agreed with the author, found the piece informative or confusing—whatever your response might be. There are no necessarily "right" or "wrong" reactions to material; instead, response essays are usually evaluated on the basis of how well you demonstrate an understanding of the reading and how clearly you explain your reactions.

Sometimes teachers grade response essays the same way they grade any other assignment. Other times they assign ungraded response essays—usually as a way to help students develop material for graded essays. Still other teachers combine response essays with other types of papers; for example, they ask students to summarize then respond to a reading, or to respond to a reading then critique it. Sometimes teachers will specify which aspects of the text they would like you respond to in your essay (for example, the author's thesis or use of figurative language); other times they will leave the choice of content up to you. In short, the response essay is a very flexible assignment employed widely by teachers in college. Writing this type of paper helps you understand your personal reaction to what you read: what you think about the topic, how you judge the author's ideas, how the words on the page affect you as a reader.

Effective response essays demonstrate a strong connection between the source text and your reaction. Your responses are triggered by what you read, by certain words on the page. It is important to keep that connection strongly in mind as you compose your response essay. First, you need to put into words your responses to the source text. Second, you need to identify which words on the page triggered those responses. Third, you need to determine, then explain for your reader, why and how those words triggered those responses.

In writing this type of essay, you cannot simply state your response and move on: "I liked this. I didn't like that." "This interested me; that puzzled me." Instead, you must develop and explain your response: what, *exactly,* is your response; what part of the text triggered it; what, *exactly,* is the relationship between the words on the page and your reactions to them? While the idea of "developing" your response may seem odd, remember that you are writing for a reader, not just for yourself. You want your reader to be able to understand and appreciate both your response and what led you to have it. Clearly, writing a response essay is more difficult than it might first appear.

QUALITIES OF A GOOD RESPONSE ESSAY

Part of what makes a good response essay difficult to write is that it must be honest, informed, clear, and well supported.

- *Honest*—it reflects your true responses.
- *Informed*—it reflects an accurate and thorough understanding of the source text.
- *Clear*—it makes sense to your readers.
- *Well supported*—it demonstrates a close link between your responses and the source text itself.

HONEST

A response essay should focus on your sincere, thoughtful reactions to what you read. You want to identify your responses to the material and explore their relationship to the text itself: What gives rise to your reactions? How do they affect your reading of the author's work? These essays are highly subjective— you focus on *your* reactions to the text. Consequently, you should not pretend your responses are other than what they truly are. If you found a work boring, for example, do not claim that you found it intriguing simply because you think that is the way you are *supposed* to respond.

INFORMED

Can your responses, then, ever be "wrong"? In one sense, they cannot—your responses are your responses. That does not mean, though, that all responses to a reading are equally informed. If, for example, your response is based on a misunderstanding of the source text—if you criticize an author for saying something she never said—then your response is misguided. Responses can also be naive, shortsighted, or biased. These responses are not, in a sense, "wrong," but neither are they very insightful. Informed response essays are based on a clear understanding of the source text: the more you know about a topic, author, or reading, the more likely your response will be informed.

Take, for example, an experience I had a few years ago. I asked a group of students to respond to a satirical political essay before we discussed the piece in class. The students who recognized the satire produced fine response essays. However, the students who did not understand that the author was being satirical terribly misread the piece and produced misguided essays. Their responses were honest—the responses accurately reflected their reading of the text—but they were not informed.

CLEAR

When your readers finish your response essay, they should understand (1) how you reacted to the reading and (2) how your reactions are tied to the source text. Problems with clarity often arise from weak content, weak organization, or poor word choice.

Problems with clarity involving **content** occur when the person writing the response essay fails to state clearly the nature of his or her response, fails to identify which aspect of the source text gave rise to that response, or fails to explain the relationship between his or her response and those aspects of the text. Without all three being clearly stated and explored, readers are often left confused about the nature of your response to the reading.

Other problems with clarity involve **organization.** Be sure that your essay has a fully developed opening and closing section and a clearly stated thesis. A good response essay also explores only one reaction at a time and provides clear transitions between the various sections of the paper. Problems with clarity can occur when you shift too quickly from discussing one response to discussing another—without a good transition, the change of focus might not be clear to your reader.

Finally, problems with clarity often involve the **language** used in response essays. Too often students use vague language to explore their reactions—words that mean something to them but nothing to their readers. Though response essays are highly subjective, when you turn them in for a grade, they must be addressed to a more public audience. Good response essays can be difficult to write for just this reason: you have to find language that clearly and efficiently communicates to others your subjective responses to a reading.

WELL SUPPORTED

In good response essays, students support and explain their reactions to the text with specific, elaborated examples. If, for example, a student claims that she was offended by an author's illogical assertions, she should quote some of those passages and explain why she finds them illogical. If another student reads the same work and finds the same passages convincing because they match his experiences, he should also quote some examples and explain why he finds them convincing. In either case, the student supports her or his responses by citing from the source text examples that gave rise to them and then clearly explaining the relationship between those examples and their responses.

WRITING THE RESPONSE ESSAY

CAREFULLY READ THE MATERIAL

The problem with many response essays is that the students have not *fully* understood the source text before they begin to write. Some students respond to only part of the reading, without indicating they understand how the material fits into the author's overall thesis. As a result, their responses often seem limited or even biased; their work tends to ignore important issues raised in the source text. Other students simply misread the source text—basing their response on something the author neither wrote nor intended.

Therefore, when you are assigned to respond to a reading, read it several times and briefly summarize it before you write your essay (see Chapter 5 for advice on writing summaries). Summarizing the piece first can help ensure that your response will be based on a full and accurate understanding of the text's content, structure, tone, and thesis.

EXPLORE YOUR RESPONSES TO THE READING AS YOU ANNOTATE THE TEXT

To develop material for your response essay, as you read and annotate the text, note your responses briefly in the margin of the piece. Sometimes just jotting down a key word or two will do; other times you may need to write out a question you have. Even punctuation marks, such as exclamation points or question marks, can help you keep track of your reactions. When you are finished, expand on these notes at the end of the reading or on a separate sheet of paper. Your goal is to capture in a few sentences your overall response to what you have just read. These notes will form the basis of your response essay. In deciding what to mark and what kinds of comments to write as you read the source text, try answering the following questions.

How Do You React Emotionally to What the Author Has Written?

Your subjective, emotional reaction to a reading is a good place to start generating material for a response essay. Does the text make you angry? Excited? Bored? To explore these reactions, ask yourself several questions:

1. What, exactly, has the author written that makes you feel this way?
2. At what point in your reading did you have these reactions?
3. Which words on the page or ideas cause this response?
4. In short, what has the author done to make you respond this way? Examine the choices the writer made concerning content, organization, and style. What aspects of the text contribute to your response?

As you try to capture your responses in writing, carefully examine your reactions and, when possible, tie them to specific words, passages, or graphics in the text.

How Do the Ideas Offered in the Reading Compare with Your Experience or Your Sense of Reality?

We have all had the experience of hearing or reading something that has a ring of truth or falsehood. Something in a reading makes sense to us because it squares with our experience; it sits right with what we have come to understand about the world. As you reread and annotate a reading, note which of the author's ideas you tend to agree with or question based on their match to your own experience.

There is a real danger, though, in judging what others say by the standards of our experience alone. All of us bring to a reading important but limited experiences. When an author's statements do not match our sense of reality, we should not act defensively and immediately dismiss her ideas. Likewise, simply because we tend to agree with an author does not mean we ought to accept her ideas uncritically. Writing a response essay will give you the chance to question what you believe in light of what the author writes, to understand how your experiences influence the way you react to new ideas.

How Do the Ideas Offered in the Source Match What Others Have Had to Say on the Topic?

When you read a source, you bring with you not only what you think and feel based on your own experience, but also what you know, what you have already learned from your reading and education. There is no reason to ignore this knowledge when you write your response essay. In fact, whether the source text confirms or contradicts what you already know about the topic may be one of the reasons for your reaction to the piece. Be sure to note any reactions you have based on the match between the author's ideas and those proposed by other authors you have read.

COMPOSE YOUR ROUGH DRAFT

When you write your response essay, you will need to introduce the source text, provide your reader with a brief summary of its content, then develop and clarify your reactions.

Introduce the Source Text and Give Your Thesis

When composing the opening of your response essay, you should introduce the topic of the source text, identify the title of the piece and its author, and state your thesis. A general strategy you might employ to begin your response is first to introduce the topic of the reading. Next, somewhere in the beginning of your essay you should give the full name of the author whose work you are examining along with the exact title of the source text. Your thesis for this type of essay will be a statement of your overall response to the reading, whether you found the piece "convincing," "informative," "enjoyable," "confusing," or some combination of reactions.

Summarize the Source Text

After introducing the source and stating your thesis, give a brief summary of the reading. Generally, this summary will be only a paragraph or two long, highlighting the reading's most important findings, conclusions, or arguments. In the summary, anticipate what you will address in the body of your response. For example, if you know you will be questioning the validity of some of the author's claims, summarize his claims in this part of your essay. When they come up again in the body of your response, your reader will likely remember them and will be able to follow your assertions more easily.

State and Explain Your Responses Clearly and Concisely

In the body of your essay, you explore your responses, clearly and thoroughly, one at a time. This process might sound simple, but clearly and thoroughly stating and explaining your response to a reading can be difficult primarily because it is *your* response. The language you use when describing your reaction may make perfect sense to you but might well be unclear to your reader. For instance, if you were reading someone else's response essay and the writer complained that the source text made her feel "wheezy," would you really know what the person meant? Perhaps her explanation would make it clear, but the language she uses to characterize her response may hinder her readers' ability to understand her reaction. Therefore, a first step in clarifying your response for a reader is to choose language that others can understand. Likewise, explain the terms you use. For example, if you contend that a source is confusing, explain what you mean by "confusing"— that is, whether you had difficulty understanding the writer's language, findings, structure, or some other aspect of the text.

Next, be sure to provide specific examples from the source text to help your reader understand each response. When you have a particular response to a reading, something on the page triggered it. In your essay, identify those "triggering" passages before you explain the dynamics of your response. For example, if you contend that a source text is confusing, identify and perhaps quote a passage you cannot understand, then explain what it is about the writing you find difficult to follow (the logic of the passage? the wording? the structure?).

REVISE YOUR ROUGH DRAFT

As you revise the rough draft of your response, pay particular attention to your assertions, organization, language, and support.

Review Your Assertions

When you review the assertions you make in your response essay, your primary concern is accuracy:

- Have you truly captured your reactions to the reading?
- Have you openly, honestly, and thoroughly explored your response to the material?
- Does your essay offer an accurate representation of your reaction?
- When other people read your essay, will they be able to understand and appreciate your reaction?

To check your assertions, first reread the source text and see whether you still feel the same way about it. Even a short time away from a reading may enable you to reconsider your reactions—maybe your views have changed. If they have changed, revise your essay. Also, in reviewing the source text, be sure you reread the annotations you originally made. Have you addressed the concerns, questions, and reactions you noted as you earlier annotated the piece?

Review Your Support and Explanations

As you revise your response, examine the way you illustrate and explain each of your responses. Remember that your responses should be tied to specific aspects of the source text, such as words, images, and graphics. When you compose your response, you need to explain for your reader the link between the source text and your reaction. In the body of your essay, you should state a response, point out what aspect of the reading led to that reaction (perhaps quoting the passage), then explain clearly and thoroughly how that material led you to that response. As you revise your draft, make sure you accomplish all three goals in each section of your essay.

Review Your Organization

Next, when you review the organization of your rough draft, check to be sure you have fully developed opening and closing sections and have a clearly stated thesis. In the body of your essay, be sure that you are developing only one response at a time. Often when you write your rough draft, examining one reaction will lead you to a new response, one you have not previously considered. That is one of the real powers of writing: it not only helps you capture ideas in words but often will help you generate new ideas as well. When this happens, some writers will follow that new idea even if it does not belong in that part of the essay, knowing that in the next draft they can place it elsewhere. Other writers prefer to write a note to themselves to explore that new idea later, not wanting to lose track of the idea they are currently exploring. When you review your rough draft, check to see that you are developing only one response at a time in your essay.

Finally, be sure you indicate to your reader—through paragraph breaks and transition words—when you shift focus from one response to the next. Adding these signals to your paper makes it easier for your reader to follow your line of thought. Since you are writing about *your* responses, you know when you have changed focus; your readers, though, may have a harder time recognizing the structure of your essay. Adding appropriate paragraph breaks and transitions can help.

Review Your Language

As indicated earlier, word choice—finding and choosing appropriate terms to express your reactions—can be truly problematic when you are writing response essays. First, your initial reactions to what you read may be so emotional or so abstract that you cannot put them into words. You may struggle to find appropriate language. Second, your first efforts at finding words may result in highly "private" writing; since they arise from your own knowledge and experience, the terms you use may make sense only to you. In this case, you need to find terms that can communicate your responses to others. Before you turn in the final draft of your response essay, be sure to have someone else read your work, someone you trust to give you an honest appraisal of your language. Ask that person to indicate any part of the response he or she does not understand because of the words you are using.

SAMPLE RESPONSE ESSAY

This sample essay is responding to the article "AIDS and Population 'Control' " by Gerard Piel found in Chapter 5 of this book. If you are unfamiliar with the article, read it before you read the following response essay.

A Response to "AIDS and Population 'Control' "

Overall, I found the argument presented in "AIDS and Population 'Control' " interesting and informative. Author Gerard Piel presents a clear thesis and supports it well with logical examples and sound reasoning. However, I also found parts of the essay confusing, especially some of the allusions, which makes me wonder about the intended audience of the piece.

"AIDS and Population 'Control'" examines the claim advanced by some that AIDS will serve as a check on population. Piel rejects this idea, pointing out that past epidemics have had little long-term effect on population growth. Instead, he believes that industrial development curbs overpopulation. Citing the experiences of Europe and Japan as examples, Piel puts forward the idea that as countries industrialize and improve their standard of living, birth rates fall and life expectancy rises. As a result, industrialized nations reach near-zero population growth. Piel claims such a process is now occurring in countries such as China and India— industrialization, he claims, controls population, not diseases such as AIDS.

Generally, I found Piel's argument convincing. First, he offers several examples to support his contention that famine and disease have little effect on population growth. For example, Piel points out that Europe overcame the effects of the Black Death in three centuries and that all the death and destruction associated with the two world wars again had a negligible effect on population growth. By 1970 the world's population was growing at a record pace (76). I thought these specific examples clarified Piel's position and added credibility to his thesis: he is relying on historical facts that can be verified.

His examination of industrialization and population was also interesting, but I found it more difficult to follow. For example, he refers repeatedly to the "second phase" of the "demographic shift" without fully explaining what a "demographic shift" is and without explaining how many "phases" are involved in such a phenomenon.

More informative was the analogy Piel draws between the experiences of Europe and Japan and the current condition of India and China (77–78). I know the history of Europe more thoroughly than I know the history of India and China—the comparisons he draws give me some context for understanding what is happening in the lands and cultures I know less well. Particularly compelling was his use of specific statistics—on child death rates, life expectancy rates, and fertility rates. These figures bring into sharp focus and make more concrete the current state of affairs in these countries (especially the fact that China's current fertility rate is 2.3 children per woman with 2.1 representing zero population growth) (78). What is missing, though, are some comparison figures. How have these figures changed over the past few decades? How do they currently compare to European or Japanese figures? Without more of a context, the figures Piel provides are not as effective and informative as they could be.

I had more trouble with some of Piel's allusions. He refers frequently to the work of Thomas Malthus and twice cites the words of Alfred North Whitehead. I think readers unfamiliar with the theories proposed by Malthus (that population growth will outstrip our means of production) would have a hard time following Piel's argument. I wonder what type of reader Piel had in mind when he wrote this piece. He obviously assumes his audience is well read, that they are familiar with Malthus's ideas and with European history. Readers who understand Piel's allusions will get the most out of his work. However, even if they do not catch all the references, they will still come away with a clear idea of how industrialization might affect population growth far more than will AIDS.

Summary Chart

HOW TO WRITE A RESPONSE ESSAY

1. **Carefully read the material.**

   Your goal is to form a clear understanding of what the writer has to say.

   Identify and be able to paraphrase the writer's thesis and main assertions or findings.

2. **Reread and annotate the text.**

   As you reread the material, begin to examine your responses by asking yourself the following questions:

   - *How do I react emotionally to what the author has written?*
   - *How do the ideas offered in the source text match my experience and my sense of reality?*
   - *How do the ideas offered in the text match what others have had to say about the topic?*

   Note in the margin your responses to these questions using some combination of the following:

   - *key words*
   - *questions*
   - *statements*
   - *punctuation marks*

   When you are finished, write out in a few sentences your response to the material.

3. **Compose your rough draft.**

   Introduce the topic, your source text, and the full name of the author or authors.

   Summarize the source text.

   State and explain your responses clearly and concisely one at a time.

   - *State your response.*
     For example, the material made you angry.
   - *Explain the terms you are using.*
     What do you mean by "angry"?

- *Tie that response to some aspect of the source text.*
  What material in the reading made you feel that way?

- *Explain how that material gave rise to that response.*
  Why or how did that material make you feel angry?

4. Revise your rough draft.

Review your assertions about your reactions.

- *Are they honest?*
- *Are they informed?*
- *Are they clear?*
- *Are they well supported?*

Review your organization.

- *Are your opening and closing sections constructed well?*
- *Are you addressing one response at a time?*
- *Are there clear transitions between the responses you explore?*
- *Are your responses tied to some guiding thesis?*

Review your language.

- *Are you using terms your readers are likely to understand?*
- *Are you invoking a consistent tone, not becoming too informal, too angry, or too satiric when that does not match the tone of your response as a whole?*

Review your support.

- *Have you tied each response to some aspect of the text?*
- *Have you added enough textual references to make clear the connections between the reading and your response?*
- *Have you attempted to explain those connections?*

Chapter 7

CRITIQUE

DEFINITION AND PURPOSE

While response essays focus on your personal reactions to a reading, critiques offer a more formal evaluation. Instead of responding to a reading in light of your experience and feelings, in a critique you evaluate a source text's quality or worth according to a set of established criteria. Based on your evaluation, you then assert some judgment concerning the text—whether the reading was effective, ineffective, valuable, or trivial. Critiques, then, are usually argumentative. Your goal is to convince your readers to accept your judgments concerning the quality of the reading.

These judgments will be based on certain criteria and standards. **Criteria** are certain aspects of a reading that serve as the basis of your assessment—for example, the text's style or use of evidence. **Standards** serve as the basis for evaluating a criterion—what makes a certain "style" good or bad, acceptable or unacceptable? What counts as "valid" evidence in a reading? When you critique a reading, you will employ either **general** academic criteria and standards (those used to evaluate source material in many fields) or **discipline-specific** criteria and standards (those used by scholars in a particular field of study and generally not applicable to material studied in other disciplines).

In college composition courses you may learn how to critique a source text using general evaluative criteria—for example, how to assess the quality of a reading based on its structure, style, or evidence. These criteria can help you evaluate source material in a variety of classes. In your other college courses you may learn discipline-specific evaluative criteria typically used to assess source material in that field of study. For example, in an English literature course you may learn the criteria used by scholars to critique a poem or a play; in an accounting class, you may learn to employ the criteria and standards experts in that discipline use to critique a financial report or prospectus.

Students often find the idea of writing a critique intimidating: they are not sure what the assignment is asking them to do, how to generate material for their paper, what to include in their essay, how to support their assertions, or what tone to assume. However, you are probably more familiar with this type of writing than you realize since you are often exposed to one special form of critique: the movie review. If you ever listened to Siskel and Ebert argue over a film, you are familiar with the basic structure of a critique. If you ever discussed the strengths and weaknesses of a movie and tried to get a friend to go see it (or to avoid it), then you have already engaged in critique. Examining how a film critic writes a review of a movie can help you understand how to write a critique of a reading.

THE FILM REVIEW AS CRITIQUE

First, consider the nature of a movie critic's job: he watches a film, analyzes and evaluates what he sees, forms some judgment based on that analysis and evaluation, then writes his review, trying to clarify and defend his judgments with specific references to the film and clear explanations of his assertions. In writing his review, the critic does not address every aspect of the film; he addresses only those aspects of the movie that best support his judgment of it. If, for instance, he thought a film was wonderful, he would address in his review only the aspects of the film that, in his opinion, made it exceptional—for example, the direction, the photography, and the acting. If he thought the film was uneven—some parts good, other parts weak—he would offer in his review examples of what made the film effective (maybe the plot or the lighting) and examples of what made it ineffective (maybe the musical score and the special effects).

Think about the way you discuss a film with someone. Maybe the conversation runs something like this:

> "So, did you like the movie?"
>
> "Yeah, pretty much. I wasn't too sure about some of the dialogue—sounded pretty lame sometimes—but the special effects were good and the acting was ok."
>
> "The acting was just 'ok'? What didn't you like? I thought the acting was great."
>
> "Well, there was that scene early in the film, right before he shot the guy; I just didn't buy it when he…"

In this conversation, one friend asserts a position about the film, is challenged, then begins to defend or explain her view. To convince her friend to accept her judgment, she will likely discuss specific aspects of the film she believes best illustrate her views.

Most of us are accustomed to talking about movies, television shows, or CDs this way—we form and defend judgments about what we see, hear, and read all the time. However, we are usually more comfortable evaluating movies than we are critiquing arguments, book chapters, or lab reports. First, when it comes to movies, we are probably familiar with many of the source texts—we have seen lots of films—and most of us feel we can knowledgeably discuss what we have seen; we can generate, fairly easily, lots of examples from a movie to support our views. Second, we know *how* to talk about films: we know how to identify and discuss particular aspects of a movie—certain criteria—that influence our judgment. We know that when we analyze a movie we can address the dialogue, the acting, the special effects, and so forth. Finally, we know the standards usually applied to evaluate various aspects of a film; we know what passes for good dialogue, good acting, good special effects, and so on. In short, when we discuss a movie, we know how to *analyze* it (what parts to focus on for review), *evaluate* it (what kinds of questions to ask of each part when assessing its quality), and *defend* our assertions (how to examine specific scenes from the film that support our judgments).

These are the same basic skills you employ to critique readings in college. To critique readings, you need to engage in:

- *Analysis*—break readings down into their essential parts.
- *Evaluation*—assess the quality of those various parts.
- *Explanation*—link your judgments to specific aspects of the readings and make those connections clear and convincing to your reader.

Even though you have probably engaged in this process quite often when discussing movies or television shows, you may have a hard time using these skills to critique readings. First, you are probably less familiar with how critiques look and sound than you are with how movie reviews look and sound. When you are assigned to write a critique, no model may come to mind. Second, the readings you are asked to critique in college can be hard to understand. You cannot critique a reading until you are certain you know what it has to say. Finally, you are probably less familiar with the criteria and standards used in college to analyze and critique readings than you are with the criteria and standards used to review films. When you are asked to critique a philosophical essay on the nature of knowledge, do you know how to break that reading down into its key parts and what kinds of questions to ask of each part to determine its quality? When asked to critique a chapter of your history book, do you know what to look for, what questions to ask? Learning how to critique readings such as these is a central goal of your college education, a skill you will obtain through practice in many different disciplines.

Examining how a movie critic organizes a review can also help you understand how to structure a critique. For example, a critic typically opens her review with a "thesis" that captures her overall assessment of the film. This thesis may take the form of a statement early in the review, a graphic placed beside the review—for example, five stars or two stars—or frequently a comment at the end of the review. Sometimes the critic will love the film; she will give it five stars and a rave review. Sometimes she will hate the movie; she will give it one star and a terrible review. Still other times she will have a split decision; she will give it two and a half stars and in her review acknowledge the strengths and weaknesses of the movie. Next, the critic will typically offer a brief summary of the film so her readers can follow what she has to say in the review. Then, in the body of the review, she will address only the aspects of the film that best illustrate or defend her thesis: she will introduce a particular element of the film (for example, the special effects), comment on its quality (claim they were especially effective), describe a specific example or two from the film (perhaps the climactic battle scene), and explain how that specific example illustrates or supports her judgment (what made the special effects in that battle scene especially good).

Writing a critique involves much the same process. After reading the text, you'll form a judgment of its quality or worth based on some set of criteria and standards. This judgment will form the thesis of your critique, which you will explain or defend in the body of your essay, with specific references to the reading. As you draft your thesis, keep in mind the range of judgments open to the film critic. To critique a reading does not necessarily mean only to criticize it. If you honestly think a reading is weak, based on your evaluation of its various parts, then say so in your thesis. If, however, you think the writing is quite strong, say that. If your judgments fall somewhere in the middle—some parts are strong while others are weak—reflect *that* in your thesis. Your thesis should reflect your carefully considered opinion of the reading's overall quality or worth, whatever that judgment may be.

Next, you will offer a brief summary of the text so your reader can follow what you later have to say about the piece. In the body of your critique, you will choose for examination only the parts of the reading that best illustrate or defend your thesis: you will introduce a particular aspect of the reading (for example, its use of statistical evidence), describe a specific example or two from the reading (perhaps the way statistics are used to support the author's second argument), and explain how that specific example illustrates or supports your judgment (what makes the statistical evidence especially compelling in this section of the text).

Your goal, then, in writing a critique mirrors in many ways the goal you would have in writing a movie review. Your task is to analyze and evaluate a reading according to a set of established criteria and standards, pass judgment on the reading's quality or worth, then assert, explain, and defend that judgment with specific references to the reading.

WRITING A CRITIQUE

Writing a critique typically involves five steps:

1. Read and annotate the text.
2. Analyze and evaluate the piece: break it down into its primary parts and judge the quality of each part.
3. Write your thesis and decide which aspects of the reading you will focus on in your essay.
4. Compose your rough draft.
5. Rewrite your critique.

This is only a general guide. Throughout college you will learn much more specific, specialized ways to critique readings.

STEP I—CAREFULLY READ AND ANNOTATE THE SOURCE TEXT

Before you start to write a critique, you first need to develop a clear understanding of the reading you are about to analyze and evaluate. The material you read in college is often challenging; you have to work hard to understand exactly what the author is asserting. However, this work is unavoidable: it makes little sense to evaluate a piece of writing when you are not completely sure what point the author is attempting to make. As you annotate a reading for a critique, keep in mind the following suggestions.

Note the Author's Thesis, Primary Assertions, and Primary Means of Support

Be sure that you mark the author's thesis, highlight and summarize each major point the author makes, and highlight and summarize how the author supports each idea, argument, or finding. Are the thesis and primary assertions clearly stated? Does the thesis direct the development of the paper? Are the assertions supported?

Note the Author's Use of Graphics, Headings, and Subheadings

What graphics does the author provide? What are their function? How do the headings and subheadings organize the piece? Are the headings and graphics effective? How so?

Note the Author's Diction and Word Choice

Consider the kind of language the writer is employing. Is it formal or informal? Is it overly technical? Is it appropriate? Do you notice any shifts in diction? Are some sections of the text more complicated or jargon laden than others? Note any strengths or weaknesses you see in the author's language.

Note the Author's Tone

What seems to be the author's attitude toward the topic? Is he being serious, comical, or satiric? Does the tone seem appropriate, given the writer's topic and thesis? Are there any places in the text where the tone shifts? Is the shift effective?

Note the Author's Audience

When you finish the piece, determine what the writer seemed to assume about his or readers. For example, is the writer addressing someone who knows something about the topic or someone likely reading about it for the first time? Is the author assuming readers agree or disagree with the position being forwarded in the piece? Judging from the content, organization, diction, and tone of the piece, which type of reader would tend to accept the author's position and which would tend to reject it?

Note the Author's Purpose

Decide, in your own mind, the primary aim of the piece. Is the author attempting to entertain, inform, or persuade readers? Where in the text has the author attempted to achieve this aim? How successful are those attempts? Note at the beginning or end of the reading your comments concerning the author's purpose.

Summarize the Piece

After you have read and studied the text, write a brief summary of the piece, either at the end of the reading or on a separate sheet of paper (see Chapter 5 for tips on summarizing a reading).

When you have finished reading, rereading, and annotating the source text, you should have a clear understanding of its content, organization, purpose, and audience. Try to clear up any questions you have about the reading before you attempt to critique it. You want your critique to be based on a thorough and clear understanding of the source text.

STEP 2—ANALYZE AND EVALUATE THE READING

Think back to the process of putting together a movie review. When a movie critic watches a film, she forms a judgment of its quality based on certain things she sees or hears. As she watches the movie, she will examine and judge certain aspects of the film, including its:

acting	scenery	lighting
direction	costuming	plot
special effects	dialogue	action
theme	pacing	makeup
cinematography	stunts	music

Her evaluation of these various elements of the film—either positive or negative—will form her overall judgment of the movie, her thesis.

What, then, should you look for when analyzing a reading, what parts of a text should you be isolating for evaluation as you read and reread the piece? In part, the answer depends on the course you are taking: each discipline has generally agreed-on ways of analyzing a reading. As you take courses in anthropology or physical education, you will learn how experts in those fields analyze readings. However, analyzing certain general aspects of a reading can help you better understand material in a wide variety of classes. Regardless of the course you are taking, you might start to analyze a reading by identifying its:

- thesis and primary assertions or findings,
- evidence and reasoning,
- organization, and
- style.

Once you have analyzed a reading, isolating for consideration its essential elements, your next task in writing a critique is to evaluate the quality of each element. Here, writing a critique differs from writing a response essay. In a response essay, your goal is to articulate your personal, subjective reaction to what you have read. In a critique, though, you are expected to evaluate the reading according to an established set of standards. Think about the movie critic's job again. Most reviewers employ similar criteria and standards when evaluating a film. If a reviewer decides to critique the musical score of a film, she knows the types of evaluative questions one usually asks about this aspect of a movie: How did the music contribute to the overall mood of the film? Was it too intrusive? Did it add humor or depth to the scenes? Did it heighten drama? Was it noteworthy because of the performers who recorded it? Her answers to these questions will lead to her final assessment of this particular aspect of the film. (Of course, another reviewer employing the same criteria and applying the same standards could come to a different judgment concerning the quality of the music in the film; for example, one reviewer might think it heightened the drama in a particular scene while another might think that it did not.)

In college, you will quickly discover that the criteria and standards used to evaluate readings vary from discipline to discipline. Teachers often employ evaluative criteria unique to their field of study, especially in upper-level courses in which the professor is preparing students to enter a profession. In lower-level courses designed to introduce you to a field of study, you may encounter a different sort of problem. Teachers in different fields may be asking you to employ the same or similar criteria, but their standards are very different. Suppose, for example, you are asked to evaluate the style of a particular reading in both an education and an English course. Your job is the same—determine, stylistically, whether this is a well-written essay. Your answer might be different in each class.

According to the stylistic standards advocated by the school of education, you might have before you a well-written essay; according to the standards advocated by the English department, though, the same piece of writing might not fare so well. As always, work closely with your teacher when evaluating a reading to be sure you are applying an appropriate set of criteria and standards.

Below are a series of questions you can ask to begin your analysis and evaluation of a reading's thesis, assertions, evidence, reasoning, organization, and style. They are meant to serve only as general guidelines. Your teacher may have much more specific questions he would like you to ask of a reading or evaluative criteria he would like you to employ. Together, analysis and evaluation enable you to critique a reading. After breaking a reading into its essential parts and judging their effectiveness, you will form the thesis of your critique—a judgment of the reading's quality or worth—which you will develop and defend in your essay.

Analyzing and Evaluating a Reading's Thesis and Primary Assertions or Findings

Sometimes identifying an author's thesis can be relatively easy—you can point to a specific sentence or two in the text. Other times, though, an author will not state his thesis. Instead, the thesis is implied: some controlling idea is directing the development of the piece even though the author never puts it into words. If this is the case, you will need to identify and paraphrase this controlling idea yourself and evaluate it as if it were the thesis.

Many times, identifying the author's primary assertions or findings can be easy, too. For example, if the author has made effective use of paragraph breaks, topic sentences, headings, or graphics, you can usually locate his primary assertions fairly easily. However, do not rely on these means alone to identify the author's main ideas. Not every source text is well written. Often, important assertions get buried in an article; key findings may be glossed over. As you analyze a reading, make up your own mind about its primary assertions or findings independently of what the author may assume to be the case. Also, be sure to distinguish between primary assertions and their evidence or support. Very often a student will identify as a primary argument of a reading some statistic or quotation that the author is using only as a piece of evidence, something to support the actual assertion he is trying to make. In short, to analyze a reading's thesis and primary assertions, consider the following questions:

- What is the author's thesis? Is it stated or unstated? If stated, highlight it; if unstated, paraphrase it.
- What are the primary assertions in the reading? Highlight each one and paraphrase it in the margin of the text.
- What is the primary means of support offered to illustrate or defend each assertion? Again, highlight this material.

In determining the quality of a reading's thesis and primary assertions or findings, you can begin by questioning their clarity, effectiveness, and organization. The thesis, whether stated or implied, should direct the development of the piece. Each major finding or assertion should be clearly stated and linked to that thesis through the effective use of transitions, repetition of key terms, or headings. To evaluate an author's thesis and findings, you might begin by asking the following questions. If your answers are positive, you can likely claim that the author has effectively presented and developed his thesis; if your answers are negative, be sure to articulate exactly where the problems exist.

- Is the thesis clearly stated? Does it control the organization of the piece? Is it consistently held or does the author shift positions in the essay?
- If the thesis is implied rather than stated, does it still serve to direct the organization of the piece? Are you able to paraphrase a comprehensive thesis on your own, or does the material included in the piece preclude that?
- Are the author's assertions or findings clearly stated?
- Are the author's assertions or findings somehow tied to the thesis?

Analyzing and Evaluating a Reading's Evidence and Reasoning

Here you identify two separate, but related, aspects of a reading: (1) the evidence an author provides to support or illustrate her assertions and (2) the author's reasoning process or line of argument.

First, try to identify the types of **evidence** the author uses to support her thesis. (At this point do not try to evaluate the effectiveness of the evidence—that comes later.) The types of evidence used to support a thesis vary greatly in academic writing, so again be cautious when using these guidelines to analyze the readings in any particular course. However, to begin your analysis of the evidence an author employs, you might try asking yourself this series of questions:

- In supporting her assertions or findings, what kinds of evidence has the author employed? Has the author used any of these forms of evidence:

statistics	empirical data	precedent
expert testimony	emotional appeals	case histories
personal experience	historical analysis	analogies

- Where in the article is each type of evidence employed?
- Is there a pattern? Are certain types of evidence used to support certain types of claims?
- Where has the author combined forms of evidence as a means of support?

Analyzing an author's **reasoning process** is more difficult because it is more abstract. First, you identify how the author uses evidence to support her thesis and how she develops and explains her ideas, her line of reasoning. Second, you examine the assumptions an author makes concerning her topic and readers. As she wrote the piece, which aspects of the text did she decide needed more development than others? Which terms needed clarification? Which argument or explanation needed the most support? In analyzing the author's reasoning process, these are the kinds of questions you might ask:

- In what order are the ideas, arguments, or findings presented?
- What are the logical connections between the major assertions being made in the piece? How does one idea lead to the next?
- What passages in the text explain these connections?
- What assumptions about the topic or the reader is the author making?
- Where in the text are these assumptions articulated, explained, or defended?

Standards used to assess the quality of an author's evidence and reasoning will vary greatly across the disciplines. For example, you might want to determine whether an author offers "adequate" support for his or her thesis. However, what passes for adequate support of a claim will be quite different in an English class from what it will be in a physics course or a statistics course: these fields of study each look at "evidence" and the notion of "adequacy" very differently. In other words, a good general strategy to employ when critiquing a reading is to determine the adequacy of its evidence; however, how that strategy is implemented and what conclusions you reach employing it can vary depending on the course you are taking. Part of learning any subject matter is coming to understand how scholars in that field evaluate evidence; therefore, answer the following questions thoughtfully:

- Does the author support her contentions or findings?
- Is this support adequate? Does the author offer enough evidence to support her contentions?
- Is the evidence authoritative? Does it come from legitimate sources? Is it current?
- Does the author explain *how* the evidence supports or illustrates her assertions?
- Has the author ignored evidence or alternative hypotheses or explanations for the evidence she offers?
- In developing her position, are there any problems with unstated assumptions? Does the author assume something to be the case that she needs to clarify or defend?
- Are there problems with logical fallacies such as hasty generalizations, false dilemmas, or appeals to false authorities?
- Has the author addressed the ethical implications of her position?
- Is the author's reasoning a notable strength in the piece? Is it clear and convincing?

Your answers to these questions will help you determine whether there are serious problems with the evidence and reasoning employed in the reading.

Analyzing and Evaluating a Reading's Organization

Here you want to identify how the author orders the material contained in the reading. As the author develops a set of findings or ideas, lays out his reasoning for the reader, offers examples and explanations, what comes first? Second? Third? How has the author attempted to mold these parts into a coherent whole? When analyzing the organization of a reading, you might begin by considering the following questions:

- In what order are the ideas or findings presented?
- How has the author indicated that he is moving from a discussion of one point to the discussion of another point?
- What is the relationship between the thesis of the piece (stated or unstated) and the order in which the assertions or findings are presented?
- How has the author tried to help the reader understand the organization of the reading? Identify where in the text the author has used any of the following to help guide his readers through the text:

headings and subheadings	repetition of key terms
transition words or phrases	repetition of language from the thesis
transition paragraphs	repetition of names or titles

If any aspect of a reading's organization makes it difficult for you to understand the author's message, you may want to examine it in your critique. Clearly explain the nature of the problem and how it damages the reading's effectiveness. Likewise, if the organization is especially strong, if it significantly enhances the reading's clarity or effectiveness, you can point that out in your critique and explain how it helps the text. Here are some questions to consider when evaluating the source text's organization:

- Is there a clear connection between the major assertions of the essay? Does there seem to be some reason why one idea precedes or follows another?
- Are all the assertions clearly related to the overall thesis of the piece?
- Has the author provided headings or subheadings to help readers follow his line of thought? How effective are they?
- Has the author provided adequate transitions to help readers move through the writing and see the logical connection between the assertions he is making? How effective are they?

Analyzing and Evaluating a Reading's Style

Stylistic analysis is a complicated process, an academic specialty in and of itself within the field of English studies. In most of your college courses, though, when analyzing style you will likely focus on issues of clarity and convention. First, when you critique a reading, you might comment on its clarity. You will want to identify which aspects of the writer's word choice and sentence structure help you understand what she has to say or which serve to complicate your reading of the text. Other times, you may ask a different set of questions concerning style, especially in upper-division courses. Your assignment will be to assess how well an author adheres to the stylistic conventions of a discipline. For example, you might explore whether the author's language, tone, and syntax are appropriate for a particular type of writing or field of study. To begin your analysis of style, here are some questions you might ask about a reading:

- What level of diction is the writer employing (how formal is the prose)?

  formal?   conversational?
  informal? a mixture?

  Identify which words or passages lead you to this conclusion.
- What is the tone of the piece (what is the author's apparent attitude toward the topic)?

  serious?   satiric? involved?
  humorous? angry?   detached?

  Identify which words or passages lead you to this conclusion.
- What kind of language is used in the piece? Identify any passages using specialized language, emotional language, or jargon.
- What types of sentences are used in the reading?

  simple, compound, complex, complex-compound?
  long or short?
  active or passive?
  a mixture of types?

When critiquing a reading's style, you evaluate elements of the author's prose such as diction, tone, word choice, and syntax. Again, stylistic standards vary greatly across the disciplines. While teachers in various disciplines may use similar terms when describing "good" style in writing—that it should be clear and concise, for example—how they define their criteria is likely to vary. Clear and concise writing in a chemistry lab report may have little in common, stylistically, with clear and concise writing in a philosophy research report. Below are some questions that might help you begin to evaluate certain aspects of an author's style. Remember, though, that your answers may well depend on the stylistic standards accepted by a particular discipline:

- How would you characterize the diction of the piece: formal, informal, or somewhere in the middle? Is it consistently maintained? Is it appropriate? Does it contribute to the effectiveness of the piece?
- How would you characterize the tone of the piece? Is it inviting, satiric, or humorous? Is it appropriate, given the topic and intent of the piece? Does the tone enhance or damage the effect of the writing?
- Is the author's word choice clear and effective? Or does the writer rely too heavily on jargon, abstractions, or highly technical terms?

- Is the author's word choice needlessly inflammatory or emotional? Or do the words convey appropriate connotations?
- Are the sentences clearly written? Are any of the sentences so poorly structured that the source is difficult to read and understand?
- Are the sentence types varied? Is the syntax appropriate given the audience and intent of the piece?

STEP 3—WRITE YOUR THESIS AND DECIDE WHICH ASPECTS OF THE READING WILL BE THE FOCUS OF YOUR ESSAY

At this point you need to develop your thesis and decide which aspects of the reading you will use to develop your critique. To formulate your thesis, you need to decide which elements of the source text best illustrate or defend your judgment. You want your reader to understand and accept your thesis, but this acceptance can come about only if you clearly explain each claim you make about the reading and offer convincing examples from the text to illustrate and defend your contentions.

In your critique, you do not need to address every aspect of the source text. Remember how the movie critic supports her assertions about a film. No review addresses every aspect of a movie. Instead, the critic chooses to discuss in her review only those elements of the movie she thinks most clearly and effectively illustrate her judgment. Maybe she will address only the acting and direction, perhaps only the dialogue, plot, and special effects. Perhaps she will choose to mention, only briefly, the costuming and musical score, then concentrate more attention on the film's cinematography.

Follow the same line of thinking when you decide which aspects of the reading to address in your critique. To illustrate and defend your thesis, you may choose to look only at the logic of the piece and its structure. However, you may choose to ignore both of these and concentrate, instead, on the writer's style. Maybe you will decide to look briefly at the evidence the author offers, then concentrate most of your attention on the organization of the piece. Your decisions should be based on two fairly simple questions: (1) Which aspects of the reading most influenced your judgment of its quality and worth? and (2) Which aspects will best illustrate and support your thesis? Choose only those aspects of the reading for examination in your critique.

Your thesis in a critique is a brief statement of what you believe to be the overall value or worth of the source text based on your analysis and evaluation of its parts. In stating your thesis, you have several options. You can say only positive things about the reading, only negative things, or some mixture of the two. Your main concern at this point is that your thesis honestly and accurately reflects your judgment.

Also, your thesis statement can be either open or closed. In an open thesis statement, you offer your overall judgment of the piece and nothing else. In a thesis statement you offer your judgment and indicate which aspects of the [readin]g you will examine when developing your essay. Below are some sample [open] and closed thesis statements for a critique—positive, negative, and mixed.

Positive Thesis Statement

Open

Jones presents a clear, convincing argument in favor of increased funding for the school district.

Closed

Through his use of precise examples and his accessible style, Jones presents a clear and convincing argument in favor of increased funding for the school district.

Negative Thesis Statement

Open

Jones's argument in favor of increased funding is not convincing.

Closed

Because there are numerous lapses in reasoning and problems with the organization, Jones's argument in favor of increased funding is not convincing.

Mixed Thesis Statement

Open

Though uneven in its presentation, Jones's argument in favor of increased funding for the school district is, finally, convincing.

Closed

Even though there are some problems with the organization Jones employs in his report, his use of expert testimony makes his argument for increased funding for the schools ultimately convincing.

STEP 4—WRITE YOUR ROUGH DRAFT

While there are many ways to structure a critique, the suggestions that follow can serve as a general guide.

Introductory Section

- Introduce the topic of the reading.
- Give the title of the piece and the name of its author.
- Give your thesis.
- Summarize the source text.

In the opening section of your critique you should introduce the topic of the reading and give your reader its exact title and the full name of its author. You will also include here your thesis and a brief summary of the reading (one or two paragraphs long). The exact order you choose to follow when covering this material is up to you. Some writers like to begin with the summary of the source text before giving their thesis; some prefer to give their thesis first. Overall, though, your introductory section should only be two or three paragraphs long.

Body

- Examine one element of the reading at a time.
- Cite specific examples of this element from the reading.
- Explain your evaluation of each example you offer.

State the Criteria and Your Judgments

In the body of your critique you will explain and defend the judgment you made in your thesis, focusing on one aspect of the reading at a time. Topic sentences in a critique usually indicate the element of the reading you will be examining in that part of the essay and whether you found it to be a strength or liability—for example, "One of the real strengths of the essay is the author's use of emotional language."

Offer Examples

Whatever aspect of the reading you are examining—logic, word choice, structure—give your readers specific examples from the source text to clarify your terms and demonstrate that your judgment is sound. For example, the student who hopes to prove that the author's use of emotional language is one of the reading's strengths will need to quote several examples of language from the text he believes is emotional. Offering only one example might not be convincing; readers might question whether the student isolated for praise or criticism the single occurrence of that element in the text.

Explain Your Judgments

After you have specified the aspect of the reading you are examining in that part of your critique and have offered your readers examples from the text, you will need to explain and defend your judgment. After the student mentioned above cites a few specific examples of the author's emotional language, he will need to explain clearly and convincingly *how* that language strengthens the author's writing. Simply saying it does is not good enough. The student will have to explain how this type of language helps make the author's article clearer or more convincing.

In this section of the critique you will likely develop and explain your unique perspective on the reading. Suppose you and your friend are critiquing the same reading. You could both agree that it is effective and could even choose to focus on the same elements of the reading to defend and illustrate this judgment; for example, you could both choose to focus on the author's use of evidence. The two of you will probably differ, though, in your explanation of how and why the author's use of evidence is strong. You will offer your individual assessments of how the writer effectively employed evidence to support his thesis.

Conclusion

- Wrap up the paper.
- Reassert the thesis.

In your concluding section, try to give your reader a sense of closure. Consider mirroring in your conclusion the strategy you used to open your critique. For example, if you opened your essay with a question, consider closing it by answering that question; if you began with a quotation, end with a quotation; if you opened with a story, finish the story. You might also consider restating your thesis—your overall assessment of the piece—to remind your readers of the judgments you developed in the body of your essay.

STEP 5—REWRITE YOUR CRITIQUE

In rewriting your critique, check to make sure your work is accurate, thorough, organized, and clear.

- *Accurate*—it reflects your true assessment of the source text.
- *Thorough*—you completely explain your assertions.
- *Organized*—readers can easily follow the development of your critique.
- *Clear*—you have explained all the terms you need to explain and supported any assumptions that might reasonably be questioned.

Check for Accuracy

When reviewing your work, first check for accuracy. You want to be sure that your essay reflects your honest assessment of the source text. Starting with your thesis, look through your essay to make sure the assertions you make, the supporting material you employ, and the explanations you offer accurately reflect your point of view.

Check the Development of Your Assertions

Next, make sure you have been thorough in developing your critique. Check to be sure you have offered examples from the source text to support and illustrate your claims and that you have explained your reasoning clearly and completely. Add material—quotations, examples, and explanations—where you think they are needed.

Check the Organization

As you review the organization of your critique, make sure your thesis guides the development of your essay. Are you examining only one aspect of the reading at a time? If not, move material around to improve the organization in your essay. Have you provided adequate transitions to help your reader move through the piece? Do you repeat key terms or provide transition words that remind your reader of your thesis or signal the relationship between the various assertions you make?

Check for Clarity

Check your critique for clarity. Have you used any terms that need to be defined? Have you made any assertions that readers would find unclear? Have you made any assumptions that need to be explained or defended? When necessary, change the content, word choice, or sentence structure of your essay to make your ideas more accessible to your readers.

READING

The essay "Clear Message to Teens: 'It's OK to Have Sex' " appeared in the *Chicago Tribune* on September 10, 1989. Following the essay is a sample critique that analyzes and evaluates it.

Clear Message to Teens: "It's OK to Have Sex"

Joan Beck

Joan Beck *is a columnist for the* Chicago Tribune.

Whatever his intentions, the message that New York City Schools Chancellor Joseph Fernandez is proposing to give students in the city's 120 high schools is clear: It's OK to have sex.

Fernandez has asked the city Board of Education to agree to make free condoms available to all 261,000 high-school students, regardless of their age. Not in a school-based health clinic. Not in connection with sex education. Not just if they have a parent's permission.

Simply, free condoms for the asking from male and female staff volunteers during the school day.

The Board of Education is expected to give its approval next month.

What has persuaded Fernandez to take such a controversial step is concern about AIDS. New York City has the nation's highest rate of AIDS cases among adolescents, and 20 percent of all teens in this country who have the deadly disease live there.

But it's hard to jump from those facts, however worrisome, to giving out condoms free in all the New York City high schools.

The number of cases of AIDS diagnosed among teens is still small compared with the national toll. Of the 154,917 cumulative cases of AIDS reported to the Centers for Disease Control by the end of October, only 604 were diagnosed among 13- to 19-year-olds.

Not all these teens acquired the AIDS virus through sexual activity. Drug users who share needles now account for a substantial and growing percentage of AIDS cases.

Does that mean Fernandez will next propose handing out clean, free needles in the schools?

What Fernandez should remember is that the lessons adults think they are teaching children aren't necessarily the messages young people pick up.

The chancellor may think he's warning students to be responsible about sex. But what the teens are most likely to hear is that the school says it's all right for high-schoolers to have sex and that sex has school backing, right up there with reading, writing and arithmetic.

How can parents teach teen-agers moral values and counsel them against premature sexual activity, for which they are probably not psychologically ready, and which may have consequences they are unprepared for? The school will be telling these adolescents it expects them to be having sex.

By giving out condoms—and at least tacit permission to be sexually active—the schools also will be making it harder than ever for girls to say no. Teen-agers who don't want to be rushed into sex for very good reasons already have lost most of the backing they used to get from society.

Little in popular culture now supports premarital abstinence. And boys who customarily pressure girls with everyone-does-it, what's-the-matter-with-you? arguments will now be able to point out that even the school makes that assumption.

Fernandez tries to counter criticism about handing out condoms—without counseling or sex education—by saying, "People at any age have ready access to condoms at supermarkets and drugstores without the benefit of an educational or counseling component." But since access to condoms is so easy at supermarkets and drugstores, why is it necessary for the schools to hand them out? Any teen who is reluctant to make a public purchase would probably be even less likely to ask for them at school.

There are other problems. Condoms are not a totally sure protection against the AIDS virus any more than they are 100 percent effective in preventing pregnancy. At best, they offer only safer sex, not safe sex—a distinction that is easily lost on adolescents. They also require responsible, unfailing use, a self-discipline that many teen-agers seem unable to muster for a variety of reasons.

Little clear evidence exists that efforts to reduce teenage pregnancies by encouraging the use of contraceptives have been successful on a large scale, even when they have involved much more sex education and counseling than New York City high-schoolers get.

Yet, almost no efforts are being made—except by parents and churches—to persuade teens that the only sure protection against pregnancy and sexually transmitted AIDS is abstinence.

Fernandez may be correct in assuming that sexual activity among teens of high-school age is so pervasive that it justifies his condom plan. But it is also possible that expecting students to be sexually active will increase the number of them who are—and could even raise the incidence of adolescent pregnancy and AIDS.

Before the city's Board of Education approves Fernandez's plan, it might pause to consider how poorly the New York schools—and most other big, urban systems—succeed in their traditional task. When the schools can't even do a good job of teaching academics, it's grasping at straws to expect they can be effective in reducing AIDS and teen pregnancies.

The real problem is that we are reduced to grasping at straws.

SAMPLE CRITIQUE

Beck's Essay Not Convincing

Joan Beck wrote "Clear Message to Teens: 'It's OK to Have Sex' " in response to a proposal by New York City School Chancellor Joseph Fernandez to distribute free condoms to high school students on demand without parental permission. In her essay Beck criticizes the plan, claiming that it will not help prevent the spread of AIDS or curb the number of unwanted pregnancies and may even harm students by implicitly sending the message that the school system endorses premarital sex. Though on the surface many of Beck's criticisms seem valid, a closer reading shows that they frequently rest on unsupported assertions and questionable ethical stands. As a result, Beck's essay presents an unconvincing case against Fernandez's proposal.

Beck offers several reasons for her stand against dispensing condoms to New York City high school students on demand. First, she believes that if one of the motivations for the program is to stem the spread of AIDS, then the plan will fail: dispensing condoms to high school students, Beck maintains, will have a negligible effect on the AIDS crisis. Second, she believes the proposal sends the wrong message to students, giving implicit official consent to premarital sex. Third, Beck holds that high school students will be too embarrassed to ask for condoms from a high school staff member. Finally, Beck questions whether dispensing condoms will actually help reduce the rate of teenage pregnancies, and proposes instead that the program may actually increase the number of students who contract AIDS or become pregnant.

Though on the surface, Beck's criticisms may seem valid, careful analysis shows that her claims often lack sufficient grounds and raise disturbing ethical questions. A close examination of just one claim—that the Fernandez proposal will have a negligible effect on the AIDS crisis in New York—demonstrates the problems inherent in most of Beck's argument.

Beck believes a concern over AIDS was the primary motivation for the program: "What has persuaded Fernandez to take such a controversial step is concern about AIDS. New York City has the nation's highest rate of AIDS cases among adolescents, and 20 percent of all teens in this country who have the deadly disease live there" (112). While acknowledging that New York City has a problem with teenage AIDS cases, Beck believes Fernandez's proposed solution is too extreme. As support, she says the number of AIDS cases among teenagers "is still small compared with the national toll" (112), citing statistics from the Centers for Disease Control that show that of the 154,917 confirmed cases of AIDS, "only 604" of the victims were 13 to 19 years old. Beck holds that since a growing number of teens now get the disease from dirty drug needles, not from unprotected sex, Fernandez's proposal does not adequately address the problem.

There are two major problems with Beck's position, however: her efforts to shift the grounds of the argument and the ethical stand inherent in her position. First, Beck shifts the grounds of the argument to avoid statistical evidence that casts doubt on her position. After acknowledging that 20 percent of all teens in the country who have contracted AIDS live in New York City, she shifts attention to the number of teens who have AIDS in terms of the total number of AIDS victims. She wants her readers to consider only the 604 teens who have AIDS in the United States, not the 20 percent of them who live in New York City—604 nationwide does not seem to be as alarming a statistic as 20 percent of the nation's total living in one location. However, such a shift helps Beck avoid the need to present a logical argument against the Fernandez proposal in terms of the crisis currently facing the New York school system. Readers must ask themselves if the School Board's actions are appropriate given the 20 percent figure (the number of students who are in their schools), not the 604 figure (the number of students nationwide). Without addressing Fernandez's proposal on these grounds, Beck's argument is weakened since it purposely avoids a central issue in the debate.

Second, and perhaps more disturbingly, Beck seems unaware of the ethical implications of her unstated warrants. Her argument runs something like this: since a comparatively "small" number of teens nationwide have AIDS, "only 604," schools do not need to make readily available to them one form of birth control that, though not perfect, will at least give them some form of protection from the disease. This position is ethically questionable for a number of reasons. First, Beck seems rather callous toward the suffering of those 604 teenagers, as if having only 604 teens dying a horrible, lingering death somehow shows that as a nation we have the AIDS crisis under control and need not consider radical steps to help prevent further infections. Second, Beck's warrant fails to consider how quickly the disease can spread through sexual contact. She claims without any grounds that "drug users who share needles now account for a substantial and growing percentage of AIDS cases" (112). Even if this assertion is true, Beck is admitting that many if not most teens still contract AIDS through sexual activity, a majority that proper condom use may help protect. If distributing condoms in a high school can help prevent a 605th student from contracting the disease, perhaps the proposal deserves consideration.

Because Beck often fails to support adequately her contentions about the relationship between AIDS and condom distribution and fails to address adequately the ethical implications of her position, her argument is not convincing. Some of Beck's criticisms may be well founded: some teens might be embarrassed to pick up condoms at school, and some students might interpret the New York City program as endorsing premarital sex. However, both of these problems could be addressed by the school system through education and counseling. They, alone, do not discredit Fernandez's proposal.

ADDITIONAL READING

Condom Availability Promotes Health, Saves Lives

Margaret Pruitt Clark

Margaret Pruitt Clark is Executive Director of The Center for Population Options headquartered in Washington, D.C.

In 1990 a group of high school students in Cambridge, Mass., received intensive training to learn to counsel their peers about HIV/AIDS and how it is transmitted. They hoped friends would take their message of prevention to heart. They were convinced it was a message that could save lives.

But feelings of frustration and futility gradually replaced their natural optimism. Despite their best efforts, they continued to hear stories of friends and classmates risking their lives and futures through unprotected intercourse, unknowing or nonchalant about the dangers of sexually transmitted diseases, pregnancy, and even AIDS.

How could they get the attention of these other young people? How could their friends know the facts about AIDS and still have unprotected sex? What could keep them from foolishly, needlessly, thoughtlessly, throwing away their lives?

With the idealism and courage of young people who believe in a cause, the students started handing out plain white envelopes containing condoms and written materials about AIDS prevention. They weren't sure what to expect from school authorities and realized the reaction could be harsh. But they were willing to take the risk because of what was at stake.

The actions of this student group and others who collected signatures on a petition to the school board opened an important debate in the community. Ultimately, the Cambridge school board altered an existing policy and permitted the school clinic to make condoms available to sexually active students.

Growing Awareness

No longer is condom distribution in schools a novel idea, though it continues to generate controversy. A growing number of communities are adopting policies and developing plans to help young people understand the seriousness of the risks they face and reduce risk-taking behavior.

A surprising but important benefit of the controversy over school condom availability programs is the way it has engaged entire communities in the debate and increased public awareness at the local level.

Schools are conducting surveys of teenage students to determine their level of risk-taking. Students themselves also are being heard on this issue, sometimes for the first time. Parents and community members are becoming involved in the early stages of the debate, and their help is being enlisted in designing the programs. Typically, school condom availability programs involve collaborative efforts among schools, health agencies, and youth-serving organizations.

The stakes in the controversy are considerable. According to the national school-based Youth Risk Behavior Survey by the Centers for Disease Control (CDC), 31.9 percent of ninth-grade girls and 48.7 percent of ninth-grade boys have had sexual intercourse. By the time they are seniors, the figures rise to 66.6 and 76.3 percent, respectively.

Another survey of inner-city black males found an average age of first intercourse under 12 years old. The younger the age at which an individual becomes sexually active, the more likely he or she is to have multiple partners, substantially increasing the risk of acquiring a sexually transmitted disease, including the AIDS virus.

Two and one-half million adolescents are infected with sexually transmitted diseases, and one in 10 teenage girls becomes pregnant every year. A recent study by CDC at the National Children's Medical Center in Washington, D. C., shows a five-fold increase since 1987 in the number of HIV-positive adolescents who are treated there. Since this study involved a limited population, we can assume that these known cases are just the tip of the iceberg.

Deserve Protection

When faced with the facts, most adults agree the threat to young people has reached crisis proportions and that strong measures are required to control the spread of HIV among adolescents. Every tool at our disposal must be used to help students make healthier choices. Every one of our institutions, not just the schools, must be mobilized in the effort to control the triple threat of pregnancy, sexually transmitted diseases, and AIDS.

While only sexual abstinence and abstinence from intravenous drugs and other judgment impairing substances, including alcohol, guarantee nontransmission, teens who are exposed to risks need and deserve the best means possible for protecting themselves: knowledge, skills, and access to latex condoms. School personnel can and should provide these to in-school youth.

Condoms are legally available to teen-agers in a variety of settings, and condom use among sexually active teen-agers is increasing. Nevertheless, in 1988 only 26 percent of sexually active teen women reported condom use at last intercourse. Young people often cite confidentiality, cost and access as reasons for failing to use contraceptives. Other reasons include a lack of transportation, embarrassment, objection by a partner, and lack of perceived risk of pregnancy and infection.

School condom availability programs, whether as part of comprehensive health services at the school site or in the context of school-based HIV/AIDS and sexuality education, address each of these barriers and help to establish condom use as a norm with both peer and cultural acceptance.

The ground-breaking proposal by New York City Schools Chancellor Joseph Fernandez to make condoms available upon request in all 120 public high schools moved the issue of condoms in schools onto the national stage. Part of the goal of this program is not just to make condoms available, but to change adolescent culture.

The comprehensive HIV/AIDS education program in New York seeks to make condom use the norm rather than the exception for sexually active young people and to provide a setting in which adolescents can talk openly about their behavior and their concerns with adults they trust.

Students' fear of being judged, embarrassed, sanctioned, or "hassled," as one student put it, needs to be overcome for the programs to be effective. Recent news coverage about the program suggests that since the novelty has worn off, most teen-agers are using the program to ask questions and get counseling.

Community Backing

Since December 1990, the Center for Population Options' (CPO) national School Condom Availability Campaign and Clearinghouse has monitored developments across the country and provided information, assistance, and referrals to communities. In many cities, such as Baltimore, Chicago, and Portland, Ore., condoms are available through school-based health centers that provide primary health care to students, CPO is aware of almost 50 (out of more than 300) school-based health centers that provide condoms to sexually active students.

These programs have the strong support of the communities they serve. Surveys conducted by Baltimore and Portland health officials (prior to decisions by local policy-makers to permit condoms to be dispensed in the clinics) showed a majority of parents in both cities support condom availability for sexually active students.

In some schools with no health facility on site, condoms are made available by specially trained school staff or local health professionals as part of school- or districtwide AIDS/HIV prevention and education programs. School officials in Los Angeles, San Francisco, and Philadelphia approved both clinic-based and education-based programs. These are now being implemented.

Earlier this year the District of Columbia announced a citywide campaign to control the spread of AIDS, including condom availability in all 16 public high schools. With one in 57 D.C. males between the ages of 20 and 64 infected with HIV and one in 67 babies being born to mothers with HIV, there is no room for cautious response. As one D.C. City Council member put it, "Abstinence is preferable, but AIDS kills." One thousand and six hundred students signed petitions asking for condoms in their schools.

School condom availability programs are not limited to urban school systems. One of the first programs started in 1988 in Commerce City, Colo., a district with 6,000 students, nearly half living in poverty. This program uses specially trained, volunteer teachers who are available to students at times and locations posted prominently in the school.

In addition, the Massachusetts Board of Education last year passed a resolution to become the first state agency urging all school districts to consider making condoms available as part of HIV prevention and education for students. As of early summer, 10 local school boards had approved the concept and now are planning or implementing a program.

Single Answer

Schools contemplating condom distribution have many issues to resolve, such as whether availability will be part of comprehensive health services or part of an intensive HIV/AIDS and sexuality education program. How will costs be covered? What sort of education and counseling will be provided to students? Who will actually be trained to give out the condoms? How, ultimately, will the effectiveness of the program be evaluated?

No one would argue that making condoms available in high schools alone will eliminate the threat of AIDS and adolescent pregnancy or miraculously change adolescent behavior. Yet easy access to latex condoms is an important strand in the safety net of services, care, and education for teen-agers.

ADDITIONAL READING

Apply Peer Pressure, Not Latex, against Casual Sex

Edwin J. Delattre

Edwin J. Delattre is Dean and Olin Scholar in Applied Ethics at Boston University's School of Education.

We are told by condom distribution advocates that school distribution of condoms is not a moral issue but rather an issue of life and death. We are told by the same people we have a moral obligation to do everything in our power, at all times to save lives.

The incoherence—indeed, contradiction—between these claims reflects the failure of condom distribution advocates to perceive that all life-and-death issues and all questions of what schools do in the interest of their students are moral questions.

If our only moral duty were to save lives—at whatever cost to other ideals of life—we would raise the legal age for acquiring a driver's license to at least 25; reduce speed limits to 35 mph or less; mandate annual physical examinations; outlaw tobacco and foods that contribute to bad health; and so on.

Even if saving lives were our only moral concern, distributing condoms in schools is not the best way to save lives. Abstinence has greater life-saving power than any piece of latex can have. We have a duty to make clear to students the danger they face if they become sexually involved with someone who may be HIV positive and has not had the decency to seek out a medical test. That person is, in principle, willing to kill.

We have a duty to explain to students that it is morally wrong to cause needless suffering and to be indifferent to the suffering we may cause.

Indulgent Behavior

Condom distribution in our schools promotes casual sex, casual indifference to the seriousness of sexual life, and casual disregard and contempt for others. Casual sex is promiscuous sex.

Where promiscuity is calculated, it is crudely exploitative and selfish; where it is impulsive, it is immature. A person who is promiscuous treats others as objects to be used for gratification, ignoring the possibility of pregnancies that may result in an unwanted child whose lot in life will be unfair from the beginning.

Those who are promiscuous usually exert peer pressure in favor of their form of indulgence, just as drug users do. Such persons say condoms make sex "less dangerous," that sexual activity is only a health issue and not a moral issue.

That leaves to us, the teachers, the duty to tell our students about the rate of failure of condoms in preventing pregnancy when used by young unmarried women—36.3 percent. The Family Research Council stresses this figure is probably too low in protecting against AIDS, since the HIV virus is 1/450 the size of a sperm and is less than 1/10 the size of open channels that routinely pass entirely through latex products such as gloves.

The behavior of health professionals with respect to "less dangerous" sex ought to be described to students as well. The Richmond, Va., *Times-Dispatch* reported recently on a speech given by Dr. Theresa Crenshaw, a member of the national AIDS Commission and past president of the American Association of Sex Education, Counselors, and Therapists, to an international gathering of 800 sexologists.

"Most of them," Crenshaw said, "recommended condoms to their clients and students. I asked them if they had available the partner of their dreams and knew that person carried the virus, would they have sex, depending on a condom for protection? No one raised their hand. After a long delay, one timid hand surfaced from the back of the room. I told them that it was irresponsible to give advice to others that they would not follow themselves.

The point is, putting a mere balloon between a healthy body and a deadly disease is not safe."

By distributing condoms to children and adolescents, we convey the false message that we do not care about the moral dimensions of sexual life, and that there is no reason for them to care either. Those who tell them, and us, that we are not faced with a moral issue betray the young to expediency.

Misguided Messages

Condom distribution advocates will reply that sexual activity among the young is inevitable, even natural. To protect themselves from pregnancy, AIDS, and other sexually transmitted diseases, students must use condoms. At the same time, these advocates deny that the availability of condoms will increase sexual activity.

But if we teach the young we expect them to be sexually active, they are likely to expect it of themselves. We have no right to exhibit such low expectations—or to encourage the young in sexual activity that is promiscuous and, thus, necessarily devoid of the emotional and spiritual intimacy that anchor genuine love.

We must ask ourselves whether we really want to encourage the young to engage in sexual activity that, by its nature, undermines the sanctity of the family as the model of loving sexual intimacy between adults committed to one another and to their offspring.

And for those who are sexually promiscuous—whether to aggrandize themselves, or exert power over others, or gain prestige or physical pleasure or peer approval—does it follow that we should give them the condoms in the high school?

Even if promiscuity with condoms and dental dams is physically less dangerous than promiscuity without them, should we be in the business of distributing them? Filtered cigarettes are less harmful than unfiltered ones, but we do not distribute free filtered cigarettes.

We should instead stand on the side of peer pressure against casual sex, because it is morally right and because it has the power to save lives.

Some condom distribution advocates insist that we defer to experts in health care on the subject. They claim these experts do not try to tell us what we should do as educators, and we should not tell them what to do in matters of health.

This argument is based on the false premise that what health officials do in the high school contains no educational lessons. Health and social service providers attempt to teach students the high school is an appropriate condom distribution site, while dismissing as irrelevant questions of morality and educational mission. In this, they exceed their competence.

Furthermore, as if qualified not only in ethics but also in law, these health professionals and social service personnel dismiss the prospect of legal liability for our institutions. Yet it is well understood by all of us that condoms are quite fallible.

On this weak foundation of flawed arguments about educational policy, about ethical life, and about the law, too many school boards across the country have voted in favor of the distribution of condoms in their schools. In doing so, they have made it possible for students to believe that even a questionable expediency is more important than mature judgment, personal restraint, and respect for the well-being of other people—and they have placed teachers and administrators in a position that runs counter to sound educational policy.

Necessary Limits

In these schools, it is necessary to make the best of bad policy by imposing requirements on the distribution of condoms.

- First, only the most reliable condoms manufactured should be distributed, whatever their cost.
- Second, indemnification should be provided for the school and the city for all malpractice or other legal liability.
- Third, the high school should send a letter to all parents describing the services offered by the health clinic and informing them condoms do not make sex safe.
- Fourth, under no circumstances should any teacher or school administrator be involved in the distribution of condoms.
- Fifth, these condoms should be distributed only in conjunction with qualified counseling in their use and qualified instruction in ethics—both to be provided by health personnel in the clinic. The instruction should first be prepared in general form in writing—in English and other languages—for review and approval by those qualified in such matters.
- Sixth, the counseling should include instruction about all sexually transmitted diseases and their consequences, not only in suffering and possible death of those infected but also in endangering pregnancies and in harming or killing offspring. This instruction should include education about all conditions under which AIDS can be transmitted by intercourse and oral sex, by transfusions, by shared use of contaminated needles, by intrusive medical treatments performed by afflicted health care professionals, and by other varieties of behavior against which condoms and dental dams afford no protection.
- Seventh, students should be given a written examination, and be required to pass it, on these subjects before receiving condoms.
- Eighth, no student should ever be excused from classes or study periods to receive such counseling and instruction. Only lunch period or time

before and after school should be available for this purpose—in keeping with the educational mission and priorities of the schools.

- Ninth, any student who requests condoms, and is not exempt by statute from requirements of parental consent for medical treatment, should be made to bring a signed letter from a parent or guardian approving distribution of condoms to this daughter or son—and explicitly absolving the school and city and all of their personnel from all legal liability for any consequences—all liability. The letter should be confirmed by telephone or by a written receipt sent by return mail.

If the parent or guardian cannot, for any reason, provide such a letter, then legally satisfactory approval should be given in person, witnessed and recorded. All letters and visitation and telephone logs should be kept permanently on file to safeguard against legal actions.

Responsible Actions

If we are forced to distribute condoms, we should do so in a way that shows our understanding of the duties and aspiration central to a life well and honorably lived—the respect for others and the effort to make the best possible people of ourselves.

Students should understand we are not willing to grant free rein to peer pressure that obstructs their self-interest and jeopardizes their happiness. They should understand we cannot save their lives—only they can do that for themselves—and we are working to advance their ability to do so, in the short run and in the long run, as they assume progressively greater responsibility for their own destinies.

I cannot forget the youngest in a group of students who spoke publicly in favor of condom distribution in the local high school. Although she had not yet reached high school age, she beseeched us to distribute condoms in the high school because if we did not, students would die. The sincerity of her belief was clear in her tone and in her eyes, which glistened with tears.

I want that child to be told the truth.

I want her to learn that those students do not have to die in youth; that many of her peers will not die of sexually transmitted disease but will learn to avoid casual sex because it is irreducibly dangerous and because it diminishes self-respect; that untimely sexual activity is not inevitable unless individuals make it so, by their own decisions and actions; that there are many safeguards against destructive diseases available to the young; and that the most trustworthy of these are not condoms and dental dams.

I want her to learn that among the better safeguards are a due regard for personal safety, an unwillingness to put loved ones at risk, a rejection of promiscuity as a way of life, and a choice of friends and possible spouses who deserve trust and love.

High-Risk Gamble

These safeguards also include the courage to rise above adverse peer pressure, the maturity of self-determination, the acquisition of habits of learning that open the doors of opportunity and dramatically expand the domain of future friendships and loves, and the patience to defer gratification until it is timely, healthy, and warranted.

And I want students to know that betting their life—or letting someone else bet their life—on a condom is a gamble only one in 800 experts on sexual behavior is willing to risk, and if our own students behave otherwise, they make a mockery of the commitment they expressed over and over again to saving lives.

If we fail to do all this, we will have been incompetent and immoral teachers. Such incompetence would be far more shameful than being forced to distribute condoms, and every student, every citizen, deserves to learn that we know it.

Summary Chart

WRITING A CRITIQUE

1. **Carefully read and annotate the source text.**

   - *Read and reread the text.*

   - *Identify the author's intent, thesis, and primary assertions or findings.*

   - *Write an informal summary of the piece.*

2. **Analyze and evaluate the reading, breaking it down into its parts and judging the quality of each element.**

   Identify and evaluate the author's logic and reasoning.

   - *Is the thesis clearly stated, and does it direct the development of the text?*

   - *Are the author's primary assertions reasonable and clearly tied to the thesis?*

   - *Are there problems with logical fallacies?*

   - *Are the author's positions or findings logically presented?*

   Identify and evaluate the text's evidence.

   - *Does the author support his or her assertions or findings?*

   - *Is the support offered adequate to convince readers?*

   - *Is the evidence authoritative?*

   - *Is the evidence current?*

   - *Does the author explain how the evidence supports his or her assertions or findings?*

   - *Has the author ignored evidence or alternative hypotheses?*

   Identify and evaluate the text's organization.

   - *Is there a clear connection between the assertions developed in the essay?*

   - *Are the assertions or findings tied to a guiding thesis?*

   - *Does there seem to be a reason for one assertion following another, or do they seem randomly organized?*

Identify and evaluate the text's style.

- *Is the author's diction consistently maintained?*
- *Is the author's word choice clear and effective?*
- *Is the author's tone consistent and effective?*
- *Are the author's sentences clear?*

3. **Formulate your thesis and choose the criteria you will include in your essay.**

- *Draft a thesis, a brief statement concerning the overall value or worth of the source text.*
- *Choose which elements of the reading you will focus on in your critique.*

4. **Write your rough draft.**

- *Introduce the topic, source text, and your thesis.*
- *Establish your evaluative criteria and your judgments of them.*
- *Offer examples to substantiate each of your criteria and judgments.*
- *Explain your judgments, clarifying how the examples you provide support your assertions.*

5. **Rewrite your critique.**

Check to make sure your writing is accurate.

- *Does your writing honestly reflect your judgment?*
- *Does your writing misrepresent the author?*

Check to make sure your writing is thorough.

- *Do you cover all the aspects of the source text you need to cover?*
- *Do you clearly and thoroughly explain and support your assertions?*

Check to make sure your writing is organized.

- *Does your thesis statement guide the development of your essay?*
- *Have you provided transitional devices to help lead your reader through your work?*

Check to make sure your writing is clear.

- *Is your terminology clear?*
- *Are your sentences clear?*
- *Are your examples and explanations clear?*

Chapter 8

SYNTHESIS

DEFINITION AND PURPOSE

In a synthesis, you combine information from two or more readings to support a position of your own. Your aim in the paper can be expository (to convey information) or argumentative (to convince readers that your thesis is correct). In either case, when writing a synthesis, you combine material from two or more readings with your own knowledge and reasoning to explain or support your thesis.

College writing assignments often require you to synthesize material. In some courses the assignment will be direct and clear: "Compare what Author A and Author B have to say about topic X. How are their views alike and how are they different?" Other times the assignment might be more subtle: "Authors A, B, and C all address topic X. Which do you find most convincing?" Completing either assignment would require you to form and defend a thesis by drawing information from two or more readings.

To write a synthesis, you first need to sort through the readings to find information you can use in your paper. Being able to annotate readings thoroughly is essential. Second, you need to find the best way to organize this material around your own thesis and the demands of the assignment. Third, you need to find a place in the essay for your own ideas, findings, or arguments. Composing a synthesis usually involves more than just stringing together quoted and paraphrased material from other writers. Fourth, as you write your paper, you need to keep straight who receives credit for which ideas. Through proper documentation, you need to clarify for your readers when you are drawing on the work of a particular author and when you are developing material yourself. Finally, as you revise your work, you need to keep clearly in mind the rhetorical situation of the assignment. In your efforts to work with other people's ideas, you cannot afford to lose sight of your reader's needs and the purpose of the assignment.

TYPES OF SYNTHESIS ESSAYS

Synthesis essays can assume many different forms in college, some rather specialized and sophisticated. One way to begin sorting through all this variety is to recognize that for the most part the assignments you receive will ask you to compose either an **informative** or an **argumentative** synthesis.

The goal of an informative synthesis is to communicate clearly and efficiently information you have gathered from two or more readings. You do not defend a position of your own in this type of paper or critique the source texts. Your primary aim is to summarize the material in the readings and convey the information to your readers in a clear, concise, organized fashion. In contrast, the goal of an argumentative synthesis is to convince your reader to accept your thesis, an argument you are presenting on either the quality of the readings or the topic they address. You use the material in the source texts to support your thesis—sometimes summarizing the readings, sometimes critiquing them.

Either type of synthesis can be organized in a variety of ways. Often writers will choose to employ either a **block** or an **alternating** format. When you use a block format to structure your synthesis, you discuss only one source text at a time. With an alternating format, you switch back and forth between readings as you develop your thesis point by point.

Before examining each type of synthesis in more detail, read the following reviews of the movie *Forrest Gump*. As you read these reviews, consider what they have in common and how they are different: What is the reviewer's opinion of the film? What aspects of the movie does he examine to support his judgment? How convincing is his argument?

The Fool on the Hill

Brian D. Johnson

Brian D. Johnson *reviews films for* Macleans.

The story unfolds in whimsical flashbacks, narrated in a slow-talking southern drawl by a simpleton sitting on a bench. Forrest Gump (Tom Hanks) was born stupid, but his mother (Sally Field) feels he has as much a right to the

American Dream as anyone. In fact, Gump does astonishingly well. To escape local bullies, he learns to "run like the wind," which leads to a football scholarship. He goes on to become a Vietnam War hero, a world Ping-Pong champion and a shrimp magnate.

For the film-makers, however, Gump's job is to serve as a deadpan witness to history in the making. With serendipitous timing, he keeps showing up on the scene of important events. And through computer doctoring of archival clips, director Robert Zemeckis shows Gump making small talk with luminaries ranging from John Lennon to John F. Kennedy. The movie unfolds as a montage of baby boom experience: Elvis, assassinations, Vietnam, hippies, Black Panthers, and moon landing, Watergate, cocaine, AIDS. All the hits of the '60s, '70s, and '80s. No touchstone is left unturned.

But the narrative is so programmed it is like watching software. *Forrest Gump* is a medley of sound bites—clever, cute, amusing, silly, sentimental—and irritatingly phoney. Meanwhile, to underscore every shift in the action, Zemeckis has assembled a sound track of vintage pop songs with plodding literalism.

Zemeckis, the special-effects wizard who directed *Back to the Future* and *Who Framed Roger Rabbit?*, often overpowers his actors. Hanks is endearing as Gump, and Gary Sinise valiantly tries to stay real as his Vietnam buddy, Lt. Dan, who loses his legs in combat. But as Jenny, Gump's heartthrob, Robin Wright gets lost in a whirlwind of costume changes as her character keeps step with the times by becoming a folksinger, a stripping hippie, a radical and a drug addict.

The movie strikes an odd balance between novelty and formula. Zemeckis sets about healing wounds with an Oliver-Stone-lite version of the modern American tragedy. Through Gump's uncomprehending eyes—shades of Dustin Hoffman's autistic hero in *Rain Man*—he renders it meaningless. As an exercise in high-powered manipulation, the movie works: audiences may find it irresistible. But *Forrest Gump* is, quite literally—to quote Shakespeare—"a tale told by an idiot full of sound and fury, signifying nothing."

Forrest Gump

David Ansen

David Ansen *reviews films for* Newsweek.

In the course of "Forrest Gump" you will discover how it came about that the title character, a sweet-natured simpleton from rural Alabama with a two-digit IQ, taught Elvis how to move. That's just for starters. Forrest (Tom Hanks) is an idiot for all seasons, and his life story encompasses—and sometimes brings about—most of the major events of four stormy decades of American life. You'll see how this boy with braces on his legs became a Crimson Tide football star and a Vietnam War hero. How he met JFK, LBJ and inadvertently caused the downfall of Richard Nixon. How he came to be playing Ping-Pong in China, met the Black Panthers and ended up on the cover of *Fortune*. You'll see him chatting with John Lennon on "The Dick Cavett Show." Forrest was even the guy who inspired the bumper sticker S—T HAPPENS.

As Hollywood summer movies go, this picaresque fable is definitely not the same old same old. Adapted from Winston Groom's comic novel by Eric Roth, directed with great flair and technical brilliance by Robert Zemeckis, "Forrest Gump" is inventive, sometimes hilarious, and it pushes so many nostalgia buttons you can't help but stay engrossed even when the tale starts to ramble. Yet the whole seems less than the sum of its parts.

Forrest himself is like a combination of Candide, Rain Man, Zelig, Chauncey Gardiner and the guy from "Regarding Henry." Hanks, who can do no wrong as an actor, turns this fantastical conceit into funny, touching flesh and blood; even his elbows are eloquent. As the troubled, beautiful Jenny, the abused hometown girl he loves with dogfish devotion through his life, Robin Wright gives a sketchy role grace and gravity. And in a season top-heavy with special effects, "Forrest Gump's" are truly remarkable. Everyone will be astonished by the "Zelig"-like insertions, which place the hero inside archival footage, shaking hands with Kennedy, popping up next to George Wallace, talking with Tricky Dick. No less impressive are the effects you may not recognize: using digital computer technology to create vast crowds at a Washington anti-war rally, or to amputate the legs of Gary Sinise's embittered Lieutenant Dan, the officer Forrest saves in battle and later teams up with in the shrimping business. Zemeckis, Ken Ralston and Industrial Light & Magic did state-of-the-art effects together in "Who Framed Roger Rabbit" and "Death Becomes Her," and their work here is groundbreaking. And a little scary—we've entered an era where photographic reality can't be trusted.

But what does "Forrest Gump" add up to? For all its ambition, the movie ends up using great historical events in the service of a dubious sentimentality. As satire, it's surprisingly toothless, especially coming from the man who directed the gleefully savage "Used Cars" (1980). As a tear-jerker, which unfortunately is what it ultimately becomes, it left me unmoved. Roth's screenplay significantly departs from the Groom novel in its maudlin resolution of the love story, and the more it focuses on the lovers the less psychologically credible it becomes. The movie wants to use Forrest Gump every which way—as dunce, as idiot savant, as the one pure soul in an impure world, as faithful lover. It's a tribute to Hanks and Zemeckis that this all-purpose symbol is as fetching as he is. The world according to Gump is certainly an enjoyable place to visit. But its core is disappointingly soft and elusive.

Forrest Gump

Peter Travers

Peter Travers *reviews films for* Rolling Stone.

Forrest Gump is a movie heart-breaker of oddball wit and startling grace. There's talk of another Oscar for Tom Hanks, who is unforgettable as the sweet-natured, shabbily treated simpleton of the title. The Academy is a sucker for honoring afflicted heroes. In Hollywood, it's always raining rain men. Credit Hanks for not overplaying his hand. He brings a touching gravity to the role of an idiot savant from the South who finds strength in god, country, his childhood pal, Jenny (Robin Wright), and his good mama (Sally Field). When Forrest falls a few IQ points shy of minimal school requirements, Mama knows who to sleep with to bend the rules. Her son has a gift. As Forrest makes his pilgrim's progress from the '50s to the '80s, he becomes a college football star, a Vietnam war hero, a shrimp tycoon and even a father.

Taking a cue from *Zelig*, director Robert Zemeckis places Forrest in a vivid historical context—he talks with JFK, LBJ and Nixon, among other luminaries. The effects dazzle, though never at the expense of the story. Winston Groom, who wrote the 1986 novel, saw Forrest as a modern Candide, an optimist in the face of strong opposing evidence. But Groom is no Voltaire, and neither is screenwriter Eric Roth (*Mr. Jones, Memories of Me*), who blunts his satire with choking sentiment. It's Hanks who brings humor and unforced humanity to the literary conceit of Forrest, though the slim actor scarcely resembles the 6-foot-6-inch, 240-pound bruiser of the book.

In a college dorm with Jenny, who lets him touch her breast, the virginal Forrest ejaculates instantly, losing her interest and his self-respect. In the Army, Forrest saves his captain (Gary Sinise), whose legs are later amputated, and the captain resents him. Forrest is everything we admire in the American character—honest, brave, loyal—and the film's fierce irony is that nobody can stay around him for long.

Zemeckis doesn't fall into the trap of using Forrest as an ad for arrested development. He knows the limits of a holy fool who can't understand the hypocrisy of postwar America that his picaresque epic so powerfully reveals. The peace-love pretensions of the '60s are skewered as neatly as the greed decades that follow. But there is something of Forrest that Zemeckis would like to see rub off on us: his capacity for hope. It's an ambitious goal in this age of rampant cynicism. Godspeed.

INFORMATIVE SYNTHESIS

DEFINITION

Your goal in writing an informative synthesis is to combine material on some topic you have gathered from two or more readings into a clear, organized essay. After finishing your essay, a reader should have a better understanding of the topic and should know the position of the various authors whose work you include. You are not trying to show how one author is correct in what she says and another is wrong. Neither are you trying to advocate a position of your own on the topic. Instead, you are trying to present other people's ideas or findings as clearly and concisely as you can.

For example, if you were writing an informative synthesis of these three *Forrest Gump* reviews, you would want to summarize what each critic had to say about the movie or at least about certain aspects of the film—the acting, the scenery, and the direction, for instance. In fact, a good way to write this paper would be to isolate for examination certain aspects of the film all three critics address—that way you could draw direct comparisons among the reviews. While you point out for your reader any important similarities or differences you see in the various reviews, you would not argue that one critic is correct in his review of the film and that the others are misguided, nor would you comment on the quality of the writing or argument in any particular review.

To compose an informative synthesis, you employ many of the same skills needed to write summaries. As with writing summaries, you may encounter a number of problems when composing an informative synthesis:

1. Because of their content, language, or structure, the source texts themselves might be hard for you to understand. Because you need to form a clear understanding of the readings before you write about them, you need strong critical reading skills to write a successful synthesis.

2. You will often be looking for subtle differences among readings—not just different arguments or findings authors put forward, but slightly different interpretations of data, slightly different uses of terminology, slightly different emphases. Because a synthesis involves multiple source texts, when you examine a reading you plan to use in your paper, you also have to keep in mind the material contained in the readings you have already read. The more readings you are working with, the harder it is to keep track of the material contained in each and the easier it is to overlook the subtle differences between them.

3. You need to stay as objective as possible when examining the source texts and writing your essay. You do not editorialize in an informative synthesis: your goal is *not* to comment on the topic of the readings or on the quality of their writing. Instead, you need to be open-minded when reading them, to pull out from them material relevant to your thesis, and to present that material as clearly, concisely, and fairly as possible. As when you

are writing a summary, remaining neutral can be difficult, especially when you feel strongly about a topic and must include in your informative synthesis ideas that disturb or anger you.

4. Organizing an informative synthesis can also be challenging. You need to decide how to construct your thesis so it adequately guides your reader through your work, how to order the information you include in your paper, and how to employ transitions within the body of your essay.

5. Supplying proper documentation in an informative synthesis can be problematic. One paragraph of your paper may contain information you have drawn from several different authors. Learning how to document such passages properly can be trying; remembering to do it is crucial. Improper documentation can lead to problems with clarity and plagiarism.

WRITING AN INFORMATIVE SYNTHESIS

Because writing an informative synthesis can be challenging, it is best to break the process down into a series of more manageable steps:

1. Analyze the assignment.
2. Review and annotate the readings.
3. Formulate a thesis and organizational plan.
4. Write your rough draft.
5. Revise your draft.

Remember that this method of writing a synthesis will not work for everybody. We all have our preferred way of writing papers, which can vary according to the type of essay we are composing and the time we have to complete the assignment. For example, some writers like to complete a rough draft before they write their thesis, while others must have a thesis in hand before they begin to write; some will rewrite a paper several times before they turn it in for a grade, while others revise very little. So use these directions as a rough guide for writing an informative synthesis. The important principle to keep in mind is to complete your paper in a series of steps, no matter the nature or order of those steps.

Analyze the Assignment

Read the assignment carefully to make sure your instructor is asking you to write an informative rather than an argumentative synthesis. If you have any doubt, ask your teacher to clarify the assignment. Make sure you understand how many sources you are required to consult when researching the topic or to include when writing your paper. Also, check on the type of source texts your teacher expects you to use if you are required to collect the readings yourself. Some instructors will want you to use only "academic" sources—material written by experts in the field.

Review and Annotate the Readings

Once you have assembled the readings that will serve as the basis of your synthesis, read through them several times with your assignment in mind. In most cases, you will look for specific information in each reading, passages that address the topic of your paper. Thoroughly annotate the reading and then summarize it. As you work with the material, remember to be fair and open-minded. Consider how the author's perspective on the topic is similar to or different from what other authors have written and decide whether you think it should be included in your essay.

Formulate a Thesis and Organizational Plan

Your thesis in an informative synthesis serves an important function. More likely than not, it will indicate the topic of your essay and indicate how you will structure your synthesis: what you will discuss and in what order you will discuss it. Always keep in mind the rhetorical function of your thesis statement. When people read your paper, they need to know early on what you will be discussing and will look to your thesis as a guide.

Your thesis for an informative synthesis can be either open or closed. In an open thesis you indicate the topic and general structure of your paper:

> Peter Travers, David Ansen, and Brian D. Johnson offer quite different views of *Forrest Gump*, not all of them positive.

When writing this paper, you might employ a block format—discussing what one reviewer had to say before moving on to the next. In outline form, your paper might look something like this:

Opening Section

Introduce the topic

Give thesis

Section on Peter Travers Review

Summarize his critique of the film

Section on David Ansen Review

Summarize his critique of the film

Section on Brian D. Johnson Review

Summarize his critique of the film

Conclusion

In writing an informative synthesis, you can also choose to employ a closed thesis. With a closed thesis you list the specific issues you will address in your essay. However, you have to be careful not to put too much information in your thesis—doing so will only lead to cluttered prose. A possible closed thesis statement for the paper described above might read something like this:

> Peter Travers, David Ansen, and Brian D. Johnson disagree about the quality of *Forrest Gump*, offering conflicting judgments concerning the movie's acting, special effects, and message.

With this thesis you might choose to employ an alternating structure, discussing what each critic has to say, in order, about the movie's acting, special effects, and message. In outline form, the paper might look like this:

Opening Section

Introduce the topic

Give thesis

Acting in *Forrest Gump*

Travers's views

Ansen's views

Johnson's views

Special Effects in *Forrest Gump*

Travers's views

Ansen's views

Johnson's views

Messages in *Forrest Gump*

Travers's views

Ansen's views

Johnson's views

Conclusion

If, however, you choose to employ a block format to develop this closed thesis, in outline form your paper might look like this:

Opening Section

Introduce the topic

Give thesis

Section on the Travers Review

His views on the film's acting

His views on the film's special effects

His views on the film's message

Section on the Ansen Review

His views on the film's acting

His views on the film's special effects

His views on the film's message

Section on the Johnson Review

His views on the film's acting

His views on the film's special effects

His views on the film's message

Conclusion

Alternating and block formats have their particular strengths and weaknesses. The alternating format allows you to compare and contrast the views of different writers fairly easily. In this paper, for example, you would be able to present each critic's judgments of the film's acting, special effects, and message in its own section. If you were using a block format, you might discuss Travers's views of the acting on page one of your paper and might not discuss Johnson's comments about the acting until page five or six. Your reader would have a hard time remembering Travers's views by the time you discussed Johnson's. Using a block format allows you to give your readers a good sense of the general argument presented by each author. Instead of having the discussion of his opinions spread throughout your paper, each critic's work is developed in a single section of your essay. Using the block format, you give your readers a thorough view of the author's work before you move on to the next source text.

Regardless of the structure you employ, your job in writing an informative synthesis involves more than summarizing what each critic has to say. In writing this paper, you would not be arguing a position of your own concerning *Forrest Gump*. Instead, you would point out for your readers important similarities and differences among the views advanced by the critics.

Once you have designed your thesis, you need to go back through the readings, consult your annotations, and locate material you want to include in your essay. Preparing an informal outline can be quite helpful at this point. In your outline, indicate the focus for each part of your paper, the material you will draw from the readings to develop that section of the essay, and the ideas you will contribute.

Write Your Rough Draft

The introductory section of an informative thesis should, first, capture your reader's interest. You might consider opening your paper with an interesting anecdote, a case history, an important statistic, or a telling quotation from one of the readings. Writing an effective opening gives you the chance to be imaginative and creative. A second goal of the opening section of your synthesis is to introduce the topic of your essay. The title of the synthesis should give your reader some indication of your essay's topic, but you want to be sure to clarify the topic in your opening section. Finally, the introduction to your essay should contain your thesis statement. Whether your thesis is open or closed, you need to include it in your introduction to serve as a guide to the rest of your synthesis.

In the body of your essay, you will follow the structure supplied by your thesis, explaining ideas one author or issue at a time. If you were writing an informative synthesis using the three reviews of *Forrest Gump* as your source texts, in the body of your paper you would summarize, paraphrase, and quote what each critic has to say about the movie, including in your essay material that best captures each critic's views and illustrates your thesis. However, not all the material in your informative synthesis will come from the readings. You have significant contributions to make, too. Besides quoting, paraphrasing, and summarizing what various authors have to say, you will contribute transitions, elaborations, clarifications, and connections.

For example, in one paragraph of your essay, you may introduce the issue to be discussed, introduce a reading by giving the author's name and qualifications as well as the title of the article, quote a relevant passage from the piece, restate the author's ideas in your own words to clarify them, point out how the author's stance differs from the author you discussed in the previous paragraph, and provide a transition to your next paragraph. If you devote a sentence to each of these tasks, your paragraph will be six sentences long, with only one sentence coming directly from the reading. The rest of the material in the paragraph comes from you.

When concluding your informative synthesis, you want to reiterate the main issues or findings you have covered in the body of your essay and give your work a sense of closure. You might want to look back at your opening strategy and reemploy it in your conclusion, if possible. For example, if you opened your paper with a quotation, consider ending it with a quotation. If you began with a question, conclude with the same question, perhaps answering it this time. If you began with a story, come back to the story in your conclusion.

Revise Your Draft

Revising a synthesis takes time. In fact, it is probably best to revise your paper in several stages. First, you might check the **content** of your essay. Here you have two concerns. First, reread what you have written to make sure you are being true to your own intentions. You might ask the following questions of your manuscript:

• Does my thesis accurately reflect my understanding of the readings?
• Have I said in my paper what I wanted to say?

- Have I covered all of the material I hoped to cover when annotating the readings?
- Have I covered the ideas I discovered as I wrote the essay, ideas I did not plan on addressing but developed as I wrote?

A related goal is to review the content of your essay in light of the assignment. Here the questions you ask might include:

- Have I met the demands of the assignment?
- Have I adequately covered the ideas contained in the reading?
- Have I avoided editorializing or arguing a particular position?
- Have I kept my reader in mind? Would this essay make sense to someone who knows little or nothing about the readings? Do any ideas need more development or explanation?

Next, you might review the **organization** of your essay. Here you are concerned with the quality of your thesis statement, topic sentences, and transitions. These are some of the questions you should be asking:

- Does my thesis guide the development of the essay? Put another way, does my essay follow the format suggested or outlined by my thesis?
- Do I have clearly stated topic sentences introducing the major sections of my essay? Are these topic sentences tied to the thesis?
- Have I supplied enough transitional devices to guide my reader through my synthesis, especially when I move from discussing one author to discussing another?

Finally, revise with an eye toward **accuracy** and **clarity**. Here your concerns are word choice, sentence structure, and documentation. Again, you need to ask yourself a series of questions as you review your work, making needed changes when any of your answers are no:

- In choosing words, have I remained as fair and objective as possible?
- Have I successfully avoided jargon and highly technical terms when such language would not be appropriate for my audience?
- Are my sentences easy to read?
- Have I varied the type and length of my sentences?
- Have I quoted material accurately and properly?
- Have I paraphrased material accurately, properly, and fairly?
- Have I documented material thoroughly and properly?

You may need to revise your informative synthesis several times to address adequately all of these concerns.

ARGUMENTATIVE SYNTHESIS

DEFINITION

In an argumentative synthesis, you use material from the readings to support and illustrate an argument of your own, usually concerning the quality of writing in the source texts or an issue they address. If your argument centers on the quality of the readings, you might argue that one is better written or more convincing than the others. If, however, your teacher asks you to present an argument on the issue the readings address, you will draw on the material in the readings to support your thesis.

For a number of reasons, writing an argumentative synthesis can be challenging:

1. As with the informative synthesis, the sources you consult when gathering information for this type of essay can be difficult to read. They will often present complex arguments themselves or employ terminology or research methodologies new to you. Being able to read this material critically is essential if you hope to write a successful argumentative synthesis.

2. As you read these source texts, you will need to critique them. For example, if you are arguing that one is better written than another, you will have to critique both to determine the relative strengths and weaknesses of each. If you are using the readings to develop an argument of your own on the topic they address, again you will have to critique the source texts to determine the quality of the arguments and information in each. You want to base your argument on the best available material.

3. When you compose your argumentative synthesis, you have to be concerned, first, with the content and quality of *your* argument. You need to decide if the material you are including in your paper will achieve the desired effect on your reader—will your audience be convinced by your argument? At the same time, since you are working with source texts, you have to pay close attention to the way you are using other people's findings or arguments to be sure you are fairly representing their work.

4. Part of composing an argumentative synthesis is deciding how best to order the claims, evidence, findings, or arguments you present. You need to decide which ideas or arguments you will present in which order and to provide effective transitions between and within the major sections of your argument.

5. In supporting your argument with source material, you will need to be quoting, summarizing, and paraphrasing other people's ideas, arguments, and findings. As a result, documentation becomes a challenge. You will need to be explicit and clear in acknowledging the source of the information you use to support your assertions.

WRITING AN ARGUMENTATIVE SYNTHESIS

Because argumentative syntheses are so complex, writing them in a number of steps or stages is often helpful. Here are some of the steps you might consider following when writing an argumentative synthesis:

1. Analyze the assignment.
2. Annotate and critique the readings.
3. Formulate a thesis and organizational plan.
4. Write your rough draft.
5. Revise your draft.

Analyze the Assignment

Some teachers will not specify the type of argument they want you to present in your synthesis. If this is the case, you will need to decide for yourself whether you want to focus on the quality of the writing in the readings or on the issue they address. However, if a teacher specifically asks you to focus your argument on the quality of the source texts, his assignment might include directions such as these:

> Review the readings in Chapter 6 of the textbook. Which author do you believe presents the most convincing case? Why?

* * * * *

> Review the readings in Chapter 6 of the textbook. Which piece is better written? How so?

In the first assignment, the teacher wants you to analyze, evaluate, then compare the **arguments** presented by the various writers, arguing that one presents the best case. In the second assignment, the teacher wants you to analyze, evaluate, then compare the **styles** of the various writers, arguing that one produces the best-written text.

However, when a teacher wants you to take a stand on the topic the readings address, her directions may read something like this:

> Review the readings in Chapter 6 of the textbook. Where do you stand on the issue? Present an argument in favor of your position using the readings for support.

Here the teacher wants you to read the articles, think about the arguments presented by each author, reflect on your own knowledge and feelings concerning the topic, then present an argument in which you assume and defend a position of your own on the issue.

Once you have determined the type of argument the teacher wants you to write, check the assignment to determine the number and types of sources the teacher wants you to use in your paper. Sometimes instructors specify a certain number of readings you must use in your paper, asking you, for example, to base your paper on four to six sources. Other times teachers specify the types of readings you have to use: those provided in class, those you find or own in the library, academic sources only, and so on. If you have any questions about the number or type of readings you need to use in your synthesis, be sure to check with your instructor.

Annotate and Critique the Readings

As you begin to collect the readings you plan to use when writing your argumentative synthesis, you need to annotate and critique them (see Chapter 7 for advice on critiquing readings). First, annotate each reading, identifying its thesis, primary assertions, and evidence. Next, analyze and critique the content and structure of each reading. If you base your argument on other authors' faulty writing or reasoning, your essay will likely reflect their weaknesses; likewise, if you base your argument on solid, well-written sources, your argument will likely be stronger. The questions you want to ask of a reading include:

- What, exactly, is the main point of this reading?
- How has the author supported his ideas, arguments, or findings?
- How well has the author explained or supported his ideas, arguments, or findings?
- Do I find the reading convincing? Why or why not?
- How have the structure and tone of the piece influenced my reaction?
- What is the quality of the writing?
- How do the author's ideas, arguments, or findings compare with those found in the other sources I have read?

Place your annotations in the margins of the reading, on sheets of paper, or on index cards. If you use paper or index cards, be sure you copy all the bibliographic information you will need to complete a reference list entry on the source, in case you use any of that material in your paper. In an argumentative synthesis, all quoted, paraphrased, or summarized material needs to be documented.

Formulate a Thesis and Organizational Plan

Formulating a clear thesis statement is an essential step in writing a successful argumentative synthesis. Your thesis statement tells your reader the position you plan on advancing in your paper and will likely indicate the structure of your essay. Put another way, your thesis statement establishes in your readers' minds certain expectations concerning the content and form of your paper. When you satisfy those expectations, your reader will have an easier time following your argument; if you do not, however, readers may feel your work is confusing and disorganized. So you need to spend some time forming and refining your thesis statement.

In an argumentative synthesis you advance a position of your own, on either the quality or the topic of the readings. If you are focusing on the quality of the readings themselves, you can assume a number of different positions. For example, you may argue that one author is most convincing:

> While Travers, Ansen, and Johnson each present insightful critiques of *Forrest Gump*, Travers alone presents a convincing argument explaining why the film became so popular.

Or you may argue that one author's work is better written than another's:

> While Ansen and Johnson both criticize *Forrest Gump* for offering viewers empty sentimentality, Johnson presents a much better argument supporting his interpretation.

In either case, the thesis sets out the position you will be developing in your paper.

As with other types of essays, thesis statements for argumentative syntheses can be either open or closed. While both of the examples above are open thesis statements, they could easily be modified to give the reader a better indication of what exactly will be covered in the paper:

> While Travers, Ansen, and Johnson each present insightful critiques of *Forrest Gump*, through his clear examination of the acting in the film and the director's message, Travers alone presents a convincing argument explaining why the film immediately became so popular.

* * * * *

> While Ansen and Johnson both assert that the effect of *Forrest Gump* relies on empty sentimentality, Johnson presents a much better argument supporting his interpretation by examining in detail specific scenes from the film and effectively comparing the movie to more critically acclaimed films.

If, however, your goal in composing an argumentative synthesis is to argue a position of your own on the topic of the readings, your thesis will read a little differently, something like this (employing an open thesis):

> Though reviewers seem divided in their judgments concerning *Forrest Gump*, it is an important American film.

Or, perhaps this (employing a closed thesis):

> Though reviewers seem divided in their judgments concerning *Forrest Gump*, its special effects and message make it an important American film.

Using either thesis statement, this final argument could be structured in a number of different but related ways. First, you might choose to employ the **block format**, structuring your paper around the views of the critics, agreeing or disagreeing with their assessments of the film's importance. In outline form, your paper might look something like this:

Opening Section

Capture reader interest

Introduce the topic

Introduce the film

Give thesis—*Forrest Gump* is an important American film

Summary of Film (Optional)

Discussion of Ansen Review

Introduce review—title, author, place of publication

Summarize review—what Ansen says about the film's importance

Critique review—how Ansen is or is not correct in his assertions

Tie criticisms to specific passages in review

Fully explain or defend criticisms

Develop your argument

Discussion of Johnson Review

Introduce review—title, author, place of publication

Summarize review—what Johnson says about the film's importance

Critique review—how Johnson is or is not correct in his assertions

Tie criticisms to specific passages in review

Fully explain or defend criticisms

Relate to Ansen's views (if applicable)

Develop your argument

Discussion of Travers Review

Introduce review—title, author, place of publication

Summarize review—what Travers says about the film's importance

Critique review—how Travers is or is not correct in his assertions

Tie criticisms to specific passages in review

Fully explain or defend criticisms

Relate to Johnson's and Ansen's views (if applicable)

Develop your argument

Conclusion

In the opening section of this paper, you would introduce the topic of the paper, introduce the film you will be discussing, and offer your thesis in a way that captures your readers' interest. In the body of the paper, you would critique the work of all three movie critics, focusing your attention on their judgments concerning the importance of *Forrest Gump*. You would summarize and then critique what each has to say about the film's significance, advancing your position through your criticisms of the reviewers' positions. Finally, you would need to tie your praise and criticism of the authors' views to specific passages in their work, explain clearly in your own words whether or not their claims are valid, and tie all of this to the thesis you are advancing.

You may choose, instead, to employ the **alternating format**, structuring your paper around various aspects of the film rather than around the individual reviews. In this case, your paper might reflect this structure:

Opening Section

> Capture reader interest

> Introduce the topic

> Introduce the film

> Give thesis—that the film's acting, special effects, and message make *Forrest Gump* an important American film

Summary of Film (Optional)

Discussion of Why Acting Makes the Film Important

> Describe remarkable acting in the film—specific examples from film

> Argue why acting makes film important

>> *Presentation of your argument*

>> *Support from reviewers—when appropriate*

>> *Critiques of reviewers—when suitable or helpful*

Discussion of Why Special Effects Make the Film Important

> Describe special effects—specific examples from film

> Argue why special effects make film important

>> *Presentation of your argument*

>> *Support from reviewers—when appropriate*

>> *Critiques of reviewers—when suitable or helpful*

Discussion of Why Message Makes the Film Important

> Describe message—specific examples from film

> Argue why message makes film important

>> *Presentation of your argument*

>> *Support from reviewers—when appropriate*

>> *Critiques of reviewers—when suitable or helpful*

Conclusion

In the opening section of this paper, you would again introduce the topic of the essay, give the title of the film, and offer your thesis, trying at the same time to capture your readers' attention and interest. In the body of your essay, you would examine two aspects of the movie, one at a time, explaining why each makes *Forrest Gump* an important American film. In defending your position, you would discuss specific scenes from the movie and refer to the critics' reviews for support—quoting, paraphrasing, summarizing, and critiquing the work of authors who agree and disagree with the position you are advocating in your thesis.

Once you have drafted at least a preliminary thesis for your paper and have some sense of the assertions that will serve as the focus of your synthesis, you will need to return to the readings to locate material to include in your essay. Remember that the focus of an argumentative synthesis should be the argument you are advancing, not the material from the readings. In other words, your first responsibility is to develop a sound argument—the source material serves to illustrate or support *your* assertions.

Write Your Rough Draft

When you feel you are ready to begin writing your rough draft, be sure you have in front of you all of your source texts and notes. Some students like to begin writing immediately—they need to see some of their ideas in writing before they can decide on a final thesis or organize their paper. Other students have to begin with a clear thesis and outline in hand. Follow the method of composing that is most comfortable and successful for you.

When writing your essay, you will support your argument with material from the readings. You can use source material to give your readers background information on the topic (quote or paraphrase material you think your reader needs to know to understand your argument), to support your assertions (quote or paraphrase material that substantiates or illustrates your claims), or to acknowledge opposing views (quote or paraphrase material that calls into question your assertions; you then must decide whether to refute, accommodate, or concede to these different perspectives).

Revise Your Draft

Revising your argumentative synthesis to make it ready for others to read is a time-consuming process again best approached in a series of steps. First, revise to improve the **content** of your paper, focusing on the quality and clarity of the argument you are advancing. Here are some questions you might ask about your draft as you revise to improve its content:

- Have I clearly indicated the point I want to prove?
- Have I clearly indicated the reasons I believe others should accept my position?

- Have I supported each of those reasons with expert testimony, statistics, or some other means of support as well as with clear explanations?
- Have I acknowledged opposing views in my paper when necessary? Have I found ways of refuting, acknowledging, or conceding to them?

Next, review the **organization** of your essay, asking these questions:

- Is the thesis statement clearly worded, and does it control the structure of the essay?
- Have I provided clear transitions between the major sections of my essay?
- Are there clear connections between the material I draw from the readings and my own elaborations and explanations?

Finally, when checking the **accuracy** and **clarity** of your work, ask yourself:

- Have I chosen words that are clear yet contribute to the effect I wanted to elicit from my readers?
- Are my sentences clearly structured with adequate variety?
- Have I quoted and paraphrased material accurately and properly?
- When incorporating quoted or paraphrased material in my synthesis, have I supplied enough background information on the source text so the material makes sense to my readers?
- Have I defined all the terms I need to define?
- Have I documented all the material that needs to be documented?

THE ELEMENTS OF ARGUMENT

As you develop, draft, and revise your argumentative synthesis, pay particular attention to the three basic elements of any argument: **claims**, **grounds**, and **warrants**. According to British philosopher Stephen Toulmin, in *The Uses of Argument* (1958), every argument involves an assertion (the claim) that is supported by evidence (the grounds) and that rests upon a particular set of assumptions or line of reasoning (the warrant). Effective arguments employ clear, limited claims; reliable, appropriate grounds; and fully developed, explicit warrants. Understanding each of these elements can help you compose more effective argumentative syntheses.

A **claim** is an assertion you want your readers to accept. The most general claim in your essay will likely be your thesis; for example, "In his review, Brian D. Johnson offers a more effective, thorough critique of *Forrest Gump* than David Ansen offers in his review." If this were the thesis of an essay you were writing, you would likely support the thesis with other claims or "because" statements: Johnson's review is more effective than Ansen's review *because* he balances criticism with praise and employs more powerful language and comparisons. There are two supporting claims here: (1) in his review Johnson balances criticism with praise, and (2) he employs more powerful language and comparisons than Ansen employs. If you were writing an argumentative synthesis with this thesis, in the body of your essay you would need to support these two claims with valid grounds or evidence and effective warrants or explanations.

The **grounds** are the evidence for a claim. Grounds can include expert testimony, examples, experimental findings, personal experience—whatever is appropriate and effective given the audience and purpose of the assignment. For example, if you were writing an argumentative synthesis that compares Johnson's review of *Forrest Gump* to Ansen's review, the grounds for your thesis might include specific paraphrased or summarized examples from each author's work to support or illustrate your claims, direct quotations from the reviews, or even examples drawn from the film itself.

Warrants are a little harder to understand because they tend to be more abstract. Simply stated, though, a warrant is a line of reasoning, set of assumptions, or explanation that links a claim to its grounds. When writing an argumentative synthesis, you have to do more than simply make a claim and support it with grounds. You also need to explain how, in your view, those grounds do, in fact, support that claim. Grounds do not speak for themselves; you need to explain how the evidence you provide supports your claim. Suppose, for example, you want to support your claim that Johnson uses more powerful language in his review than Ansen uses in his review. To prove your point, suppose you offer as grounds the following example: "In his review, Johnson calls the film's sentimentality 'irritatingly phony.'" Are you ready to move on to your next claim? Have you sufficiently argued or supported this claim by citing an example from the text? No. What's missing here is your warrant—before you move on to your next claim, you have to *explain why* or *how* language like "irritatingly phony" (your ground) makes Johnson's writing more powerful than Ansen's writing (your claim). As you try to do this, you will probably find that citing only one example is insufficient. You may have to cite more examples from Johnson's review to prove your point and compare them directly to language from Ansen's essay. In the end, you will need to explain exactly how these examples support your claim. You will need to provide warrants for your argument.

When you compose an argumentative synthesis from source texts, most of your claims and most of your grounds will be based on what you read. Your teacher may give you several readings to study or require you to collect them on your own outside of class. In either case, you will be asked to study the readings carefully, critique them, form an argumentative thesis, and explain or defend a position in your essay. As you revise your work, remember that good claims are clear and limited—they employ specific, unambiguous language and avoid sweeping generalizations. "There are several good things about Johnson's review" is not a clear claim. What does the writer mean by "good" or by "things"? Likewise claims like "Johnson's review is the best piece of writing ever produced" or "There is absolutely no value at all to Johnson's review" are not sufficiently limited. They are so sweeping that defending them will prove difficult. As you draft and revise your argumentative synthesis, be sure all of your claims (including your thesis) are clear and limited.

Good grounds are relevant, reliable, and appropriate. As you defend or illustrate a claim be sure the evidence you employ is relevant to the assertion you are making. Writing an argumentative synthesis can be confusing since you will be working with multiple texts and multiple claims. As you select the evidence you will use to support a particular claim, be sure it clearly relates to that claim and not to some other assertion you are making in your essay. Also, be sure the grounds are reliable. Draw on the skills you developed when writing critiques of readings. For example, be sure you examine the author's credentials and possible biases, the publication's credibility and biases (especially if you find the material online), and the date of publication. You may have a valid claim to make in your synthesis, but your argument will fail if you support it with unreliable evidence. Finally, be sure your grounds are appropriate for the assignment and audience. As you write papers in classes across the curriculum, you will discover that what counts as valid grounds in one class may not count as valid grounds in another. Learning what grounds are appropriate for arguments in any field of study is part of learning how to reason like a member of that discipline. Analyze the essays you read in class to determine the kinds of evidence successful authors in that field of study utilize in their arguments and ask your instructor for help if you ever question the appropriateness of evidence you plan to use in an essay.

As you evaluate the warrants you employ in your argumentative synthesis, be sure they are fully developed and explicit. Do not expect your grounds to speak for themselves or for your readers to supply missing warrants on their own. Instead, as you develop your essay, explain those connections thoroughly and clearly. Strong warrants offer readers a glimpse of the way your mind works. Warrants make your writing unique: two or more writers may make similar claims and support them with identical grounds, but their warrants will almost always be different. Reasoning from grounds to claims is an individualized process. Our warrants are usually based on our life experiences, education, social status, and assumptions about the world. Fully developed, explicit warrants make your synthesis more effective, individualized, and interesting.

One final word about composing an argumentative synthesis from readings concerns the variety of ways you can employ material from source texts as evidence for your claims. Most writers know that they can support a claim by quoting, paraphrasing, or otherwise alluding to the work of authors who agree with that position. Citing authorities who support the claims you make improves your work's credibility. However, there are other ways to use source material to support an argument. For example, consider citing authorities who *disagree* with the claim you are making. Incorporating counter-examples into your argumentative synthesis can be effective if you employ them correctly. First, acknowledging alternative positions increases your credibility as a writer. It demonstrates your knowledge of the subject matter, your fairness, and your confidence in your own position. However, just citing counter-examples alone will not help you achieve these benefits; instead, you must integrate them into your essay by refuting them, conceding to them, or accommodating them. When you *refute* them, you offer a fair summary of the opposing view then demonstrate how that position is wrong, problematic, or otherwise flawed. You can then demonstrate how your position is better. When you *concede* to an opposing view, you acknowledge how and when the opposition might be right in their assertions. However, you then demonstrate how that fact does not seriously damage your own position or thesis. Finally, when you *accommodate* an opposing view, you explain how that position and your own may be equally correct and how, by combining them, one might gain a better, more comprehensive understanding of the issue. In short, be imaginative in your use of source material as grounds in an argumentative synthesis. Just be sure the grounds you use are linked to your claims with strong warrants.

ARGUMENT AND PERSUASION

Most rhetoricians draw a distinction between argument and persuasion. Argument, they maintain, involves demonstrating the credibility of a position; persuasion involves moving readers to accept or act on that position. The most commonly acknowledged agents of persuasion are logos (logic), pathos (emotion), and ethos (character). That is, people can be persuaded to accept or act on a position in an argument if the writer sufficiently appeals to their logic or to their emotions or if they feel the writer has sufficient credibility or character to sway their views.

In an argumentative synthesis, successful appeals to *logos* largely depend on the quality of your claims, grounds, and warrants. Clear, qualified claims supported by valid grounds and clear, reasonable warrants will go a long way toward persuading a reader that your position is reasonable enough to accept or act on. As discussed above, however, such writing rarely happens by accident. It results from careful, critical revision.

Successful persuasive appeals to *pathos* can be difficult to achieve but can be very effective. When composing an argumentative synthesis, consider which examples or quotations might have the most significant emotional impact on your readers. Consider what moves you as a reader—examples of injustice that need to be righted, threats to your security or well being, humor? Employing pathos to persuade a reader is tricky because it can have the opposite effect if used incorrectly or clumsily. Pathos can quickly turn into *bathos*, or unintentionally comic appeals to emotion. However, when used sparingly and appropriately, emotionally charged grounds or language can prove very persuasive.

Finally, there is *ethos*, perhaps the most difficult appeal to understand. In one sense, ethos is closely linked to logos because it has to do with the credibility of the claims, grounds, and warrants you employ in your synthesis. Ethos involves trust and character: do you demonstrate through the quality of the claims, grounds, and warrants you employ in your writing that you are a trustworthy, knowledgeable, fair-minded individual? If you do, then you may persuade some readers to accept your position through your own ethos as a writer. This is why including alternative points of view in your writing is so important—doing so increases your ethos or credibility in the eyes of many readers.

Ethos, though, also has to do with quality of your own prose. Even if you have a synthesis with strong claims, grounds, and warrants, you will lose your credibility as a writer if your prose is marred by misspellings, grammatical problems, typos, or other surface errors. Most readers will feel that they cannot trust authors who are careless with their writing; if the authors are so sloppy with word choice, syntax, spelling, or punctuation, how sloppy have they been with their research, reasoning, and documentation? Carefully proofreading your work before you present it to an audience is an essential aspect of ethos. Persuasion depends on trust, and you may lose the trust of your readers—and your credibility as a writer—if your argumentative synthesis is full of easily correctable errors.

SAMPLE INFORMATIVE AND ARGUMENTATIVE SYNTHESES

Below are three synthesis essays drawing on the three reviews of *Forrest Gump*. One synthesis is informative, and two are argumentative. The first argumentative synthesis focuses on the quality of the arguments presented in the reviews; the second presents the writer's own argument concerning the film, using the reviews to support or clarify the writer's thesis. As you read the essays, consider how each is structured and how each uses material from the source texts to give readers a better understanding of the film, the critics' views, and the writer's thesis.

SAMPLE INFORMATIVE SYNTHESIS

Three Reviews of Forrest Gump

How much do you trust critics when choosing a movie to go see? Do you only see films that get favorable reviews, or are you more likely to follow friends' advice when picking a movie? Often there is a huge difference between the public's opinion of a film and the critics' views. This difference is clear, for instance, in the case of Forrest Gump, one of the most popular films of 1994. The public seemed to love the film; however, the movie received only mixed reviews from some of the media's better-known critics. The range of critical response to the film is clearly illustrated in the reviews written by Peter Travers for Rolling Stone, David Ansen for Newsweek, and Brian D. Johnson for Macleans. While Travers generally praises Forrest Gump, Ansen and Johnson question its quality, all three critics focusing their comments on the film's acting, special effects, and message.

First, all three critics comment on the actors in the film, including Tom Hanks (Gump), Robin Wright (his girlfriend, Jenny), and Gary Sinise (his friend and business partner, Lt. Dan). Travers praises the movie's actors, especially Hanks, calling his work "unforgettable," noting that he brings "a touching gravity to the role" through "humor and unforced humanity" (131). Ansen generally agrees with Travers's praise of Hanks. Ansen writes that Hanks turns his character into "touching flesh and blood" (130). He also has praise for Wright, saying she "gives a sketchy role grace and gravity" (130).

However, Johnson presents quite a different view of the acting. He believes director Robert Zemeckis, by relying so heavily on special effects, "overpowers his actors" (129). Thus, while he terms Hanks's characterization of Gump "endearing," Johnson is less enthusiastic about Sinise, who "valiantly tries to stay real as his Vietnam buddy, Lt. Dan," and criticizes Wright for getting "lost in a whirlwind of costume changes" (129).

Travers, Ansen, and Johnson are equally split in their views of the film's special effects. Both Travers and Ansen point out that Zemeckis builds on the earlier work of Woody Allen in Zelig; using trick photography, Zemeckis splices into his film old footage that enables Gump to "meet" many famous people. Travers believes the special effects are an unqualified success: "The effects dazzle, though never at the expense of the story" (131). Ansen has even higher praise. He terms the effects "groundbreaking," calling them "remarkable" and "impressive," even "a little scary—we've entered an era where photographic reality can't be trusted" (131). Johnson, though, questions the effectiveness of such "computer doctoring" (129). He believes all the special effects disrupt the narrative of the film, resulting in "a medley of sound bites—clever, cute, amusing, silly, sentimental—and irritatingly phoney" (129). According to Johnson, the spliced-in scenes become so predictable and technological that watching the film "is like watching software" (129).

Finally, all three critics offer quite different interpretations of the film's message and importance. Travers believes Zemeckis has put together an important, serious film about America's values and history. He praises the director for not offering an oversimplified view of Americans: "Forrest is everything we admire in the American character—honest, brave, loyal—and the film's fierce irony is that nobody can stay around him for long" (131). According to Travers, Zemeckis satirizes American values of the '60s as much as he satirizes those of the '80s while still maintaining a sense of optimism, "a capacity for hope" in "this age of rampant cynicism" (131).

Ansen, however, is far less certain about the message the film is trying to convey. If the movie started out to comment on history, Ansen believes it falls into "dubious sentimentality" (130). As a potential tear-jerker, the film left him unmoved. If it was meant to be satiric, Ansen thinks it is "surprisingly toothless" (130). In the end, Ansen believes Zemeckis spreads Gump too thin: as an all-purpose symbol, representing so much in America, Gump ends up representing nothing. Ansen closes his review by commenting, "The world according to Gump is certainly an enjoyable place to visit. But its core is disappointingly soft and elusive" (130).

Johnson echoes Ansen's criticisms of the film's message. He believes Zemeckis's goal is "healing wounds," addressing the same "modern American tragedy" that Oliver Stone has explored (129). However, he thinks that the film ultimately fails to achieve this end. Because of the scattered plot, the frenetic pace, and the overpowering special effects, Johnson claims Hanks's superb portrayal is ultimately "meaningless" (129). According to Johnson, the film succeeds on only one level: "As an exercise in high-powered manipulation, the movie works: audiences may find it irresistible" (129). In the end, though, "Forrest Gump is, quite literally—to quote

Shakespeare—'a tale told by an idiot full of sound and fury, signifying nothing'" (129). For Johnson, the film, despite its technical achievements, has very little to offer its audience.

Even though Forrest Gump proved to be a highly successful film, winning Academy Awards for Hanks and Zemeckis as well as being named Best Picture of 1994, most film critics echoed Ansen and Johnson, not Travers. While most critics praised Hanks and acknowledged the quality of the special effects, they were much less certain about the film's message. Despite these criticisms, though, the film enjoyed great commercial success and popular approval, raising interesting questions about the different standards employed by critics and the general public when evaluating movies.

SAMPLE ARGUMENTATIVE SYNTHESIS (FOCUSING ON THE QUALITY OF THE READINGS)

The Message of Forrest Gump?

Forrest Gump was one of the most popular films of 1994. Even though it won several Academy Awards—including one for Best Picture—the movie was not a hit among most film critics. Some reviewers praised the film, but many more gave it only a lukewarm response while many others severely criticized it. Reviews that reflect the range of negative opinion are "Forrest Gump," by Newsweek film critic David Ansen, and "The Fool on the Hill," by Macleans critic Brian D. Johnson. Ansen's review notes both positive and negative aspects of the film, but in the end he believes the film's weaknesses outweigh its strengths. Johnson's review, however, is almost entirely negative. One aspect of the film both men severely question is its meaning or message; however, through effective word choice and comparisons, Johnson presents a much better argument to support his criticisms.

In his review, Ansen comments positively on several aspects of Forrest Gump. He has particularly strong praise for the acting of Tom Hanks ("Hanks, who can do no wrong as an actor, turns this fantastical conceit into funny, touching flesh and blood; even his elbows are eloquent") and for Hanks's costar, Robin Wright, who "gives a sketchy role grace and gravity" (130). Ansen was equally impressed with the film's special effects, both "the 'Zelig'-like insertions, which place the hero inside archival footage" and the other, less noticeable computer-enhanced scenes, such as the anti-war rally at the Washington Monument. Ansen calls the special effects "groundbreaking" (130).

However, in the end, Ansen questions the film's message: "the whole seems less than the sum of its parts" (130). Ansen believes that as a piece of historical drama, the film collapses into "dubious sentimentality"; that as satire, it is "toothless"; and that as a tear-jerker, it is unmoving. In the end, he believes Zemeckis overplays his hand with

Gump, having the character symbolize so many aspects of late-20th-century America that the character ends up truly symbolizing nothing. Overall, Ansen finds the film "disappointingly soft and elusive" (130).

In his review, Brian D. Johnson notes many of the same weaknesses in Forrest Gump, but he does not balance his criticism with praise. While he calls Hanks "endearing" as Gump, Johnson claims Robin Wright "gets lost" in her role as Gump's girlfriend, Jenny, and instead of expressing admiration for the special effects, Johnson claims they "overpower" the actors (129). However, most of his criticism is aimed at the film's message. Johnson finds the film essentially vacuous, closing his review with the claim, "Forrest Gump is, quite literally—to quote Shakespeare—'a tale told by an idiot full of sound and fury, signifying nothing'" (129).

While Ansen and Johnson both criticize the film's message, Johnson produces a much more effective critique through his use of powerful language and comparisons. First, Johnson's criticisms are couched in language much more negative and powerful than Ansen's. For example, while Ansen considers the film's sentimentality "dubious" (130), Johnson terms it "irritatingly phoney" (129). Though he wonders how the special effects contribute to the film's message, Ansen still calls them "groundbreaking" (129). Johnson, though, simply complains about the "computer doctoring of archival clips" (130). Johnson also uses sarcasm to question the effect of the film, pointing out with amazement that Gump does "astonishingly well" in life because of "serendipitous timing" (129). He criticizes the film's plot as being "clever, cute, amusing, silly, sentimental" and the sound track as "plodding" (129). In the end, Johnson believes the bad acting, overreliance on special effects, and sentimentality render the film "meaningless" (129). Johnson's harsh language and satire present a much more effective critique of the film's message than the one Ansen produced.

Johnson also supports his judgment quite well by comparing Forrest Gump to other, more critically acclaimed films. For example, both Ansen and Johnson point out how Zemeckis used similar special effects in earlier films, such as Who Framed Roger Rabbit? However, Johnson goes on to point out that Zemeckis is using these special effects to explore themes already successfully explored by Oliver Stone, calling Zemeckis's work "Oliver-Stone-lite" (129). Likewise, he compares Hanks's work as the dim-witted Gump to Dustin Hoffman's work as the "autistic hero in Rain Man" (129), implying that Hanks's efforts pale in comparison.

Through his use of negative language, satire, and effective comparisons, Johnson presents a thorough, effective critique of Forrest Gump's message. He notes many of the same weaknesses Ansen points out, but develops and explains his criticisms much more effectively. Forrest Gump continues to be a popular movie—video sales are going well. However, unlike these critics, many people find the movie not just entertaining but also inspiring, seeing in Forrest Gump a message of hope, courage, and love.

SAMPLE ARGUMENTATIVE SYNTHESIS
(FOCUSING ON THE TOPIC OF THE READINGS)

Forrest Gump: An Important American Film

Even though Forrest Gump won several Academy Awards—including one for Best Picture—the movie was not an unqualified hit among film critics. While some reviewers praised the film for the quality of its acting, writing, and special effects, others questioned its value and significance. For many of these critics, the film offered technical flash but little more; they were unimpressed with the film's acting, direction, or message. However, time may well prove these latter critics to be wrong in their assessment. Because of its groundbreaking special effects and message of hope and survival, Forrest Gump is likely to be recognized as one of the most important end-of-the-century American films, one that will likely be studied by film scholars and film students for years to come.

Forrest Gump's special effects have generated the most critical comment—both positive and negative—and rightly so. The film's innovative special effects will help ensure its status as a significant work. Director Robert Zemeckis, who in earlier films such as Who Framed Roger Rabbit? gained a reputation for technical innovation, broke new ground in Forrest Gump. Using advanced computer graphics, for example, he incorporated old news footage into his film, enabling the title character, Forrest Gump (played by Tom Hanks), to meet and converse with John F. Kennedy, Richard Nixon, and John Lennon. As reviewer David Ansen noted, a similar technique was employed by Woody Allen in Zelig (130). However, the quality of Zemeckis's effects go well beyond that achieved by Allen: the grafting is almost seamless. Whereas Zelig frequently appears behind or beside celebrities and political figures of the past, Gump interacts with them. As Ansen comments, the effect is a bit unnerving: "we've entered an era where photographic reality can't be trusted" (130).

However, Forrest Gump's special effects achieve more than just remarkable realism; Zemeckis uses them to support the film's characters and theme in important, innovative ways. In his review "The Fool on the Hill," Macleans reviewer Brian D. Johnson contends that the special effects sometimes "overpower" the actors (129). In reality, though, Zemeckis's effects tend to support, not overpower the actors. Consider, for example, how Zemeckis employed blue screen imaging technology to "amputate" the legs of Gary Sinise, who played Gump's Vietnam commanding officer, Lt. Dan. Sinise's ability to portray Lt. Dan's anguish and anger is clearly enhanced by the realistic effects achieved by Zemeckis's technology. On screen, Lt. Dan's legs are clearly and simply gone, enabling viewers to understand and share his sense of loss and frustration in the hospital, as well as his sense of triumph at Gump's wedding celebration. The special effects in Gump set important new technical standards, but they also establish new standards in supporting a film's characters and themes.

These themes and the film's message also make Forrest Gump an important American film, though again, many critics disagree. For example, Brian D. Johnson, quoting Shakespeare, calls Gump "'a tale told by an idiot full of sound and fury, signifying nothing'" (129), and even David Ansen, who praised the film's acting and special effects, says that at its "core" Forrest Gump "is disappointingly soft and elusive" (130). However, to determine whether these critics are correct in their criticisms, one must first determine the meaning and intent of this tale, what, at its core, the film is trying to communicate.

In Forrest Gump Zemeckis explores what it means to be an American in the second half of the twentieth century. Gump, slow-witted and soft spoken, witnesses or participates in most of the key historical and cultural events of the past fifty years: he teaches Elvis to dance, plays football for Bear Bryant, survives Vietnam with honor, triggers the discovery of the Watergate break-in, instigates the jogging craze, and buys Apple stock early. Through fate or luck or both, Gump not only survives the turbulent years that killed so many others, but thrives. At the end of the film he is a rich, successful businessman with a beautiful son. Why?

Throughout the film, Zemeckis makes the point that Gump flourishes because of his innate goodness. In this film, some good deeds do go unpunished, faith is rewarded, hope is vindicated. Gump represents much that is right with humans. First, he remains loyal to his friends and family. By keeping his promise to Bubba, a Vietnam buddy, Gump becomes a millionaire in the shrimping business. Through his steadfast love for Jenny, Gump gains a loving son. Second, Gump follows his heart, always trying to do what is right. By remaining steadfast to his values, Gump avoids the plagues that eventually doom Jenny and inadvertently outsmarts "Tricky" Dick Nixon.

However, while Gump's simplicity and sincerity guide him through life and in some ways protect him, Zemeckis points out that Gump's good nature cannot shield him from all of life's pain and suffering. Gump loses his mother, Bubba, and Jenny. His Vietnam experiences are horrible. He must endure years of loneliness in his old house; in public, he faces the ridicule and humiliation frequently cast upon fools. Yet, in the end, Gump prevails, a sad, kind, and wise man.

While many film critics have dismissed Forrest Gump's message as simplistic and outdated, the sheer popularity of the film indicates otherwise: it created an audience for itself through the power of its message. As human beings, we need to be reminded of what is positive in us, reminded about our potential for goodness. Forrest Gump delivers this better vision of humanity which, as Peter Travers notes in his review, is "an ambitious goal in this age of rampant cynicism" (131).

Forrest Gump is and will remain an important American film. Through his use of special effects, Zemeckis has produced a visually remarkable movie. More significantly, though, Forrest Gump presents a vision of what is good and enduring about humanity. As we watch Gump's life unfold in memory, we have to reflect on his remarkable success: how can such outcomes be explained? In working out our answers, we come closer to the true core of this film—its vision of hope, endurance, and charity.

Additional Reading

Teenage Suicide

National Alliance for the Mentally Ill

*Founded in 1979, the **National Alliance for the Mentally Ill** is a non-profit advocacy group for people who suffer from severe mental illness and for their families.*

Most everyone at some time in his or her life will experience periods of anxiety, sadness, and despair. These are normal reactions to the pain of loss, rejection, or disappointment. Those with serious mental illnesses, however, often experience much more extreme reactions, reactions that can leave them mired in hopelessness. And when all hope is lost, some feel that suicide is the only solution. *It isn't.*

According to the National Institute of Mental Health, scientific evidence has shown that almost all people who take their own lives have a diagnosable mental or substance abuse disorder, and the majority have more than one disorder. In other words, the feelings that often lead to suicide are *highly* treatable. That's why it is imperative that we better understand the symptoms of the disorders and the behaviors that often accompany thoughts of suicide. With more knowledge, we can often prevent the devastation of losing a loved one.

Now the eighth-leading cause of death overall in the U.S. and the third-leading cause of death for young people between the ages of 15 and 24 years, suicide has become the subject of much recent focus. U.S. Surgeon General David Satcher, for instance, recently announced his *Call to Action to Prevent Suicide, 1999*, an initiative intended to increase public awareness, promote intervention strategies, and enhance research. The media, too, has been paying very close attention to the subject of suicide, writing articles and books and running news stories. Suicide among our nation's youth, a population very vulnerable to self-destructive emotions, has perhaps received the most discussion of late. Maybe this is because teenage suicide seems the most tragic—lives lost before they've even started. Yet, while all of this recent focus is good, it's only the beginning. We cannot continue to lose so many lives unnecessarily.

Some Basic Facts

- In 1996, more teenagers and young adults died of suicide than from cancer, heart disease, AIDS, birth defects, stroke, pneumonia and influenza, and chronic lung disease combined.

- In 1996, suicide was the second-leading cause of death among college students, the third-leading cause of death among those aged 15 to 24 years, and the fourth-leading cause of death among those aged 10 to 14 years.
- From 1980 to 1996, the rate of suicide among African-American males aged 15 to 19 years increased by 105 percent.

It is a hopeful sign that while the incidence of suicide among adolescents and young adults nearly tripled from 1965 to 1987, teen suicide rates in the past ten years have actually been declining, possibly due to increased recognition and treatment. *(1996 is the most recent year for which suicide statistics are available.)*

Suicide "Signs"

There are many behavioral indicators that can help parents or friends recognize the threat of suicide in a loved one. Since mental and substance-related disorders so frequently accompany suicidal behavior, many of the cues to be looked for are symptoms associated with such disorders as depression, bipolar disorder (manic depression), anxiety disorders, alcohol and drug use, disruptive behavior disorders, borderline personality disorder, and schizophrenia.

Some common symptoms of these disorders include:

- Extreme personality changes
- Loss of interest in activities that used to be enjoyable
- Significant loss or gain in appetite
- Difficulty falling asleep or wanting to sleep all day
- Fatigue or loss of energy
- Feelings of worthlessness or guilt
- Withdrawal from family and friends
- Neglect of personal appearance or hygiene
- Sadness, irritability, or indifference
- Having trouble concentrating
- Extreme anxiety or panic
- Drug or alcohol use or abuse
- Aggressive, destructive, or defiant behavior
- Poor school performance
- Hallucinations or unusual beliefs

Tragically, many of these signs go unrecognized. And while suffering from one of these symptoms certainly does not necessarily mean that one is suicidal, it's always best to communicate openly with a loved one who has one or more of these behaviors, especially if they are unusual for that person.

There are also some more obvious signs of the potential for committing suicide. Putting one's affairs in order, such as giving or throwing away favorite belongings, is a strong clue. And it can't be stressed more strongly that any talk of death or suicide should be taken seriously and paid close attention to. It is a sad fact that while many of those who commit suicide talked about it beforehand, only 33 percent to 50 percent were identified by their doctors as having a mental illness at the time of their death and only 15 percent of suicide victims were in treatment at the time of their death. Any history of previous suicide attempts is also reason for concern and watchfulness. Approximately one-third of teens who die by suicide have made a previous suicide attempt. It should be noted as well that while more females attempt suicide, more males are successful in completing suicide.

Causes

While the reasons that teens commit suicide vary widely, there are some common situations and circumstances that seem to lead to such extreme measures. These include major disappointment, rejection, failure, or loss such as breaking up with a girlfriend or boyfriend, failing a big exam, or witnessing family turmoil. Since the overwhelming majority of those who commit suicide have a mental or substance-related disorder, they often have difficulty coping with such crippling stressors. They are unable to see that their life *can* turn around, unable to recognize that suicide is a permanent solution to a temporary problem. Usually, the common reasons for suicide listed above are actually not the "causes" of the suicide, but rather triggers for suicide in a person suffering from a mental illness or substance-related disorder.

More recently, scientists have focused on the biology of suicide. Suicide is thought by some to have a genetic component, to run in families. And research has shown strong evidence that mental and substance-related disorders, which commonly affect those who end up committing suicide, do run in families. While the suicide of a relative is obviously not a direct "cause" of suicide, it does, perhaps, put certain individuals at more risk than others. Certainly, the suicide of one's parent or other close family member could lead to thoughts of such behavior in a teen with a mental or substance-related disorder.

Research has also explored the specific brain chemistry of those who take their own lives. Recent studies indicate that those who have attempted suicide may also have low levels of the brain chemical serotonin. Serotonin helps control impulsivity, and low levels of the brain chemical are thought to cause more impulsive behavior. Suicides are often committed out of impulse. Antidepressant drugs affecting serotonin are used to treat depression, impulsivity, and suicidal thoughts. However, much more research is needed to confirm these hypotheses and, hopefully, eventually lead to more definite indicators of and treatment for those prone to suicide.

How to Help

Since people who are contemplating suicide feel so alone and helpless, the most important thing to do if you think a friend or loved one is suicidal is to communicate with him or her openly and frequently. Make it clear that you care; stress your willingness to listen. Also, be sure to take all talk of suicide seriously.

Don't assume that people who talk about killing themselves won't really do it. An estimated 80 percent of all those who commit suicide give some warning of their intentions or mention their feelings to a friend or family member. And don't ignore what may seem like casual threats or remarks. Statements like "You'll be sorry when I'm dead" and "I can't see any way out," no matter how off-the-cuff or jokingly said, may indicate serious suicidal feelings.

One of the most common misconceptions about talking with someone who might be contemplating suicide is that bringing up the subject may make things worse. This is not true. There is no danger of "giving someone the idea." Rather, the opposite is correct. Bringing up the question of suicide and discussing it without showing shock or disapproval is one of the most helpful things you can do. This openness shows that you are taking the individual seriously and responding to the severity of his or her distress.

If you do find that your friend or loved one is contemplating suicide, it is essential to help him or her find immediate professional care […]. Don't make the common misjudgment that those contemplating suicide are unwilling to seek help. Studies of suicide victims show that more than half had sought medical help within six months before their deaths. And don't leave the suicidal person to find help alone—they usually aren't capable. Also, *never* assume that someone who is determined to end his or her life can't be stopped. Even the most severely depressed person has mixed feelings about death, wavering until the very last moment between wanting to live and wanting to die. Most suicidal people do not want death; they want the pain to stop. The impulse to end it all, though, no matter how overpowering, does not last forever.

If the threat is immediate, if your friend or loved one tells you he or she is going to commit suicide, you must act immediately. Don't leave the person alone, and don't try to argue. Instead, ask questions like, "Have you thought about how you'd do it?" "Do you have the means?" and "Have you decided when you'll do it?" If the person has a defined plan, the means are easily available, the method is a lethal one, and the time is set, the risk of suicide is obviously severe. In such an instance, you *must* take the individual to the nearest psychiatric facility or hospital emergency room. If you are together on the phone, you may even need to call 911 or the police. Remember, under such circumstances no actions on your part should be considered too extreme—you are trying to save a life. An overwhelming majority of young people who hear a suicide threat from a friend or loved one don't report the threat to an adult. Take all threats seriously—you are not betraying someone's trust by trying to keep them alive.

Other Serious Considerations

Don't automatically assume that someone who was considering suicide and is now in treatment or tells you that he or she is feeling better is, in fact, doing better. Some who commit suicide actually do so just as they seem to be improving. One reason for this may be that they did not have enough energy to kill themselves when they were extremely depressed, but now have just enough energy to go through with their plan. Another reason for suicide during a seeming improvement is that resigning oneself to death can release anxiety. While it's not good to monitor every action of someone who is recovering from suicidal thoughts, it is important to make certain that the lines of communication between you and the individual remain open.

While it may seem a bit obvious, it should also be mentioned that it is extremely advisable to bar teens who are suicidal from access to firearms. Nearly 60 percent of all completed suicides are committed with a firearm. And while having a firearm does not in itself promote suicidal behavior, knowing that one is accessible may help a troubled teen formulate his or her suicidal plans.

Additional Reading

Complex Set of Ills Spurs Rising Teen Suicide Rate

Jessica Portner

Jessica Portner writes for Education Week.

Two teenagers burst into their Colorado high school one year ago this month and gunned down 13 people. But nearly lost in the avalanche of reaction to the shootings at Columbine High School was the fact that the young men were also on a suicide mission.

The high school seniors had meticulously planned their own deaths—down to the last bullet and explosive—for nearly a year. They fashioned homemade pipe bombs and attached them to their bodies, apparently intending to blow themselves up along with the school. But instead, after shooting their victims, they turned their weapons on themselves, punching bullets into their own heads.

"They wanted to do as much damage as they possibly could and then go out in flames," John Stone, the Jefferson County, Colo., sheriff, said that day.

By committing mass murder, Dylan Harris, 18, and Eric Klebold, 17, joined a small group of other American teenagers. In their suicides, however, they had plenty of company.

For every adolescent who opened fire at schools from West Paducah, Ky., to Springfield, Ore., in the past few years, thousands more shot themselves, slit their wrists, or gulped down pills in suicides or attempts.

In the 1998-99 school year, eight students committed homicides in schools, and 26 students died in violent incidents on school grounds. That same year, an estimated 2,700 young people ages 10 to 19 took their own lives.

While suicide rates among adults have steadied or even declined over the past few decades, teenage suicide rates have tripled. In 1960, the suicide rate among 15- to 19-year-olds was 3.6 per 100,000. But by 1990, 11.1 out of every 100,000 teenagers 15 and older committed suicide, according to the U.S. Centers for Disease Control and Prevention.

In 1997, more than 30,000 suicides were recorded in the United States; about 9 percent of those were committed by people age 19 or younger. "Where it used to be your grandfather, now it's your son," said Tom Simon, a suicide researcher at the CDC. He added that more Americans under age 19 now die each year from suicide than from cancer, heart disease, AIDS, pneumonia, lung disease, and birth defects combined.

Likely Victims

Which teenagers are most likely to take their own lives? Federal statisticians say the surge in suicides among the nation's youths is fueled by unprecedented increases in such deaths in certain populations. For example, suicide rates among 10- to 14-year-olds have nearly doubled in the past few decades. And black teenagers are now more than twice as likely to kill themselves as they were just 20 years ago. But white teenagers, particularly boys, still tower over their peers in their rates of self-destructiveness.

For every teenager who commits suicide, 100 more will try. Every year, one in 13 high school students attempts suicide, a 1997 federally funded Youth Risk Behavior Survey found. Half of all high school students report they have "seriously considered" suicide by the time they graduate, the survey says. That's an estimated 700,000 American high school students annually who attempt to kill themselves, and millions who say they have contemplated doing so.

According to a report released last fall by the U.S. Department of Education, *Indicators of School Crime and Safety, 1999*, a quarter of the deaths that occur on school grounds are actually suicides. Students who kill themselves on school property tend to do so in highly public venues—such as their classrooms or the school parking lot. Of the 34 students who died violently at school in the 1997-98 school year—the year of the multiple killings in Springfield and West Paducah—nine were suicides.

Teenage girls attempt suicide three times as often as boys do, but males are four times more likely to finish the job. This gender gap, reported in the 1997 survey, reflects the fact that boys tend to employ more lethal means, such as firearms and hanging; girls favor more survivable methods, such as overdosing on pills.

Girls attempt suicide more than boys, experts say, because their act is an effort at communicating their desperation. Boys tend to keep their emotions hidden. "Girls cry out for help, while boys are taught to be tough and never to act like a 'girl,'" said Dr. William Pollack, a professor of psychiatry at Harvard University and an expert on adolescent mental health. As a result, Dr. Pollack said, "boys are so ashamed of their feelings they figure they'd be better off dead" than express their pain.

A small percentage of the increase in teenage suicide rates could reflect improvements in reporting over the past few decades, according to Lloyd Potter, an epidemiologist and suicide expert at the CDC. But, Mr. Potter said, rates have been and continue to be artificially low because suicides are often masked or misclassified.

A child's suicide is often camouflaged by parents who rearrange the site of the death or hide suicide notes. And some medical examiners classify a death as a suicide only when a note is found, something that occurs in less than a third of all cases.

"There's no doubt there are families who don't want it to appear on the death certificate, and the coroner obliges them," said Dr. Tom Shires, a trauma surgeon with the National Suicide Prevention Institute in Las Vegas. In some states, Dr. Shires added, the person designated to determine the cause of death may be a lawyer or a justice of the peace with no medical training who is ill-equipped to investigate such cases.

Dr. Shires, who is compiling a comprehensive database on suicide attempts among people of all ages, added that police are often complicit in the undercount of suicides. Law-enforcement officers across the country so consistently record single-car collisions—even those showing no skid marks on the pavement—as accidents that doctors have coined a term for them: autocides. Such misclassification disproportionately affects youth suicide rates because the category of "unintentional injuries," primarily from automobile accidents, represents the leading cause of death for 15- to 19-year-olds in the United States.

Another way suicide is hidden from the record books, say experts who study gangs, is that some teenagers who want to escape gang life but see no way out choose to die the "honorable" way by provoking police to fire at them.

"We call that 'suicide by cop,'" said Gloria Grenados, a psychiatric social worker at Bell High School in Los Angeles, a school whose students are nearly all affiliated with a gang, she said. "There are kids [that survived] who literally tell me they ran to meet the bullets because they so much wanted to die."

Taking note of such subterfuges, U.S. Surgeon General David Satcher recently called suicide "the nation's hidden epidemic." Suicide, Dr. Satcher said as he launched a suicide-prevention campaign last fall, must be destigmatized and addressed as a public-health problem.

Impulsive Youths

Young people are more vulnerable than adults to thoughts of suicide, experts say, because they often don't comprehend in a rational sense that death is final. Suicide notes collected by researchers show children fantasizing about what they will do when they are dead. Young people often see suicide as the end of their problems, not their existence. "The developmental stage of adolescence is consistent with not thinking of the long- or short-term consequences of behavior," said Mr. Simon of the CDC.

Another tenet of child development is that adolescents are risk-takers by nature who change friends, clothing styles, and attitudes constantly and for no apparent reason. Such impulsivity still rules when teenagers want to chuck more than their wardrobes. But those traits are most often coupled with environmental stresses before a young person decides to commit suicide.

The impetus for inner turmoil in the hearts of American adolescents in recent years cannot be gleaned from superficial clues such as whether a teenager plays violent video games, listens to Marilyn Manson CDs, or dons black trench coats, school psychologists say. Young people, they say, rarely wear their angst so conveniently on their sleeves.

In his 1991 book, *The Enigma of Suicide,* journalist George Howe Colt writes that searching for a single cause for suicide is as futile as "trying to pinpoint what causes us to fall in love or what causes war."

Finding an answer to the riddle of self-murder is not like tracing the origins of a disease to a single genetic marker. Suicide is more akin to a multicolored tapestry whose yarn must be unraveled strand by strand.

Looking for Reasons

Sociologists and mental-health experts point to a tangle of cultural, psychological, and medical factors that have in the past 30 years fueled teenagers' heightened self-destructiveness: a higher divorce rate, parental abuse, poor impulse control stemming from exposure to television, the availability of handguns, lack of access to mental-health services, and a general sense of isolation and alienation from caring adults both at home and at school.

Some experts argue that the leading reason why young people are more at risk for suicide now than they were a generation or two ago is the decline of the traditional family unit. The teenage suicide rate began its climb just as the divorce rate started to surge upward in the 1970s. Half of U.S. marriages now end in divorce, compared with 28 percent in the 1960s; 70 percent of children who attempt suicide have parents who are divorced. In addition, the percentage of children living with two parents declined from 85 percent in 1970 to 68 percent in 1996, federal statistics show.

The dissolution of a two-parent family, whether from divorce, desertion, or the death of a parent, makes children more vulnerable, experts say. Ultimately, though, it's the quality of the parenting, not the constitution of the family unit, that matters most, children's advocates say. Whether married, divorced, or single, most parents are now working more than in the past and, as a result, have far less free time to spend with their children.

"We are benefitting in this society from everyone working, women working, the gross-national-product productivity per dollar increasing," said Kevin Dwyer, the president of the National Association of School

Psychologists. "But now kids are growing up without the supports they had in the past." The term "latchkey kid," for children left to fend for themselves at home after school, was coined in the 1980s.

To fill the parenting void and the decreasing ratio of caring adults to children, television increasingly has become children's stalwart companion after school. Parents spend an average of just two minutes a day communicating with their child, while the TV set spends an average of 3½ hours a day with that child, Mr. Colt writes in his book.

Studies are mixed on how exposure to media images of murders and assaults affects children's behavior, though many youth advocates are convinced that violent television shows, movies, and computer games inflame destructive tendencies. More than 86 percent of television shows and movies depict characters who solve interpersonal problems with violence, according to NASP.

By the end of elementary school, the average child will have witnessed more than 100,000 acts of violence on television, including 8,000 murders, according to the Center for Media Education in Washington.

Served the common fare of shootouts and knifings on TV, children come to believe that violence is an appropriate solution to problems, Mr. Dwyer said.

In today's media-saturated, high-velocity society, youths with poor impulse control are given the message that it's only natural that they should want everything yesterday.

While the video-game industry rejects the idea that some of its games are virtual training classes for potential gunmen, some recent, controversial studies contend that playing violent video games helps youths' dexterity with real firearms and desensitizes them to the visceral realities of violence. In one recent study, high school students interviewed after suicide attempts expressed surprise that their actions were so painful because it didn't look that way on TV.

The Media Factor

Some research suggests that the news media may foster children's self-destructive and violent behavior simply by reporting horrific events.

A 1986 study by Madelyn Gould, a professor of psychiatry at Columbia University who examined media coverage of suicides, found that the suicide of a person reported either on television or in newspapers makes at-risk individuals who are exposed to the coverage feel that suicide is a "reasonable, and even appealing, decision."

After last year's shootings at Columbine High School, which touched off weeks of intensive coverage by the national news media, there was a spike in teenage suicides across the nation, according to several experts. In Los Angeles County alone, six students killed themselves within six weeks of the shootings. In the four of those cases in which notes were left, three mentioned Columbine as an inspiration. "If you plaster their face up on the news for 20 minutes, that's going to make the difference," said Dr. Pollack of Harvard. Media coverage of suicides isn't the reason for a child's decision to kill himself, Dr. Pollack said, but it's a contributing factor.

"These things open the floodgate," he said of news accounts. "But to flood, the waters have to already be at a high level."

Keeping afloat emotionally is challenging for many young people because the violence they're exposed to is not just on their television screens. Not surprisingly, children who suffer chronic physical or emotional abuse at home or who witness domestic violence are much more likely to kill themselves than their peers who do not witness such violence.

"A child doesn't just wake up suicidal," said Richard Lieberman, a school psychologist with the suicide-prevention unit of the Los Angeles public schools who handles distress calls from school officials 24 hours a day. "Kids are dealing with more loss. Families are under more stress."

In all areas of the country—poor, rich, urban, suburban, and rural— reports of child abuse have accelerated dramatically in the past few decades. Though a small portion of the increase is attributable to better reporting, the bulk represents a real and disturbing trend, according to federal health officials. In 1997, 42 out of every 1,000 children in the United States were reported as victims of child abuse, a 320 percent leap from 10 per 1,000 children in 1976, figures from the U.S. Department of Health and Human Services show. Newspapers regularly report stories that were once rare: children locked in basements without food; battered and bruised toddlers entering shelters; teenage girls sexually assaulted by their fathers.

Changing School Climate

While home environments in general seem to have become more hazardous, so in large part have schools, say researchers who monitor school climate. Apart from the increasing rates of assaults and shootings since the 1970s, garden-variety bullying behavior is rampant, says Dorothy Espelage, a professor of educational psychology at the University of Illinois at Urbana-Champaign. In a study published last fall, Ms. Espelage found that 80 percent of the 558 Illinois middle school students surveyed reported they had been "threatened, ridiculed, or been physically aggressive" with at least one classmate in the past 30 days.

Other experts suggest that the increased emphasis on raising academic standards and student-achievement levels adds pressure to the mix.

"We have become so focused on raising standards and testing students, and we are paying very little attention that this is working against creating a motivating environment for kids to come to school," said Howard Adelman, a professor of psychology at the University of California, Los Angeles, who runs a project to promote mental health in schools.

Of course, not every student who feels pressured at school, is harassed, or even has a chaotic home life becomes suicidal.

A suicidal teenager is often fundamentally unstable, mental-health experts say.

Currently in the United States, they note, an estimated 11 percent of children ages 9 to 17—or 4 million children—have a diagnosable mental disorder, ranging from obsessive-compulsive disorders to major depression.

The rate of depression has been rising among the young, researchers say, in part because the average age of puberty has declined, and depressive illness tends to emerge after puberty.

Clinically depressed adolescents are five times more likely to attempt suicide than their nondepressed peers, according to a 15-year study that tracked 73 depressed adolescents and compared them with peers who were not clinically depressed.

Psychiatrists who have been enlisted to analyze the motivation of the Columbine shooters point to the fact that Mr. Harris was being treated with an anti-depressant.

In a new book, *Night Falls Fast: Understanding Suicide,* Dr. Kay Redfield Jamison, a professor of psychiatry at Johns Hopkins University, says clinical depression is quite distinguishable from common adolescent angst. "In its severe forms, depression paralyzes all of the otherwise vital forces that make us human, leaving instead a bleak, fatiguing, deadened state," she writes.

In *Darkness Visible,* the author William Styron describes his own severe depression as "a hurricane of the mind." And five years before killing herself, poet Sylvia Plath said of her depressive moods: "I felt as if I were smothering. As if a great muscular owl were sitting on my chest, its talons clenching and constricting my heart."

A growing number of children are now being treated for mood disorders. In 1996, 600,000 children under age 18 with clinical depression were prescribed the antidepressants Prozac, Paxil, and Zoloft, according to IMS America, a research group in New York City. Because no long-term studies on the use of antidepressants by children have been conducted, it is difficult to determine whether such medicinal remedies can lift the suffocating darkness that Dr. Jamison describes.

Whatever the effect, the upsurge in prescribing psychiatric medications has occurred mainly in middle- and upper-class populations, in which children have more access to health care. For millions of teenagers, the last trip to any kind of doctor was for childhood inoculations.

A study released last fall by the University of North Carolina at Chapel Hill found that one-fifth of teenagers said they had had no health care in the past six months, even though they had a condition that warranted a medical visit. That situation represents a lost opportunity, suicide experts say, because family doctors can detect sudden changes in mood, sleeping patterns, and eating habits—indicators of depression.

Some depressed teenagers, who are either embarrassed to seek help or can't afford it, eschew traditional medical care in favor of illicit drugs to elevate their moods. There is a strong link between the use of illegal drugs and suicide; alcohol and certain drugs are depressants and can often have the effect of deepening one's mood. And, because they knock down inhibitions, teenagers feel freer to act on their suicidal fantasies.

Autopsies of adolescent suicide victims show that one-third to one-half of the teenagers were under the influence of drugs or alcohol shortly before they killed themselves, according to HHS statistics. The rate of overall teenage drug use has fluctuated over the past three decades, peaking in the 1970s and then receding somewhat in the 1980s. Use of marijuana and alcohol—both depressants—surged in the 1990s.

Teenagers haven't been gravitating much toward church for comfort. Religious affiliation as a buffer against the harsh realities of the world has a solid grounding in research. For example, studies have shown that elderly people who participate in church-based activities—such as social events and bingo games—have a decreased risk of mortality. That finding, researchers say, could be due as much to the balm of faith as to the fact that attending places of worship decreases isolation.

But while teenage attendance at religious services rose in the late 1990s, far fewer adolescents attend than did 20 years ago.

Means and Reasons

The burgeoning numbers of isolated, despondent teenagers now more than ever have lethal means at their fingertips.

The federal Bureau of Alcohol, Tobacco, and Firearms reports that in 1960, 90 million guns were in circulation; today, there are an estimated 200 million firearms in private hands. That's enough weaponry, if distributed among the U.S. population, for three out of four Americans to be armed. Despite state and federal laws banning possession of handguns by anyone under 18, for many young people, finding a firearm is no more complicated than pilfering from a parent's closet. Other teenagers know where to buy guns illegally on the streets.

Guns are the method of choice for suicidal youths: More than 67 percent of boys and nearly 52 percent of girls ages 10 to 19 who kill themselves use a firearm. Hanging or suffocation follows far behind—the choice of roughly 23 percent of both male and female suicide victims. Smaller percentages die by overdosing on drugs, drowning, in falls, or by slitting their wrists.

Before a youth pulls the trigger, experts say, some event usually has to set him or her off. A recent survey of 15- to 19-year-old students in Oregon who had attempted suicide found that the top three things that spurred them to act—while none was the sole reason—were conflict with parents, relationship problems, or difficulties at school.

Whatever the eventual catalyst, every suicidal youth's life story has a uniquely tragic plot. More often than not, it's a circuitous route that leads him or her toward suicide. The profiles of three youths that follow show how a particular combination of character traits, circumstances, and events conspired to usher each of them to an early death.

Additional Reading

Violent Acts of Sadness: The Tragedy of Youth Suicide

Julie Thomerson

Julie Thomerson *is a former National Conference of State Legislatures specialist in youth violence and delinquency.*

More teenagers and young adults die from suicide each year than from cancer, heart disease, AIDS, birth defects, stroke, pneumonia, influenza and chronic lung disease combined. The sad reality is that youth suicide is a growing epidemic, ending young lives and leaving heartbroken families and communities. It is currently the third leading cause of death of 15- to 24-year-olds, and the fourth leading cause of death among 10- to 14-year-olds. Nearly 4,600 kids killed themselves in the United States in 1998, and approximately 46,000 others tried. Most give warnings; some do not.

Teenage suicides seldom make the front pages. Or do they? Andrew Wurst, 14, talked to his friends about taking his own life a month before he shot and killed a teacher and wounded three students at a high school dance. Luke Woodham, 16, told investigators that he shot nine students—killing two—because he was so miserable that he "just couldn't take it anymore." He later confessed that he had wanted to die. Another teenager who had already attempted suicide asked his parents for a gun. They gave it to him. Soon after, he took it to school, wounded a fellow student, then shot and killed himself.

More recently, Jason Anthony Hoffman took a firearm and wounded five at Granite Hills High School in San Diego. He then hanged himself in jail. He had a history of mental illness and was taking antidepressants months before the shooting.

"Without exception, every juvenile I've represented in a murder case has tried to kill himself," said Hoffman's attorney, William Lafond. "Many of these kids feel helpless and depressed and don't understand why they did what they did. When they try to understand their feelings, they can't handle it."

Research shows that up to 60 percent of school shooters may have been suicidal before they shot others, and a majority of them gave clues. Most had a history of depression and were desperate to end their emotional pain, and many communicated their agony to someone else in some way.

They directed their aggression toward more than just those who hurt them. They had specific targets: themselves.

No one means to absolve these kids from responsibility for their horrific acts. They usually planned ahead, knew what they were doing, had given up on life and were not concerned about the consequences. And most planned to kill themselves before they were done.

"I didn't really see my life going on any further," Luke Woodham now says. "I thought it was all over with…I couldn't find a reason not to do it."

We focus more on troubled children killing others than the thousands of children privately taking their lives every year. In reality, youth violence is a tremendous problem, and suicide is a big part of it. For lawmakers, the questions are how to design policies to prevent young people from getting to this point of desperation, and how to intervene when they do.

What's Going On?

Suicide among children ages 10 to 14 increased nearly 100 percent between 1981 and 1998, jumping from 163 deaths per 100,000 to 317, according to the Centers for Disease Control. Suicide among African American males ages 15 to 19 rose at an even higher rate, increasing from 81 deaths per 100,000 to 164. One youth commits suicide every two hours in the United States.

There are several theories about why this happens. One is that some children are growing up without meaningful connections to adults or the support they need to successfully navigate the process of growing up. Another is that kids are impulsive and can react to a moment of crisis in their lives—such as trouble in school, relationship problems or bullying—without stopping to really think about the consequences. In some cases, impulsive behavior and access to guns is a dangerous mixture. Others blame substance abuse, media violence or copycat actions.

Depression is one of the most common problems children and adolescents face, says Mark Weist, director of the Center for School Mental Health Assistance in Baltimore, Md. "Often, mental health issues in youth are not identified, especially if they are less observable problems like depression and anxiety."

Statistics show that one in 10 young people suffers from mental illness serious enough to be impaired, but fewer than 20 percent receive treatment. Many, especially boys, keep their problems to themselves and do not seek help unless an adult intervenes. Others live in communities without mental health services or their parents distrust the help that is available. Colorado Representative Kay Alexander points out that 80 percent of kids with mental health problems also abuse alcohol or drugs. "They are often either self-medicating or the substance abuse contributes to their mental health problems," she says.

"Mental health providers need support in raising awareness, destigmatizing mental illness and treating mental health as equal in importance to physical health," says Weist. "Since Sept. 11, there is an increased awareness that mental health issues are universal. Hopefully, this will translate into more resources for effective child and adolescent mental health programs."

Part of the problem is that troubled kids often appear to be "normal," well-adjusted students, says Weist. When 15-year-old Charles Bishop ended his life by crashing a Cessna airplane into a Tampa office building in January, he had given no indication beforehand that he intended to hurt himself. And 16-year-old Jason Flatt was a popular boy with a supportive family. No one expected him to shoot and kill himself in 1997 after breaking up with his girlfriend.

"Many boys have an exterior structure that looks healthy and happy, but behind it lies more pain than we can imagine. Often, they either feel too ashamed to talk about it or have no one they can really talk to. And they usually show signs beforehand, even if no one notices," says William Pollack, acclaimed Harvard psychologist, director of the Centers for Men and Young Men, and author of *Real Boys* and *Real Boys' Voices*.

What Can Legislatures Do?

"We need to understand all the issues around why people attempt suicide," says Oklahoma Representative Darrell Gilbert. "The more we learn, the easier it is to design policy, change current laws and appropriate dollars to help with the problem."

The bottom line is that the problems are too complex for any simple solution. There is no single description of a suicidal child, and no way to make sure kids never kill themselves. But there are a variety of ways that legislatures can support practitioners, school officials and parents.

One need is more education about the risk factors for youth suicide. If teachers, parents, coaches, students and others know how to recognize the warning signs for suicide, they may have more opportunities to ask questions, listen, solve problems or aid kids in getting help. "Kids do not wake up suddenly suicidal; they get there after traveling down a long road," says Richard Lieberman, Los Angeles school psychologist. "Where we intercept these kids on the road determines what our response should be."

Each state may have different needs that can be addressed through legislation. In some cases, schools might be directed to run programs where kids role-play difficult situations and talk about better ways to work through conflict or cope with disappointment. Preliminary findings of one study suggest that mentally healthy students who practice solving life problems through role-playing with other students are less likely to get depressed or show signs of suicidal behavior. "We need funding and personnel for prevention programs in schools to teach kids valuable coping skills so that they don't travel down the path to begin with," Lieberman says.

Another approach is to improve the school environment so students feel more connected and supported. Staff can be trained to mentor children better and to stop bullying and conflict more effectively. Classes can be smaller so students get more attention and know each other better. Kids can be trained to mediate conflicts between peers.

After-school programs can also help kids stay out of trouble, learn new skills and improve their self-esteem. Some schools also take time during the school day to teach kids about suicide, although some researchers argue that this approach leads kids to think about it as an alternative when they did not before.

Other suggestions include funding mental health services for troubled students, requiring professional screening of students for early signs of suicidal behavior and restricting access to firearms.

Where lawmakers need to make the most of limited funds, it is important to make sure that prevention programs are effective and a good investment of state money. There is some research that implies that the aforementioned efforts can help reduce suicidal behavior. At the same time, there is little hard proof that individual programs are effective, even though schools report they are helping. Some researchers also suggest that certain programs may be counterproductive—such as suicide awareness—but no real data exists to show a negative impact. As a result, states can work toward ensuring better investments by requiring assessment of state-funded prevention programs.

What Are States Doing?

At this point we know that comprehensive, broad-based approaches are the most successful at preventing youth suicide. They include everyone—professionals from different disciplines, community agencies, parents, kids and others—in efforts to coordinate services, share resources and work together to help kids deal with the problems that may lead them to become suicidal. Basically, the comprehensive approach intervenes early to help young people overcome barriers to development and learning and grow up successfully.

Eighteen states have youth suicide prevention laws, and many have worked to put fairly comprehensive approaches in place. Washington uses general funds to educate the public about youth suicide and staff a 24-hour crisis hotline. Other states—Kentucky, Florida, New York, New Jersey, Connecticut, Hawaii and Maryland—fund school-based mental health programs for troubled students, including suicide risks. Louisiana is developing a statewide youth suicide prevention plan.

Oklahoma recently established a Youth Suicide Prevention Council to collaborate with community organizations, develop local resources, provide technical assistance to community programs, make policy recommendations to the Legislature and promote public awareness. The Legislature was responding to increased incidents and rising concern in Oklahoma, says Representative Gilbert, co-sponsor of the law. Lawmakers wanted to include various perspectives in planning a prevention policy, since "the more information we can find out about why teens are committing suicide, the more we can help mental health professionals and others—such as religious leaders and drug and alcohol counselors—to help kids with the emotional issues in their lives," he says.

Virginia and California passed new legislation in 2001 to supplement school-based prevention programs already in place. The Virginia Department of Health is now coordinating prevention activities throughout the commonwealth. California established a statewide suicide prevention week, recognizing it as a major public health concern, declaring it a state priority and encouraging development of treatment that works, including affordable mental health care. California legislators "wanted to increase awareness and move us toward comprehensive suicide prevention plans," says bill sponsor Senator Deborah Ortiz.

California's existing school-based prevention program includes training parents and school staff about the warning signs, providing a crisis hotline for kids and developing peer support groups. "We need to direct the resources to the schools," Ortiz says. "School personnel are the most likely to run across kids who are at risk for suicide where many others may not have enough knowledge or awareness to intervene."

Barriers to Intervention

One challenge is that all these solutions require money, creating a balancing act for state legislatures with limited budgets. But research points to prevention as a long-term investment due to the emotional and economic toll that suicide takes on the population. Aside from the loss of lifetime contributions when a citizen dies prematurely, emergency room use for suicide attempts costs states an average of $33,000 per visit. With approximately 730,000 attempted suicides per year nationwide that can be a pretty hefty price tag. To some degree, federal resources—such as Medicaid and the Maternal Child Health Block Grant—can help states pay for more prevention initiatives, but reimbursements can be difficult. And there is still some question whether and how much the state should be involved in these issues.

Senator Ortiz suggests that "it may take work to realize that there are successful programs out there, but it will take long-term, sustained resources to build awareness. We can save money by investing in prevention, but it is a hard case to make in difficult fiscal times."

Other challenges—such as the general stigma surrounding mental illness services—can make it harder for children and their families to get treatment or take part in prevention activities. Many are afraid that their information will not be kept confidential. Parents may also feel that life and death are family matters that should not be addressed at school. School officials also have a limited duty to protect students from harm and may be concerned about liability issues, especially if prevention efforts are ineffective.

"The challenge is to intervene, to get these kids what they need, and they need to be connected to different systems for different problems," says Iowa Representative Ro Foege. "Because of the variety of issues, the team approach is important. But the team needs to include parents, counselors, school nurses, social workers, community organizations and all others who deal with behavioral health. Everyone needs to come together to address the issue instead of being so fragmented."

Why Now?

Being scared and unhappy can be part of growing up. But when it gets too hard and they do not know how to cope, unhappy kids often act out their feelings—sometimes by hurting themselves or others. Suicide is ultimately a mental health problem, but there are triggers and contributing factors that lead young people to turn to suicide as a solution, rather than dealing with their problems in healthier ways.

"It is alarming that we live in a time when so many teenagers feel they have nowhere to turn," says Texas Representative Geanie Morrison. "As a society, we must do more to provide a safety net and let these children know that this is a terminal solution to a temporary problem."

There is no doubt that youth suicide is a tragic act of self-violence that wreaks havoc on the lives of young people and those they leave behind. "We have to look beyond whether we are saving money," says Montana Representative Paul Clark. "We are talking about kids' lives. We are also talking about the health of our families and society. Increases in suicidal behavior should be a red flag for legislatures."

The Federal Safe School Initiative

In response to high profile school shootings during the past decade the Secret Service and the U.S Department of Education have been working together to analyze the events and learn how to prevent them.

Because most of the young shooters told at least one other person of their intent, it is believed that some attacks could be prevented. But how?

Researchers spoke to 40 surviving school shooters to find out more about their motives and events leading up to the attacks. They learned that:

- There is no profile of a school shooter. They were all very different.
- Most attackers had easy access to guns.
- Over two-thirds of the attackers felt harassed or bullied, and many were motivated by revenge.
- Most did something before the attack that raised concern or suggested that they needed help.
- In many cases, feeling suicidal or desperate could have been a motivation for the attack.
- The risk factors for targeted violence are similar to risk factors for suicide.

"There is no profile of a suicidal child," says Marisa Reddy, one of the primary researchers on the project, "but there may be behavior along the way that could be a warning, just as there often is with targeted violence." She says researchers found that many of the school shooters had thought about or tried suicide in the past, and believes that any efforts to help them move "away from desperation and toward real hope and options for the future" will pay off.

"The best way to deal with youth suicide is through the development of a comprehensive strategy that links schools, communities and families; focuses on early identification of youth experiencing problems; and refers them to appropriate resources," says Bill Modzeleski, director of the United States Department of Education Safe and Drug Free Schools Program.

Warning Signs for Youth Suicide

- Depression
- Access to firearms
- Drug or alcohol use
- Lack of parental guidance or support
- Doing poorly in school
- Feeling disconnected to the school community
- Suicidal thoughts
- Talking about death or the afterlife when sad or bored
- Withdrawal from friends and family
- Problems with sexual orientation
- Losing interest in activities once enjoyed
- Unplanned pregnancy
- Previous suicide threats or attempts
- Low self-esteem
- Unhealthy interpersonal relationships
- Victim of sexual abuse
- Witnessing domestic violence or a victim of it
- Hopelessness
- Exposure to violence or trauma
- Impulsive or aggressive tendencies
- Giving away prized possessions

Additional Reading

Whatever Happened to Affirmative Action?

Shelby Samuelsen and Demaree Michelau

Shelby Samuelsen and **Demaree Michelau** specialize in education issues at the National Conference of State Legislatures.

A Michigan native, Jennifer Gratz worked hard in high school in hopes of attending the University of Michigan. She earned a 3.77 grade point average, was a varsity cheerleader, served in class congress and was homecoming queen. With these credentials, she thought her chances were good.

So she was surprised when she was rejected by the University of Michigan College of Literature, Science and Arts. Jennifer, a white woman, believes that her fate was the result of an unfair, race-based admissions policy. After learning about a lawsuit against the university, she joined the 1997 effort "because I do not want anyone else to be discriminated against based on the color of his or her skin," she says. "The university's admissions policy is wrong."

In December 2000, a U.S. district judge ruled in favor of the university, stating that while the school's older 1996–98 policy was unfair, standards used at the university since that year that allow the school to consider race and ethnicity in admissions were acceptable. The case is likely to be appealed.

That lawsuit represents a new phase in the debate over affirmative action that began in the 1970s. In the landmark Bakke case, the Supreme Court held that race may be used as one of several factors in determining college admissions. This practice, propelled by the civil rights movement in the 1960s, was embraced as a way to redress years of racial discrimination and oppression.

Forty years later, many still maintain that race-based college admissions help minorities overcome some of the barriers on the pathway to higher education. Members of the National Association for the Advancement of Colored People continue to promote these policies as an important mechanism for ensuring diversity in higher education.

"Affirmative action is very needed in today's society," says Florida Senator Kentrick Meek. "People are still judged based on their ethnicity and gender." He says that we don't yet live in a color-blind society. "We have to work to get to a level playing field, and affirmative action is the last frontier for equal opportunity."

Some supporters believe policies can be improved and re-evaluated, but should not be discarded. People expect colleges and universities to reflect an increasingly diverse society, and many believe affirmative action serves as a means to this goal.

Last December, a federal appeals court affirmed this when it ruled in favor of using race as a consideration for college admission. It said that the University of Washington Law School acted legally when it considered the race of applicants in its now abandoned admissions policy. This allows publicly funded schools in the 9th Circuit—including Alaska, Arizona, Hawaii, Idaho, Montana, Nevada and Oregon—to continue using affirmative action policies, but will not affect current admissions in California and Washington, where state law does not allow consideration of race.

But others argue it's time to move away from affirmative action. By the mid-1990s, ballot initiatives and litigation in several states reflected a growing public sentiment that these policies had done more harm than good. Critics contend they lead to reverse discrimination against whites and unfairly penalize white students. Jennifer's story symbolizes this backlash against current affirmative action policies in the nation's colleges and universities.

Michigan Senator David Jaye, who helped bring the lawsuit against the University of Michigan, argues the school is "stealing a college education, jobs and business opportunities from nonminority students and giving them to less qualified minority applicants."

"Qualified students are being turned away because of the color of their skin," Jaye says. "Dr. Martin Luther King Jr. must be spinning in his grave."

Why are we seeing this growing backlash? Are we as a society becoming less tolerant? Does the public believe that conditions for minorities have improved in the last 40 years to a point where affirmative action is no longer necessary?

Changes in State Policies

California, Florida, Texas and Washington have effectively removed affirmative action policies from higher education admissions in the past five years, through either statewide ballot initiatives, litigation or gubernatorial action. What caused these states to abandon their affirmative action policies? What have states and universities done in response to these changes?

In 1996 and 1998, citizen initiatives in California and Washington struck down affirmative action, barring local and state governments and public universities from using race as a determining factor in hiring, contracting or admissions.

One of the leading proponents of California's Proposition 209 is controversial himself. Ward Connerly, a Sacramento businessman and member of the University of California Board of Regents, helped wage California's campaign against affirmative action. He has also been at the forefront of similar movements in Florida and Washington. As an African American, Connerly has faced resistance from minorities who feel he has "sold out," but received support from others who agreed that it was time to move beyond race-based admissions policies.

"I want the American people to confront the issue of race," he told C-SPAN, "I want them to understand that race is a 19th century social construct that we're using in the 21st century for purposes of public policy, and we need to get out of that mode. I want black people to start being more self-reliant, to realize that we can't keep looking in the past. We had a black middle class long before affirmative action; we will have one long after affirmative action."

Soon after Californians passed Proposition 209, Hopwood vs. Texas struck another blow to affirmative action. Cheryl Hopwood, a white student, applied to and was rejected from the University of Texas School of Law in 1992. She had above average test scores, a 3.8 grade point average, and had overcome hardship while in college by raising a severely handicapped daughter and putting herself through school.

Ultimately, the 5th Circuit Court of Appeals ruled in her favor, stating that race could not be used as a criterion for admitting students to the

University of Texas School of Law. The former Texas attorney general took this to mean that race or ethnicity could not be considered in any internal school policies, including determining financial aid.

Inspired by the policy change in Texas, Governor Jeb Bush introduced the One Florida Education Plan in 2000, effectively abolishing affirmative action. Interpreted by some as circumventing the legislative process and quashing the rights of minorities won decades ago, this action prompted thousands, including the Reverend Jesse L. Jackson, to march on Florida's Capitol on the first day of the 2000 legislative session.

Maintaining Diversity

In light of this new wave of policies that end affirmative action, legislatures are forced to find alternative ways to maintain and increase racial and ethnic diversity on college campuses. Minority enrollment has decreased by 30 percent in Washington since passage of its Initiative 200. And although California numbers are more of a mixed bag, there is a general decrease of minorities on University of California campuses.

Since 1997—the last year race and ethnicity were used as a factor in admissions decisions in California—the percentage of black, Latino and American Indian students dropped from 22 percent to 16 percent in 1999, even though high school graduation rates for those groups increased slightly. California's most academically rigorous institutions, UC Berkeley and UC Los Angeles, showed a drop in minorities; however, other campuses like UC Irvine and UC Riverside increased the number of African Americans and Latinos admitted. This campus discrepancy plays into the fears that ending affirmative action will disproportionately affect minority access to the more prestigious public universities.

As a result, legislators are devising new ways to accomplish diversity, including percent plans, increased recruitment efforts and targeted scholarship programs. "A reduction in minority enrollment in Washington should be alarming to everyone," says Washington Senator Jeanne Kohl-Welles, chair of the Senate Higher Education Committee. "We simply must do all we can within the confines of the law to ensure that nobody is left on the sidelines because of inadequate access to higher education."

Percent Plans

Texas was the first state to adopt a percent plan which is intended to boost minority enrollment and provide a more equitable process for admitting students into college. This policy calls for students who graduate in the top 10 percent of their high school class, regardless of their ACT or SAT scores, to be automatically admitted to the state's public universities. Representative Irma Rangel, chairwoman of the Texas House Higher Education Committee and the Mexican American Caucus, led the effort.

She brought together what she refers to as a "dream team" of law and history professors from across the state to develop a plan to ensure that diversity was a higher education priority. While about 30 percent of Texas' total population is Hispanic, only about 13 percent of freshmen enrolled at the University of Texas-Austin and only 9 percent at Texas A&M University are Hispanic. Since higher education does not reflect the state's minority population, there is growing concern about equity in educating all Texas citizens. And in some states, like Texas, whites are expected to become a minority in the next decade. In light of these projections and changing demographics, affirmative action and other admissions policies become even more complicated.

"We knew that we could not refer to race or diversity in drafting our plan," Rangel recalls. "So we developed the 10 percent plan, which would consider all high schools across the state and keep the doors open for minority students. The 5th circuit [Hopwood] had closed the doors on them."

"Hopefully the plan will stay as is," she adds. "We have excellent reports from the admissions officers that diversity is increasing due to the top 10 percent plan. It's definitely successful."

Following Texas' lead, other states have adopted similar, but not identical, plans. The California plan guarantees admission to a University of California campus to students who rank within the top 4 percent of their high school class. Florida has instituted a program in which students in the top 20 percent are admitted.

The percent plans, however, do not necessarily work for all students. E. Lynn Rodriguez was general counsel to the Texas Higher Education Coordinating Board when the Hopwood decision was handed down and is currently general counsel to Texas Southern University.

"Alternative strategies to achieve diversity at these schools, such as the top 10 percent plan, focus on admission of undergraduates. The effect of the Hopwood decision is really on the graduate and professional school level and is much more severe," she says. This focus on undergraduate admissions leaves a gap in the recruitment and admission of minorities for graduate and professional programs.

"Percent plans may be good in theory, but can be tough in practice," says Travis Reindl, director of state policy analysis for the American Association of State Colleges and Universities. "Success in college depends greatly on the quality of high school preparation, which varies widely from school to school. Colleges and universities in states with these plans will now have to deal with these differences, which could mean remediation or other special programs for students who may be in the specified percentage but are not ready for college-level work."

Outreach, Recruitment and Preparation

Statewide recruitment programs are designed to provide academic services to students from difficult backgrounds and support them on the road to higher education, shifting the focus from race to need-based programs.

Senator Ray Haynes, a member of the California Senate Education Committee, supported the state's move away from affirmative action. "We must rise above race and gender-based remedies," he says, "and focus instead on the truly disadvantaged and those who need real help."

After ending affirmative action, both California and Washington increased the scope and depth of their recruitment programs. California's Early Academic Outreach Program serves more than 77,000 students across 105 middle schools and some 311 high schools through a variety of means: counseling, university and K-12 partnerships and education on postsecondary opportunities. The program is designed to help prepare students for college. Similarly, Washington has expanded its Early Scholars Outreach Program to provide greater academic support, including tutoring for students, starting as early as middle school.

Dennis Galligani, associate vice president of student academic services who oversees outreach for the University of California, thinks it's too early to determine whether or not the recruitment programs have been effective. He has, however, seen good results.

"California has done an excellent job in expanding and enriching the academic component of its outreach efforts," he says. "The Legislature has buoyed our efforts by increasing funding for outreach from $60 million in 1996 to $250 million in 2000. When we went to the Senate with our master plan, they told us it wasn't a matter of 'if' but just a matter of 'when.'"

Senator Kohl-Welles agrees that it will take time to see how these efforts pay off. But she believes that in Washington, it's time "to find some new solutions, including increasing the availability of advanced placement courses in all schools and eliminating unfair advantages students have [such as weighted credit for advanced placement courses] to increase their college eligibility. The limited availability of these courses is fueling concern in Washington, particularly among minority, low-income and rural families," she says. Only 60 percent (compared with 82 percent in California) of schools offer advanced placement classes, and these are primarily in wealthier districts with few minorities.

To increase the number of low-income students who are prepared to enter and succeed in college, the federal government instituted GEAR UP (Gaining Early Education Awareness and Readiness for Undergraduate Programs) in 1998. This program funds partnerships between high poverty middle schools and colleges, community organizations and businesses to work with entire grade levels of students. The partnerships provide long-term tutoring, mentoring, information on college preparation and financial aid, emphasis on core academic preparation, and, in some cases, scholarships. Currently, GEAR UP is serving nearly 450,000 students nationwide.

Scholarship Programs and Preparation

One significant stumbling block for many students is not being able to afford college. Last year, the California Legislature increased funding to $1.2 billion for the CAl Grant program. This increase sets up the largest state financial aid program in the country. The California plan represents a shift in grant funding toward need and merit. Proponents argue considering socioeconomic factors moves us beyond looking at race and aids students who need the most help financially, while still increasing diversity on campuses.

The Texas attorney general's decision to expand the Hopwood decision to financial aid may have created a different barrier. Some suggest that despite efforts to recruit minority students in Texas, many are attending college in states that still can offer race-based scholarships. They contend that this ruling decreased the amount of scholarship funding (estimated at $4 million) given to minority students. Meanwhile, colleges and universities outside Texas are taking advantage of the situation by boosting recruiting efforts to increase minority representation at their campuses since they are able to offer financial incentives encouraging minorities to attend their institutions.

Whether due to statewide ballot initiatives, litigation or by their own auspices, higher education institutions are re-examining and restructuring their admissions policies and looking at different ways to approach recruitment and retention of minority students. The future of affirmative action is uncertain, but one thing is clear. The issues of access and equity remain on the front burner of legislative agendas. Despite many varying opinions on race and representation on our college campuses, most people agree on the value of diversity and the necessity of achieving it—but the question is how we get there.

Inside Texas

The United States 5th Circuit Court of Appeals in 1996 ruled in Hopwood vs. Texas that race could not be used as a criterion for admitting students to the University of Texas School of Law. The Texas attorney general interpreted this to mean that no postsecondary institutions across the state could consider race or ethnicity in any internal school policies, including admissions, financial aid, scholarships and fellowships, and recruitment and retention. This policy stands in Texas today and also affects Louisiana and Mississippi since they are in the jurisdiction.

In response, Texas instituted several new programs to achieve diversity at the state's colleges. The University of Texas-Austin has the Longhorn Opportunity Scholarship program, which awards students $4,000 per year for up to four years of study. This program targets students at traditionally underrepresented state high schools, students from low-income families and those who might not attend college without financial aid. In addition, students receiving the scholarships get coordinated, focused mentoring during their freshman year.

The Texas Legislature also passed legislation in 1997 that automatically guaranteed students who graduate in the top 10 percent of their high school class admission into the university system regardless of their ACT or SAT scores. Once the university accepts the top 10 percent, it then considers other applicants based on 18 criteria, some of which include:

- The socioeconomic background of the applicant.
- Whether the applicant would be the first generation of his or her family to attend or graduate from an institution of higher education.

- Whether the applicant is bilingual.
- The financial status of the applicant's school district.
- The performance level of the applicant's school as determined by the school accountability criteria used by the Texas Education Agency.
- The applicant's responsibilities while attending school, including whether he or she has been employed, whether he or she has helped to raise children or other similar considerations.

Additional Reading

Q: Does Diversity in Higher Education Justify Racial Preferences?

YES: WE MUST OPEN COLLEGE EDUCATION TO STUDENTS OF ALL ECONOMIC AND RACIAL BACKGROUNDS

Shirley Strum Kenny

Shirley Strum Kenny is president of the State University of New York at Stony Brook. She chaired the commission that published the report Reinventing Undergraduate Education.

If ever there was a loaded question, it is the one stated above. First, it assumes that achieving diversity at institutions of higher learning is the reason for allowing race to be one of the factors in admission decisions. Diversity is not an end in itself. It is a means toward a much bigger and longer-range goal—a more prosperous and harmonious society.

Second, the term "racial preferences" is itself loaded—it refers to admitting African-American and Latino students, never suggesting any bias toward white students. The term assumes that those entrance qualifications that favor white students, such as high scores on standardized tests, are free of racial preference and that the tests themselves are unbiased measures of who is most likely to succeed in college. That perception is false on two counts: 1) the tests are not bias-free; and 2) they are not the best predictors of college success. Many people assume that the SAT I math and verbal tests are free of racial bias, and certainly the College Board works diligently to achieve that goal. But this does not mean the tests perfectly manage racial blindness. White students tend to do better than black students on the SATs. The assumption that some people make is that white students therefore have better qualifications for college as proven by an absolutely unbiased measure of ability. It also is true that Asian students do better on the math exam than white students, but I have not seen any articles on what that proves. Should Caucasians be considered mathematically inferior?

The emphasis on the SATs ignores the fact that they are not the best predictors of college success in any case. I repeat: SAT scores are not the best predictors of college success. In fact, the College Board does not make a claim as to their ability to predict graduation. Instead, high SAT scores are recognized as good predictors of success in the first year of college work. Yet those who argue against considering other factors seem to take the SATs as the only true prognosticator of success.

In fact, the single best predictor of overall college success is class rank at whatever high school the student attends; that has been demonstrated again and again. The No. 1 slot at the best suburban school or the worst urban institution indicates potential for success better than any other single factor, including SAT scores. Apparently the top-ranking students in any school have both the intelligence and the motivation to succeed in college.

That is why the approach of the universities of California and Texas, as well as other institutions, that have made high-school class rank their chief criterion should be congratulated. It is true that both systems switched to accepting the top 5 or 10 percent after being denied the ability to consider race as one of a number of factors in admissions. But it also is true that they have hit on a better predictor than standardized tests. Is their new policy a ruse to broaden admissions racially? Conceivably. But it also is a more accurate basis for admitting the students with the greatest probability of success.

Yet the SAT reigns. What started out as a less than perfect instrument for measuring college ability has taken on the trappings of infallibility. As a result, it has become a less effective tool. Why? Because the affluent can influence the results through investing in test-preparatory classes and tutoring. In affluent school districts teachers spend far too much valuable class time prepping for the SATs; sometimes the test preparation starts as early as sixth grade. Wealthy parents have their children tutored and retutored to take and retake the SATs—not to increase their children's intellectual abilities but to increase their chances for admissions to prestigious universities. The rich simply buy the advantages of the SAT. Many parents recognize what is happening, but they find themselves helpless against a system that worships high test scores. When everyone else's children are tutored, how can they deprive their own children? Meanwhile, students in less-affluent circumstances cannot afford tutors and usually can afford to take the SATs only once. Under those unbalanced circumstances, the SAT cannot possibly measure true ability of rich and poor, even if the questions could be perfectly devised.

The fact is there is no one sure method to predict college success. One cannot take the intellectual temperature or blood pressure of a student and measure college readiness. The success of any student will depend on many things—prior education to some extent, but more importantly native intelligence, will and determination, intellectual curiosity, inventiveness, focus and heart.

There was a time when knowing the great books and speaking European languages defined a college education—students' minds were vessels to be filled with a well-defined body of knowledge, some of which flowed from high school or prep school. That cultural polish was the requisite for a career and a civilized life. Now that definition is all but irrelevant—no students can acquire in four years all the requisite knowledge for living in the modern world; they also must be taught how to envision important questions and find the answers, how to define and solve problems. How does one measure that ability from pretesting?

Universities recognize that no one set of criteria can be used for developing a freshman class. For example, colleges traditionally balance their classes for many factors—gender, geography, major areas of interest. The exceptional cellist may slip in despite below-average math scores; the young woman in engineering may get accepted despite her verbal scores. If the football team needs a running back or a Middle East prince wants to study in America, exceptional criteria may be applied.

Every college and university has "special admits"—students who are given seats in the incoming class despite scores because of some special characteristic the institution values. They may be talented athletes or children of alumni or friends of a generous donor. Since winning basketball or football teams actually increase student applications, campuses can attempt justifications for preferential treatment of athletes. Since alumni and other donors make funding available to support students or raise faculty salaries or build new buildings, their requests are taken seriously. But what is amazing is that we do not hear protestations about these practices.

Only when race comes into the picture do Americans find themselves in a pitched battle about college acceptance. Either we pretend other exceptions do not occur, or we are not aware—although it is hard to be unaware of some of these practices.

Are there then valid reasons to consider racial factors along with those undisputed factors of gender, geography, legacies and athletic prowess? There are indeed.

First, as President George W. Bush urges us to "leave no child behind," we also must leave no capable student behind. Our economy depends on education beyond the high-school level; to maintain world pre-eminence, we are dependent on a better educational level for all our people. If we do not open the doors to college education to all races and ethnicities, we condemn ourselves to failure. If we deprive ourselves of this major and growing source of educated personnel, we will not survive as the leading world economic power. Put simply, we need these people, and we need them well-educated at the college level. We also need the buying power of college-educated professionals, who will be important in sustaining our economic growth.

Second, we need a workforce capable of serving our global industries and our increasing diversity at home. If we look first at our own country, the new census gives a loud, clear message to businesses that their U.S. clients are more diverse than ever, and their business success is dependent on cultural understanding that once seemed unimportant to the corporate bottom line. Whatever the product, American customers soon will be predominantly nonwhite.

No longer is America a melting pot; it is a richly multicultural society, and the ringing of the cash register will reward those businesspeople who respond. Universities must help corporations in their need to diversify their workforces. They must both broaden the student body and give traditional (read: white) students a better understanding of other cultures. Not only business but all professions—medicine, law, government and education—will depend on knowledge of many cultures.

Look at contemporary American literature and you see growing interest in Korean, Indian, Latino, Chinese, African and other American backgrounds. Look at fashion and you see the growing influence of these cultures on what we wear. Look at the entertainment business and recognize how many Latin-, Asian- and African-American stars are now on the scene.

Notice the color of professional sports, including the first American basketball player imported from China. American life increasingly is multicultural, and there is a reason for that—to more and more Americans, those faces look "like us." Multiculturalism is good business here and abroad.

Education cannot be left behind. Business leaders understand and support the importance of diversity in our universities. They need universities that produce a well-educated and widely diverse set of new employees for their new ventures. They encourage breadth and support efforts to bring minority students into their fields; they know they need them.

Until we can find accurate predictors of college success—and we probably never will, given the role of the human spirit—we need to understand that efforts to create interesting mixes of students are a plus, not a minus. It only has been a few decades since Ivy League universities removed their quotas for Jewish students and even more recently that they have encouraged students of color. The results have been dramatically successful as the research of Derek Bok and William Bowen illustrated in their book on the success of minorities in the Ivy League. It has been even more recently that our best universities seriously undertook the study of African-American and Latino cultures. Until our universities deal with the diversity that defines our nation—in the curriculum, in the faculty and in the student body—we will fall short of our best possibilities.

We can call that racial preferences, or we can call it fairness. We can even call it good business sense. The urgency of giving all qualified Americans opportunities for higher education, undistorted by the ability to buy tutoring for entrance exams or influence for admissions, is central to the national agenda. Our well-being depends on it.

Additional Reading

Q: Does Diversity in Higher Education Justify Racial Preferences?

NO: DIVERSITY OF VIEWPOINT, NOT RACIAL SET-ASIDES BASED ON STEREOTYPES, SHOULD GUIDE THE ADMISSIONS

Ward Connerly

Ward Connerly *is the founder and chairman of the American Rights Institute, a national, nonprofit organization, and author of* Creating Equal: My Fight Against Race Preference.

Eight-year-old Cristina Capacchione of North Carolina and 47-year-old Barbara Grutter of Michigan have something in common: Both were rejected in the name of diversity from schools to which they had applied. They, along with Cheryl Hopwood of Texas and Katuria Smith of Washington State, are at ground zero in what likely will be the most controversial Supreme Court case of President George W. Bush's first term. If the court remains consistent with the principles of the equal-protection clause of the 14th Amendment, and with its own recent rulings in similar cases, the use of racial classifications and preferences to achieve "diversity" in our nation's schools and universities will come to an end.

At issue are conflicting interpretations of the 1978 case of the Board of Regents of the University of California v. Bakke in which the Supreme Court offered only a muddled answer to the question of whether the pursuit of "diversity" in school admissions justifies racial preferences. In Bakke, a sharply divided court struck down a California medical school's admission quota for minority students. However, Justice Lewis Powell's separate opinion declared that the pursuit of a "diverse student body" was a valid reason to use race as a "plus" factor. Even though no other justice concurred with that opinion—some in the legal community have said this case gave a ruling without a decision—it has been interpreted by most of the education establishment as controlling legal doctrine. While nearly every college-admissions officer in the country has interpreted Bakke to permit them to use racial classifications and preferences, the courts have been less uniform in their understanding. Late last year in a case challenging the undergraduate-admissions policies at the

University of Michigan, a federal judge ruled that achieving racial diversity in the freshman class was so important—the legal term is "compelling"—that the school was justified in using race as an admission criterion. However, in a parallel lawsuit decided March 27, another federal judge examined the diversity rationale for admissions to the University of Michigan Law School and reached the opposite conclusion. Most legal observers now agree that, during the next year or so, it is likely the Supreme Court will revisit Bakke and sort out the conflicting legal opinions in Michigan and throughout the country.

Regardless of how the legality of racial diversity is settled by the courts in the future, race remains a polarizing social issue constantly debated in the public square, and no place more than in our nation's schools. It is there that "diversity" has become a new creed, driving everything from student admissions to faculty hiring to promotion to curriculum. Yet, according to the results of a massive "diversity" poll commissioned by the Ford Foundation a few years ago, most Americans are unsure of diversity's real meaning, let alone how it is to be implemented and achieved by our institutions of higher learning. If diversity means racial integration, then most Americans support it; but if it means a system of racial classifications and preferences that must be recalibrated periodically to reach a target goal, then most American are opposed.

Regardless of what the professional diversity retailers try to sell the public and the courts, diversity as practiced by our nation's colleges and universities is little more than a Potemkin village of strict racial proportionality. In this respect, diversity has become untethered from integration and has assumed a life of its own. For the racial-advocacy groups and their allies on the left, diversity now is integration's rival.

The University of Michigan's legal defense of racial preferences in both cases went a step further by adding the stamp of social science to its justification. A mammoth study was produced by Patricia Gurin, a University of Michigan psychology professor, that purported to prove the compelling benefits of a diverse student body. Her methodology centered on interviews with students admitted under the school's preference regime. The judge in the undergraduate case cited the study as "solid evidence" that students "who experience the most racial and ethnic diversity" exhibit superior cognitive skills.

From this "evidence," one must logically conclude that historically black colleges and universities such as Spelman, Howard and Fisk offer a less-enriching academic environment because they are nearly all-black. Yet, an article in the Weekly Standard recently noted that education researcher Ernest Pascarella's studies have concluded that the academic performance of blacks at historically black colleges is no different from that of black students at predominately white colleges.

The compelling benefits of diversity proven in Gurin's study undoubtedly would have been different if students who were rejected from the University of Michigan because of their skin color had been interviewed as well. In any event, basing racial classifications and preferences on this type of Oprah-like social-science study never can be allowed to circumvent the timeless principles of equal protection under a colorblind Constitution. If the Supreme Court accepts a study that "proves" educational and life experiences are improved by diversity, would they accept one that demonstrates just the opposite? It would not be difficult to devise a study in which the sharp racial disharmony so prevalent on some college campuses "proves" that diversity is harmful to educational development.

By defining diversity down or corrupting real diversity in this manner, the University of Michigan and dozens of other elite schools have concluded that a person's skin color dictates unique group qualities. But is this true? If so, what personality characteristics and life experiences do all black students have in common that are not found in their white classmates? Are there certain personality characteristics, cognitive distinctions and life experiences found in all Hispanics? All Jews? All Asians? If there are, what are they? Of course, when asked to list traits unique to blacks or Hispanics, the diversity mavens go silent. This is because people are individuals whose identities are shaped by innumerable characteristics and experiences. All policies that classify people and then treat them differently based on race are a form of stereotyping. Achieving diversity in this manner assumes that all minorities simply are interchangeable with one another.

Indeed, the judge's opinion in the Michigan law-school case got it correct when he wrote that "viewpoint diversity" is completely different from "racial diversity." According to the judge, "While the educational benefits of viewpoint diversity are clear, those of racial diversity are less so. The University of Michigan's witnesses emphasized repeatedly that it is a diversity of viewpoints, experiences, interests, perspectives and backgrounds which creates an atmosphere most conducive to learning. As Dean Jeffrey Lehman testified, it is primarily a 'diversity of viewpoints' that the law school seeks."

The opinion continues by accurately noting that "the connection between race and viewpoint is tenuous at best. The defendants walk a fine line in simultaneously arguing that one's viewpoints are not determined by one's race, but that certain viewpoints might not be voiced if students of particular races are not admitted in significant numbers."

In essence, what the university argued is that any black student in a college class will bring a "black" perspective to the discussion and the learning experience; it doesn't matter if he attended an impoverished inner-city high school or a chic prep school—black skin creates diversity.

By doing this, the University of Michigan has done little more than "profile" their applicants no differently than some law-enforcement officers who stop motorists for questioning because they are black or Hispanic. The American justice system doesn't allow a lawyer to use a prospective juror's race as a factor in jury selection, nor does it allow a jury to consider an individual's race during criminal sentencing. These race-based presumptions violate our sense of fairness and colorblind justice.

Achieving diversity by stereotyping students based on their skin color does not enhance anyone's educational experience—it diminishes it. It belittles the mystery and the wonder and the dignity of each individual human being.

One cannot help but recognize also that Justice Powell's racial-diversity rationale for preferences coincided with the growth of racial separateness on campus. Ethnic dorms, black graduation ceremonies and race-based student-activity centers are the norm at elite schools today. When universities bow to the creed of racial diversity, perhaps that is when students start to notice—and heed—skin color.

Fortunately, these cases are approaching the day of judicial reckoning. It would be tragic—and dangerous—if the Supreme Court allows a university to use race in admissions, even as a "tie-breaker" in a contest between qualified applicants. If it does, it will be endorsing the belief that skin color really does tell us something fundamental about an individual. This is hauntingly comparable to arguments made by former Birmingham, Ala., police commissioner Bull Connor 35 years ago.

And the wait for a resolution to this issue won't be a long one. Courts in Texas, Georgia, Washington State and Michigan are in various stages of litigation to sort out this legal confusion. Even if the high court rules in favor of colorblind principles and strikes down race-based admissions policies, the nation's real work will have just begun. Closing the academic-achievement gap between whites and Asians on the one hand, and blacks and Hispanics on the other, is the unspoken reason these policies exist in the first place.

Closing the gap is the real compelling governmental interest.

Summary Chart

SYNTHESIS ESSAYS

1. **Analyze the assignment.**

   - *Determine whether you are being asked to write an informative or argumentative synthesis.*

   - *Determine how many and what kinds of readings you are expected to use in your paper.*

2. **Review and annotate the readings.**

   - *If you are writing an informative synthesis, summarize the readings.*

   - *If you are writing an argumentative synthesis, summarize and critique the readings.*

3. **Formulate a thesis.**

   - *Decide what stance you will assume in your essay.*

   - *Decide whether you want to use an open or closed thesis statement.*

4. **Decide on an organizational plan.**

   - *Decide how to order your ideas, arguments, or findings.*

   - *Decide whether you want to use an alternating or block format.*

5. **Write your rough draft.**

   - *Follow the organizational plan implied by your thesis.*

   - *If you are writing an informative synthesis, summarize and combine sources to illustrate your thesis.*

   - *If you are writing an argumentative synthesis, combine your insights, ideas, arguments, and findings with material in the sources to support your thesis.*

6. **Revise your draft.**

   A. If you are writing an informative synthesis:

   - *Revise to improve the content of your essay.*

     - *Does your thesis accurately reflect your position and intention?*

     - *Have you communicated in your paper what you want to communicate?*

     - *Will your paper give your reader a thorough understanding of the source texts and your thesis?*

- *Have you avoided editorializing in your paper?*
- *Would your essay make sense to someone who has not read the source texts?*

- *Revise to improve the organization of your essay.*
  - *Does your thesis guide the development of your essay?*
  - *Do you provide topic sentences to introduce major sections of your essay?*
  - *Have you provided transitions that help lead your reader through your paper?*

- *Revise to improve the accuracy and clarity of your essay.*
  - *Have you used language that is as fair and impartial as possible?*
  - *Have you avoided jargon and overly technical language when they would not be appropriate?*
  - *Have you checked for sentence variety and clarity?*
  - *Have you quoted and paraphrased material properly?*
  - *Have you documented material properly?*

B. If you are writing an argumentative synthesis:

- *Revise to improve the content of your essay.*
  - *In your thesis, have you clearly stated the point you want to prove?*
  - *Have you indicated the reasons you believe others should accept your thesis?*
  - *Have you supported in some way each of your contentions?*
  - *How have you used the sources to develop your thesis?*

- *Revise to improve the organization of your essay.*
  - *Does your thesis guide the development of your essay?*
  - *Have you provided readers adequate transitions between and within the major sections of your essay?*
  - *Can readers follow the development of your argument and the relationship between your thesis and the material contained in your sources?*

- *Revise to improve the accuracy and clarity of your essay.*
  - *Does your language contribute to the effectiveness of your essay? Does it convey the appropriate tone?*
  - *Have you defined all the terms you need to define?*
  - *Are your sentences varied and clear?*
  - *Have you quoted and paraphrased material properly?*
  - *Have you documented material properly?*

Chapter 9
PLAGIARISM

DEFINITION

Plagiarism occurs when writers take credit for work that is not really theirs. Because it encompasses a wide range of errors in academic writing, from improper citation to calculated fraud, plagiarism is an especially common problem for writers unfamiliar with the conventions of source-based writing. These writers often do not realize that any material they quote or paraphrase from a reading must be documented to avoid plagiarism.

Penalties for plagiarism vary from school to school, department to department, even instructor to instructor. They can range from a warning, to a failing grade on a paper, to a failing grade for a course, to expulsion from school. The academic community takes plagiarism seriously, but with care and honesty you can avoid problems and give the authors of the readings you use the credit they deserve for their work.

FORMS OF PLAGIARISM

Plagiarism is a difficult problem to address because it can assume so many different forms and involves so many different types of errors, some more serious than others. Understanding the various forms that plagiarism can assume will help you avoid problems.

PURCHASING A PAPER

Sometimes students will decide to purchase a paper rather than write one themselves. Whether you buy one from a fellow student or from a commercial vendor, purchasing a paper and turning it in as if it were your own is clearly a form of plagiarism. You are purposely taking credit for work that is not truly yours. Your teachers expect you to do your own work. Sometimes they may ask you to work with other students to write an essay, but even then you will be expected to do your own work in the group. Purchasing a paper—or even part of a paper—from someone and turning it in as if were your own is never acceptable.

TURNING IN A PAPER SOMEONE ELSE HAS WRITTEN FOR YOU

This form of plagiarism, related to the first, occurs when two students decide to let one take credit for work the other has actually completed—a student may ask his roommate to write a paper for him then turn it in for a grade. If caught, both students may face some sort of penalty for plagiarism. In other cases, roommates taking different sections of the same class may hand in the same paper to their instructors without permission. In this case, both students have committed plagiarism. Finally there are instances where a student retrieves a paper from the "fraternity" or "sorority" file, collections of papers written for various courses kept for students to copy and turn in (high tech versions of this file are the collections of student papers kept on university computer systems). These papers may have been written by people the student has never known; however, if the student represents it as her own work, that student is guilty of plagiarism.

TURNING IN ANOTHER STUDENT'S WORK WITHOUT THAT STUDENT'S KNOWLEDGE

This form of plagiarism has increased over the past few years as more and more students write their papers on computers. Here a student searches another student's computer files for a paper, copies the paper, then turns it in as if it were his own work. Most students and instructors would likely consider this action to be a form of theft and fraud. It is clearly a form of plagiarism.

IMPROPER COLLABORATION

More and more teachers are asking students to work together on class projects. If a teacher asks you to collaborate with others on a project, be sure to clarify exactly what she expects you to do individually when preparing the final essay. Sometimes a teacher will want a group of students to produce a single paper. The members of the group decide among themselves how they will divide the labor, and all group members get equal credit for the final essay. Though the group members should help each other complete the essay, if you are asked to complete a certain task as part of the larger project, make sure you give credit to others, when appropriate, for any material that was not originally your own. Other times a teacher will want the members of the group to work individually on their own papers; the other group members serve as each other's consultants and peer editors rather than as coauthors. In this case, you should acknowledge at the beginning of your essay or through documentation in the body of your paper any ideas or material you did not develop yourself.

COPYING A PAPER FROM A SOURCE TEXT WITHOUT PROPER ACKNOWLEDGMENT

This form of plagiarism occurs when a student consults an encyclopedia, book, or journal article, copies the information directly from the reading into his paper, puts his name on the essay, and turns it in for a grade. Sometimes a student will compose an entire essay this way; sometimes he will copy only part of his paper directly from a source. In either case, copying from a reading without proper quotation and documentation is a form of plagiarism. So is copying material directly from a computerized encyclopedia. Even though your computer may come with an encyclopedia on CD, you cannot copy material from it and turn it in as your own work without proper documentation and acknowledgment.

COPYING MATERIAL FROM A SOURCE TEXT, SUPPLYING PROPER DOCUMENTATION, BUT LEAVING OUT QUOTATION MARKS

Many students have a hard time understanding this form of plagiarism. The student has copied material directly from a source and has supplied proper documentation. However, if the student does not properly quote the passage, the student is guilty of plagiarism. The documentation a student provides acknowledges the writer's debt to another for the ideas she has used in the paper, but by failing to supply quotation marks, the writer is claiming credit for the language of the passage, language originally employed by the author of the source text. To properly credit the author for both the ideas and the language of the source text, the student needs to supply both proper quotation marks and proper documentation.

PARAPHRASING MATERIAL FROM A READING WITHOUT PROPER DOCUMENTATION

Suppose a student takes material from a source, paraphrases it, and includes it in his paper. Has this student committed an act of plagiarism? The student has if he fails to document the passage properly. The language is the student's own, but the original ideas were not. Adding proper documentation ensures that the author of the source text will receive proper credit for his ideas.

Few other important concepts in writing are as poorly defined as is plagiarism. Sometimes plagiarism results from premeditated fraud—a student purposely attempts to deceive her readers. Other times it results from sloppy note taking or poor proofreading—the student simply forgets to place quotation marks around a passage or fails to supply needed documentation.

HOW TO AVOID PLAGIARISM

DO YOUR OWN WORK

Obviously, the first way to avoid plagiarism is to do your own work when composing papers—do your own research and write your own essay. This suggestion does not mean, however, that collaborating with others when you write or getting needed help from your teacher, tutor, or classmates is wrong. Many instructors will suggest or even require you to work with others on some writing projects—classmates, writing center tutors, friends. Just be sure the paper you turn in fairly and accurately represents, acknowledges, and documents the efforts you and others have put into the essay. If you get help on a paper you are writing, make sure that you can honestly take credit for the unacknowledged ideas and language it contains. If important or substantial ideas or words in the paper came from someone else, be sure to document those contributions properly. When you turn in a paper with your name on the title page, you are taking credit for the material in the essay. You are also, though, taking responsibility for that material—you are, in effect, telling your reader that you compiled this information, developed these arguments, or produced these findings and will stand behind what you have written. Taking that responsibility seriously, doing the hard work of writing yourself and composing papers that represent your best efforts, can help you avoid problems with plagiarism.

TAKE GOOD NOTES

One common source of unintentional plagiarism is poor note taking. Here is what can happen: a student goes to the library and looks up an article she thinks will help her write her paper. She reads the piece and, taking notes, copies down information and passages she thinks she might use in her essay. However, if she is not careful to put quotation marks around passages she takes word-for-word from the source, she can be in trouble when she writes her essay. If she later consults her notes when drafting her paper, she may not remember that the passage in her notes should be quoted in her paper—she may believe she paraphrased the material when taking notes. If she copies the passage exactly as she has it written in her notes and fails to place it in quotation marks in her paper, she has plagiarized the material, even if she documents it. Remember, to avoid plagiarism, passages taken word-for-word from a source must be quoted *and* documented. Therefore, be very careful when taking notes to place quotation marks around material you are copying directly from a reading. If you later incorporate that material in your essay, you will know to place the passage in quotation marks and document it.

PARAPHRASE PROPERLY

Another source of unintentional plagiarism is improper paraphrasing. When you paraphrase material, you have to be sure to change substantially the language of the source passage (see Chapter 4 for guidelines on paraphrasing material). If you do not do a good job paraphrasing a passage, you can be guilty of plagiarism even if you document the material. If in your paraphrase there are phrases or clauses that should be quoted (because they appear in your paper exactly as they appear in the source), you will be guilty of plagiarism if you do not place quotation marks around them, even if the whole passage is properly documented.

SUPPLY PROPER DOCUMENTATION

When you proofread a source-based essay, set aside time to look for problems involving documentation before you turn it in. Problems like these can be hard to detect; you need to pay close attention to finding them as you review your work. Make sure everything that should be documented is properly cited. If you ever have any questions about whether to document a particular passage or word, see your instructor. Because instructors know the documentation conventions of their particular fields of study, they can often give you the best advice. If you have a question about whether to document a passage and you cannot reach your teacher for advice, you should probably err on the side of documentation. When responding to your work, your teacher can indicate whether the documentation was absolutely necessary.

Remember, whenever you quote *or* paraphrase material, you need to supply proper documentation, indicating the source of those words or ideas. Most students remember to document quotations. Remembering to document paraphrased material can be more problematic, especially if you have been told *not* to document "common knowledge." Though this may appear to be a fairly simple guideline, in practice it can be confusing and vague. What is **common knowledge?** What qualifies as common knowledge varies from discipline to discipline in college and from audience to audience. Information that does not need to be documented in a history research paper may need to be documented in a philosophy research paper—the information is common knowledge for readers in history but not for readers in philosophy. Among one group of readers, certain facts, references, statistics, claims, or interpretations may be well known and generally accepted; among other readers, the same material may be new or controversial. For the first group of readers, documentation may not be necessary; for the second, it probably is. Again, if you ever have a question concerning whether something should or should not be documented, ask your instructor, who has expert knowledge about the discipline.

Many students express dismay over this guideline because it means that if they are writing a paper on a topic relatively new to them, they will have to document almost everything. When you are writing certain kinds of papers in certain classes, there may be no way to avoid having documented material in almost every paragraph. However, this situation is not "bad"; in fact, it is to be expected when you are writing on a subject new to you. There are ways to consolidate your documentation so the citations do not take up too much space in your essay (see the three "Consolidating References" sections in Chapter 10).

CLARIFY COLLABORATION GUIDELINES

If you are asked to collaborate with others on a project, be sure to clarify the guidelines your teacher wants you to follow. You want to be sure you know what your teacher expects of each student in the group. Are the individual members of the group supposed to work together to produce a single essay? Are the group members supposed to help each individual member of the group write his or her own paper? How much help is acceptable? Can another student supply you with the material or arguments you will use in your essay? Can others help you with the organization, perhaps suggesting how you should structure your work? Can other students write part of your paper for you? Can others revise your paper for you, changing the language when needed? Be sure you know what your teacher expects before you begin work on a collaborative project, and be sure to ask your teacher to clarify how she expects you to acknowledge and document the help you receive from others.

Summary Chart

PLAGIARISM

1. **Forms of Plagiarism**

   Purchasing a paper.

   Turning in a paper someone else has written for you.

   Turning in another student's work without that student's knowledge.

   Improper collaboration.

   Copying a paper from a source text without proper acknowledgment.

   Copying material from a reading, supplying proper documentation, but leaving out quotation marks.

   Paraphrasing material from a reading without proper documentation.

2. **How to Avoid Plagiarism**

   Do your own work.

   Take good notes.

   Paraphrase properly.

   Supply proper documentation.

   Clarify collaboration guidelines.

Chapter 10

DOCUMENTATION

DEFINITION AND PURPOSE

Proper documentation for your papers serves several functions. First, it allows your readers to know exactly where to find specific information if they want to check the accuracy of what you have written or if they want to learn more about the subject. When combined with a reference list or bibliography, proper documentation enables readers to locate information easily and efficiently. Second, documentation gives credit to others for their ideas, arguments, findings, or language. When you write from readings, you are joining an ongoing conversation—people have likely written on the topic before you began your research and will likely write on it after you have finished your essay. With documentation, you acknowledge the work of those previous authors and locate your work clearly in that conversation. Finally, as a practical matter, proper documentation helps you avoid plagiarism. Many instances of unintentional plagiarism result from improper documentation. You can avoid these problems if you take a few minutes to check the accuracy of your documentation before you turn your papers in for a grade.

TYPES OF DOCUMENTATION

In college, you will encounter two primary methods of documentation: (1) in-text parenthetical documentation and (2) footnotes or endnotes. When you use in-text parenthetical documentation, right after the quoted or paraphrased material you indicate in parentheses where that information can be found in the original source. With footnotes or endnotes, you place a raised (super-script) number after the quoted or paraphrased material, then indicate where in the source text that information can be found, either at the bottom of your page (in a footnote) or at the end of your paper (in an endnote). Over the past few years, parenthetical methods of documentation have largely replaced foot-notes and endnotes. You may still find professors, though, who prefer those older forms of documentation. Always check with your teacher if you have any questions about the type of documentation you should be using in a class.

PRIMARY ACADEMIC STYLE MANUALS

The biggest problem you will face when documenting papers in college is lack of uniform practice—styles of documentation will vary from class to class. When you write papers in college, your teacher will expect you to follow the guidelines set out in the style manual commonly used in that field of study, a set of directions writers in that discipline follow when composing and documenting papers.

Fortunately, only a few style manuals are commonly used in college. Teachers in humanities classes (English, history, philosophy, art) often follow the guidelines established by the Modern Language Association (MLA), as published in the *MLA Style Manual and Guide to Scholarly Publishing*. Teach-ers in the social sciences (sociology, anthropology, psychology, criminal jus-tice) tend to follow the rules set by the American Psychological Association (APA), which appear in *Publication Manual of the American Psychological Association*. Teachers in the natural sciences (biology, geology, chemistry) fre-quently follow the guidelines set out by the Council of Biology Editors (CBE), whose guide is entitled *Scientific Style and Format: The CBE Manual for Authors, Editors, and Publishers.* (This association was renamed the Coun-cil of Science Editors in 2000, but their style guidelines are still known as "CBE," which is how we will refer to them here.)

However, you may have a class with a sociology teacher who prefers that you follow MLA rules or a philosophy teacher who wants you to use APA style. Also, teachers within a given field may want their students to follow dif-ferent style manuals. During the same term, for example, you may be taking two education courses, with one teacher asking you to use MLA documenta-tion and the other wanting you to follow APA guidelines. If teachers do not specify the format they want you to follow, always ask them which style man-ual they want you to use when writing your paper. If a teacher voices no pref-erence, then choose one format and follow it consistently.

The APA, CBE, and MLA style manuals agree that writers should employ in-text parenthetical documentation and explanatory footnotes; however, they disagree over the exact form this documentation should assume. Though dif-ferences among the formats dictated by these style manuals may seem minor, knowing how to properly document your work helps mark you as a member of a particular academic or research community. Not knowing how may mark you as a novice or outsider.

Below are some guidelines for using APA, CBE, and MLA styles of documentation. The examples offered are not comprehensive. They may be sufficient for some of the papers you write, but you may have to use types of source texts not covered below. If you do, you can find each of the major style manuals in your college library; consult them if the following examples do not answer your questions.

A sample works cited or reference list citation for each example below can be found in Chapter 11.

APA GUIDELINES

IN-TEXT DOCUMENTATION

The APA recommends an author-date-page method of in-text documentation. When you quote material, note parenthetically the last name of the author whose work you are using, the year that work was published, and the page number in the reading where that material can be found. When you paraphrase material, you need to note the last name of the author whose work you are using and the year that work was published, but you do not need to include a specific page number in the documentation. What you include in a parenthetical citation can change, though, depending on the information you have already included in the body of your paper. For example, if the author's name has already been used to introduce the material, you do not repeat the name in the parenthetical citation.

Source with One Author

When you quote a passage from a source that has only one author, place the author's last name in parentheses, followed by the year the work was published and the page number where the passage can be found in the source text, all separated by commas. Precede the page reference with "p." if the passage is located on one page in the source text ("p. 12") and with "pp." if the passage runs on more than one page ("pp. 12–13"):

Example 1

> "The great majority of investigators believe not only that HIV is the primary cause of AIDS but also that HIV infection alone will usually cause profound immune dysfunction over time" (Greene, 1993, p. 99).

If you were to paraphrase that passage, following APA guidelines, you would not include in the documentation a specific page number, only the author and year of publication:

Example 2: Paraphrase

> Most of the scientists investigating HIV believe it causes AIDS and seriously damages a person's immune system even before that person comes down with the disease (Greene, 1993).

Note the space between the end of the quoted or paraphrased passage and the parenthetical citation. Also, the period for the sentence follows the documentation (which is not the case with block quotations). Also, remember not to repeat information in your parenthetical citation that is included in the body of your essay. For example, if you mention the author's name to introduce a quotation or paraphrase, cite the year of publication parenthetically right after the author's name and the page number right after any quoted source material:

Example 3

> According to Warner C. Greene (1993), "The great majority of investigators believe not only that HIV is the primary cause of AIDS but also that HIV infection alone will usually cause profound immune dysfunction over time" (p. 99).

Source with Two Authors

If a work has two authors, cite the last names of both authors when you refer to their work. Separate the names with an ampersand (&) if you are citing them parenthetically, with "and" if they appear in the body of your text:

Example 4

> "At the beginning of the AIDS epidemic, the large size of high-risk groups, and their lack of organization around public health issues virtually guaranteed that high levels of collective action to combat AIDS would be extremely low" (Broadhead & Heckathorn, 1994, p. 475).

Example 5: Paraphrase

> According to Broadhead and Heckathorn (1994), because the group of people most likely to be affected by AIDS was so large and tended not to focus on health issues, a poor response to the epidemic was almost certain.

Source with Three to Five Authors

The first time you refer to work from a source with three to five authors, list the last names of all the authors in the order in which they appear in the source. Again, use an ampersand before the last name when citing the authors parenthetically. In subsequent references to the work, cite the last name of the first author followed by "et al." (which means "and others"):

Example 6

> A recent study in Seattle demonstrated that a large number of gay men still engage in high-risk behavior, even though they report knowing the dangers they face (Steiner, Lemke, & Roffman, 1994).

Example 7

> A recent study in Seattle by Steiner, Lemke, and Roffman (1994) demonstrated that a large number of gay men still engage in high-risk behavior, even though they report knowing the dangers they face.

Example 8

> Steiner et al. (1994) also found that...

If shortening a citation through the use of "et al." will cause any confusion (that is, if two or more citations become identical when shortened), include all the authors' names every time you refer to their works.

Source with Six or More Authors

If a work has six or more authors, cite only the last name of the first author followed by "et al." and the year of publication:

Example 9

> A recent study in Africa confirms that among sexually active people, regular condom use helps prevent the spread of HIV and AIDS (Laga et al., 1994).

Example 10

> A recent study in Africa by Laga et al. (1994) confirms that among sexually active people, regular condom use helps prevent the spread of HIV and AIDS.

If shortening a citation through the use of "et al." will cause any confusion (if two or more citations become identical), list as many authors' last names as needed to differentiate the works, and then replace the remaining names with "et al."

Source with No Author

When a work has no author, cite the first two or three words of the title and the year of publication. If the source text is a journal article or book chapter, the shortened title will appear in quotation marks; if the work is a pamphlet or a book, the shortened title should be underlined:

Example 11

> "One quarter of a million people, mainly young, have died in America from an avoidable viral infection—five times the number who died in Vietnam" ("Clinton," 1994, p. 9).

Example 12

> In "Clinton and AIDS" (1994), the editors of *The New Republic* note, "One quarter of a million people, mainly young, have died in America from an avoidable viral infection—five times the number who died in Vietnam" (p. 9).

Because the title of the article is used to introduce the quotation in Example 12, it is not repeated in the parenthetical citation.

Sources Whose Authors Have the Same Last Name

If two authors have the same last name, differentiate them by their first initials:

Example 13

> Surveys have found that many people avoid discussing AIDS because they feel they know too little about the topic (J. Brown, 1991); consequently, a number of companies are beginning to develop programs to educate their workers (L. Brown, 1991).

Two or More Sources by the Same Author

If you are referring to two or more works by the same author, differentiate them by date of publication separated by commas. If both are included in the same parenthetical citation, order them by year of publication:

Example 14

> Because AZT has proved to be ineffective in controlling the effects of AIDS (Brown, 1993), scientists have been working hard to develop a vaccine against the virus, especially in Third World countries where the epidemic is spreading quickly (Brown, 1994).

Example 15

> A series of articles in *New Scientist* by Phillida Brown (1993, 1994) traces efforts to develop adequate treatments to combat AIDS.

Two or More Sources by the Same Author Published the Same Year

If you are referring to two or more works by the same author published in the same year, differentiate them by adding lowercase letters after the dates:

Example 16

> Two recent articles (Brown, 1994a, 1994b) trace the efforts to improve AIDS treatment in Third World countries.

The "a" article would appear first in the reference list, the "b" second, and so on. (See Chapter 11 for instructions on how to order these works in the reference list.)

Electronic Sources of Information

If you refer to the work as a whole, include the author's last name and the year of publication. If, instead, you are citing specific information in the source text, include the author's last name, the year of publication, and the page number. If the pages are not numbered, include the paragraph or section number in the source text where the material can be found preceded by the paragraph symbol (¶) or by "para.":

Example 17

> According to one expert, AIDS has killed 14 million people over the past 20 years (Underwood, 1999, para. 1).

As always, do not repeat information in the citation that is already present in your essay.

Consolidating APA-Style References

If you want to include references to two or more sources in one parenthetical citation, arrange them alphabetically by the last name of the authors and separate them with semicolons:

Example 18

> A survey of recent articles published on AIDS shows a growing interest in developing reliable research methods to test high-risk groups, such as drug abusers and prostitutes (Broadhead & Heckathorn, 1994; Carlson et al., 1994; Steiner, Lemke, & Roffman, 1994).

FOOTNOTES AND ENDNOTES

Some style manuals still advocate using footnotes or endnotes as the primary means of documenting source-based essays, but the APA suggests they be used sparingly, only to supply commentary or information you do not want to include in the body of your paper. These notes are numbered consecutively in the text with superscript numerals.

Example 19

> A survey of recent articles published on AIDS shows a growing interest in developing reliable research methods to test high-risk groups, such as drug abusers and prostitutes.[1]

The notes then appear on a separate page at the end of the paper with the word "Footnotes" centered at the top. The footnotes are double spaced in numerical order, preceded by superscript numerals. The first line of every note is indented five to seven spaces.

CBE GUIDELINES

IN-TEXT DOCUMENTATION

The documentation practices suggested by the *CBE* are much less uniform than those suggested by the APA or MLA, though in the sixth edition of its style manual, the CBE sets as one of its goals greater standardization of documentation forms. The CBE recommends that when you are preparing a manuscript for publication you consult previous issues of the journal you hope will publish your work to determine the form of documentation it employs. Periodicals in the natural sciences will likely employ, with slight variations, one of two documentation systems: the name-year system or the citation-sequence system.

The Name-Year System

This system closely resembles APA documentation. When you document material, note parenthetically the last name of the author and the year the work was published. The CBE style manual is much less explicit, though, in its guidelines for adapting parenthetical citations to suit the nature of the material being documented.

Source with One Author

When you quote material from a source, include the last name of the author, the year of publication, and the page number where the passage can be found in the reading preceded by "p" for both single- and multiple-page references:

Example 20

> "The great majority of investigators believe not only that HIV is the primary cause of AIDS but also that HIV infection alone will usually cause profound immune dysfunction over time" (Greene 1993, p 99).

Note that there is no comma between the name of the author and the year of publication. Include a comma between the year of publication and the page reference. The "p" denoting "page" is not followed by a period. Also note the placement of the period following the documentation. (In a block quotation, the period precedes the documentation.)

When you paraphrase a passage, generally you will refer not to specific page numbers but only to the author and year of publication:

Example 21: Paraphrase

Most of the scientists investigating HIV believe it causes AIDS and seriously damages a person's immune system even before that person comes down with the disease (Greene 1993).

Source with Two Authors

When a work is written by two authors, cite the last names of both separated by "and":

Example 22

"At the beginning of the AIDS epidemic, the large size of high-risk groups, and their lack of organization around public health issues virtually guaranteed that high levels of collective action to combat AIDS would be extremely low" (Broadhead and Heckathorn 1994, p 475).

Example 22: Paraphrase

According to Broadhead and Heckathorn (1994), because the group of people most likely to be affected by AIDS was so large and tended not to focus on health issues, a poor response to the epidemic was almost certain.

Source with Three or More Authors

If a source has three or more authors, give the last name of the first author followed by "and others":

Example 24

A recent study in Africa confirms that among sexually active people, regular condom use does help prevent the spread of HIV and AIDS (Laga and others 1994).

Example 25

A recent study in Africa by Laga and others (1994) confirms that among sexually active people, regular condom use does help prevent the spread of HIV and AIDS.

Source with No Author

When the author's name is not given in the source, use the term "Anonymous," followed by the year of publication:

Example 26

"One quarter of a million people, mainly young, have died in America from an avoidable viral infection—five times the number who died in Vietnam" (Anonymous 1994).

Example 27

> In "Clinton and AIDS" (Anonymous 1994), the editors of *The New Republic* note, "One quarter of a million people, mainly young, have died in America from an avoidable viral infection—five times the number who died in Vietnam" (p 9).

Sources Whose Authors Have the Same Last Name

When you are working with sources written by people who have the same last name, give their initials as well:

Example 28

> Surveys have found that many people avoid discussing AIDS because they feel they know too little about the topic (Brown WJ 1991); consequently, a number of companies are beginning to develop programs to educate their workers (Brown LL 1991).

Note the punctuation: do not include periods between or after the initials.

Two or More Sources by the Same Author

If you are referring to two or more works by the same author, differentiate them in your documentation by adding the date of publication separated by commas if needed.

Example 29

> Because AZT has proved to be ineffective in controlling the effects of AIDS (Brown 1993) scientists have been working hard to develop a vaccine against the virus, especially in Third World countries where the epidemic is spreading quickly (Brown 1994).

Example 30

> A series of articles in *New Scientist* by Phillida Brown (1993, 1994) traces efforts to develop adequate treatments to combat AIDS.

Two or More Sources by the Same Author Published the Same Year

If you are citing two or more works written by the same author published in the same year, differentiate them in your documentation by adding lowercase letters after the dates:

Example 31

> Two recent articles (Brown 1994a, 1994b) trace the efforts to improve AIDS treatment in Third World countries.

Electronic Sources of Information

If you are citing the work as a whole, include the author's name and the year of publication. If, however, you are citing only a portion of the source text, include the page number or numbers as well. If the pages in the source text are not numbered, include the paragraph number where that information can be found.

Example 32

> According to one expert, AIDS has killed 14 million people over the past 20 years (Underwood 1999, par 1).

Consolidating CBE Name-Year References

If you want to include references to two or more sources in one parenthetical citation, arrange them alphabetically by the authors' last names and separate them with semicolons.

Example 33

> A survey of recent articles published on AIDS shows a growing interest in developing reliable research methods to test high-risk groups, such as drug abusers and prostitutes (Broadhead and Heckathorn 1994; Carlson and others 1994; Steiner and others 1994).

The Citation-Sequence System

This system numbers references consecutively as they occur in your text. The first source you use you number "1," the second source "2," and so on. Usually, the number is a superscript placed after the quoted or paraphrased material. The next time you refer to that source, you repeat the same number it was first given. The superscript numbers should be one or two points smaller than the type used in the body of your paper. Some journals prefer you cite the number of the reference parenthetically:

Example 34

> Most of the scientists investigating HIV believe it causes AIDS and seriously damages a person's immune system even before that person comes down with the disease[1].

Example 35

> Most of the scientists investigating HIV believe it causes AIDS and seriously damages a person's immune system even before that person comes down with the disease (1).

Pay attention to the placement of the period at the end of the sentence: the period always follows the citation number. Also, if you refer to the authors in the body of your essay, the citation number comes right after their names, before a comma or other punctuation mark:

Example 36

According to Broadhead and Heckathorn[1], because the group of people most likely to be affected by AIDS was so large and tended not to focus on health issues, a poor response to the epidemic was almost certain.

Referring to a Specific Page

The CBE style manual does not suggest how to refer to a specific page number of a source text when using superscript numbers. When citing sources parenthetically, however, common practice among scientific journals suggests that in your citation you list the source number followed by the page number. Precede the page number with "p" when referring to material found on one or more pages in the source (if the pages are not numbered, as is commonly the case with electronic sources of information, include the paragraph number preceded by "par"). Separate the source number from the page or paragraph number with a comma:

Example 37

"At the beginning of the AIDS epidemic, the large size of high-risk groups, and their lack of organization around public health issues virtually guaranteed that high levels of collective action to combat AIDS would be extremely low" (1, p 475).

Example 38

"Few things in life are more satisfying than solving a mystery—especially if it involves 14 million deaths that have stumped the world for nearly 20 years" (2, par 1).

Consolidating CBE Citation-Sequence References

If you want to include references to two or more works in one citation, list them in numerical order, separated by commas:

Example 39

A survey of recent articles published on AIDS[1,3,7] shows a growing interest in developing reliable research methods to test high-risk groups, such as drug abusers and prostitutes.

Example 40

> A survey of recent articles published on AIDS (1,3,7) shows a growing interest in developing reliable research methods to test high-risk groups, such as drug abusers and prostitutes.

If you refer to several sources listed consecutively in the reference list, include only the first and last numbers, joined by a hyphen (for example, "1-3,7,11-13").

FOOTNOTES AND ENDNOTES

The CBE style manual discourages the use of footnotes. It suggests that if you use endnotes, designate them sequentially in the text with superscript lowercase letters, "a," "b," "c," and so on:

Example 41

> A survey of recent articles published on AIDS shows a growing interest in developing reliable research methods to test high-risk groups, such as drug abusers and prostitutes[a].

The notes then appear on a separate page at the end of the paper under a heading such as "Notes." The endnotes may be single- or double-spaced. Precede each note with the appropriate lowercase letter (*not* a superscript), a period, and a space:

Notes

a. See, for example, the articles by . . .

MLA GUIDELINES

IN-TEXT DOCUMENTATION

MLA style uses an author-page system of in-text documentation. When you quote or paraphrase material, you tell your reader parenthetically the name of the author whose work you are using and where in that reading the passage or information can be found. If your reader wants more information on this source text (for instance, whether it is a book or an article, when it was published, or what journal it appeared in), she will refer to the works cited list at the end of your paper, where you provide this information.

    The exact form of the parenthetical documentation—what information goes into the parentheses and in what order—varies depending on the type of source you are referring to and what you have already mentioned about the source in the body of your essay.

Source with One Author

When you quote or paraphrase information from a reading that has just one author, place the author's last name in parentheses, leave a space, and then indicate the page number or numbers in the source where the passage or information can be found. Whether you are quoting or paraphrasing material, the period follows the parentheses. In the following examples, pay particular attention to spacing and the proper placement of quotation marks:

Example 42

"The great majority of investigators believe not only that HIV is the primary cause of AIDS but also that HIV infection alone will usually cause profound immune dysfunction over time" (Greene 99).

Example 43: Paraphrase

Most of the scientists investigating HIV believe it causes AIDS and seriously damages a person's immune system even before that person comes down with the disease (Greene 99).

When using the MLA format, do *not* include "p." or "pp." before the page number or numbers. Again, notice that the final period is placed *after* the documentation. The only exception to this punctuation rule occurs when you block quote information, in which case the period comes before the parenthetical documentation.

Do not repeat in the parentheses information that is already included in the text itself. For example, if you mention the author's name leading up to the quotation or believe your reader will know who the author is from the context of the quotation, you do not need to repeat the author's name in parentheses:

Example 44

According to Warner C. Greene, "The great majority of investigators believe not only that HIV is the primary cause of AIDS but also that HIV infection alone will usually cause profound immune dysfunction over time" (99).

MLA style requires you to record specific page references for material directly quoted or paraphrased. If you are quoting or paraphrasing a passage that runs longer than one page in a reading, indicate all the page numbers where that information can be found:

Example 45

In deciding whether to undertake large scale or small scale tests of HIV vaccines, scientists must balance the cost of the study against their desire to obtain reliable results (Cohn 1073–74).

Source with Two Authors

If a work has two authors, list the last names of the authors in the order they appear in the source, joined by "and." If you mention the authors in the body of your essay, include only the page number or numbers in parentheses:

Example 46

> "At the beginning of the AIDS epidemic, the large size of high-risk groups, and their lack of organization around public health issues virtually guaranteed that high levels of collective action to combat AIDS would be extremely low" (Broadhead and Heckathorn 475).

Example 47: Paraphrase

> According to Broadhead and Heckathorn, because the group of people most likely to be affected by AIDS was so large and tended not to focus on health issues, a poor response to the epidemic was almost certain (475).

Source with Three Authors

If a work has three authors, list the last names of the authors in the order they appear in the source, separated by commas, with "and" before the last name:

Example 48

> A recent study in Seattle demonstrated that a large number of gay men still engage in high-risk behavior, even though they report knowing the dangers they face (Steiner, Lemke, and Roffman 565).

Source with More Than Three Authors

If a source has more than three authors, include the last name of the first author followed by "et al.":

Example 49

> In Dayton, Ohio, a group of investigators has developed an effective way to sample large numbers of drug addicts to determine their risk of acquiring HIV-1 (Carlson et al. 280).

Source with No Author

If a work has no author, parenthetically cite the first word or two of the title. If the work is a journal article or book chapter, the shortened title will appear in quotation marks. If the work is longer, the shortened title should be underlined or italicized. If you mention the title of the work in the body of your essay, you will need to include only the page number or numbers in parentheses:

Example 50

> "One quarter of a million people, mainly young, have died in America from an avoidable viral infection—five times the number who died in Vietnam" ("Clinton" 9).

Example 51

> In "Clinton and AIDS," the editors of *The New Republic* note, "One quarter of a million people, mainly young, have died in America from an avoidable viral infection—five times the number who died in Vietnam" (9).

Sources Whose Authors Have the Same Last Name

If two different authors have the same last name, differentiate them in your documentation by including their first initials:

Example 52

> Surveys have found that many people avoid discussing AIDS because they feel they know too little about the topic (J. Brown 675); consequently, a number of companies are beginning to develop programs to educate their workers (L. Brown 64).

Two or More Sources by the Same Author

If you are referring to two or more works by the same author, differentiate them in your documentation by putting a comma after the last name of the author and adding a shortened version of the title before citing the specific page reference:

Example 53

> Because AZT has proved to be ineffective in controlling the effects of AIDS (Brown, "Drug" 4), scientists have been working hard to develop a vaccine against the virus, especially in Third World countries where the epidemic is spreading quickly (Brown, "AIDS" 10).

Again, the shortened title of an article or chapter is placed in quotation marks; the shortened title of a longer work would be underlined or italicized.

Electronic Sources of Information

If the pages in the electronic source text are numbered, include the author's last name and the page number. If, instead, the paragraphs or sections in the source text are numbered, include the author's last name and the paragraph or section number or numbers (use "par." for one paragraph, "pars." for more than one paragraph). *Separate the author's last name and the paragraph numbers with a comma.* If the source text does not number pages, paragraphs, or sections, include only the author's last name.

Consolidating MLA-Style References

Many times in papers, you will include in one paragraph information you gathered from several different sources. When you document this passage, arrange the references alphabetically by the last names of the authors and separate them with semicolons:

Example 54

> A survey of recent articles published on AIDS shows a growing interest in developing reliable research methods to test high-risk groups, such as drug abusers and prostitutes (Broadhead and Heckathorn; Carlson et al.; Steiner, Lemke, and Roffman).

No page numbers are included here because the passage refers to the general topic of the articles, not to specific information in them.

FOOTNOTES AND ENDNOTES

The MLA suggests that footnotes or endnotes be used only to supply commentary or information you do not want to include in the body of your paper. Whether you are adding content notes (explanations of or elaborations on ideas you have discussed in the body of your paper) or bibliographic notes (a list of sources your readers might want to consult if they are interested in learning more about the topic you are discussing), try to keep them to a minimum because they are distracting.

Number footnotes and endnotes consecutively in the body of your essay with superscript numerals:

Example 55

> A survey of recent articles published on AIDS shows a growing interest in developing reliable research methods to test high-risk groups, such as drug abusers and prostitutes.[1]

If you are using footnotes, the citation appears at the bottom of the page on which the corresponding number appears. These notes are placed four lines below the text on the page and are single-spaced. Leave one blank line after each note. If a note carries over to the next page, place a solid typed line across the second page, two lines below the text; then continue the note two lines below that. Begin each note with the proper superscript number and indent the first line of each note five spaces or one-half inch from the left margin.

If you are using endnotes, all the citations appear in numerical order at the end of your paper on a separate page with the heading "Notes" centered one inch from the top margin. Double-space after typing this heading; then begin the citations. All the citations are double-spaced and begin with the corresponding superscript number followed by a space. Indent the first line of each note five spaces or one-half inch from the left margin.

Chapter 11

Reference Lists and Works Cited Entries

DEFINITION AND PURPOSE

A reference or works cited list comes at the end of your paper. In it you provide all of the bibliographic information for the sources you used when writing your essay. You have one entry for every source you refer to in the body of your paper, an entry that lists for your readers the information they would need to locate the source and read it themselves.

With in-text documentation you indicate where you found the specific information or language you used in your paper, usually including only the last name of the author and the page number on which the material is located. In your reference list you will give your reader much more information concerning this reading: the author's full name, the full title of the piece, and the place and year of publication. Also, while in-text documentation indicates a specific page where the material can be found, a reference list citation indicates all the page numbers of the reading.

A works cited or reference list is sometimes also called a *bibliography*, but actually the two are not the same. While the entry format for each is the same, in a bibliography you include an entry for every source you *consulted* when researching your paper; in a works cited list you include an entry only for the sources you actually *included* in your paper. Suppose you consulted ten books or articles when researching a topic for a paper but used only seven of them in your final draft. If your teacher asked you to put together a bibliography for your essay, you would have ten entries. If she asked you for a works cited or reference list, you would have only seven entries.

Putting together a works cited or reference list can be tedious and time-consuming because there are specific forms you have to follow, forms dictated by the type of source you are using and the style manual you are following. Your job is to follow these forms exactly. However, there is a reason for this uniformity. When you put together a works cited list in the proper form, you are providing a valuable service for your readers: when writers in a discipline agree to follow the same format for reference lists, readers can easily determine where to locate the sources that interest them because they know how to read the entries.

Complicating your efforts to put together a proper reference list is the fact that each field of study has its preferred ways of structuring entries. While the information in the entries generally stays the same across the disciplines, the order in which you present that information varies widely. As described in the previous chapter, teachers in the humanities tend to follow the guidelines established by the Modern Language Association (MLA), those in the social sciences typically employ the guidelines established by the American Psychological Association (APA), and those in the natural sciences often follow the guidelines established by the Council of Biology Editors (CBE).

When putting together a works cited or reference list, your best approach is to follow the guidelines and sample entries as closely as you can, placing the information from your source exactly where it appears in the model. Pay very close attention to capitalization, spacing, and punctuation.

The samples provided below follow the guidelines of the major style manuals, but they are not comprehensive. As you write a paper, you may use types of readings not covered in this chapter. If this occurs, you can obtain a copy of each style manual at your library and follow the sample entry it contains for the type of text you are employing.

APA FORMAT

SAMPLE REFERENCE LIST ENTRIES

In an APA reference list, you include the name of the author, the title, and the publishing information for all of the readings you use in the body of your essay. You include the authors' last names and the initials of their first and middle names. If a source has more than one author, list their last names first followed by their initials and a comma; use an ampersand (&) to introduce the final name. Book and journal titles are italicized; article titles are not (neither are they placed in quotation marks). In the titles of books and articles, you capitalize only the first word of the title and subtitle (if any) and any proper nouns and proper adjectives. The format for listing the publishing information varies by the type of source, so pay close attention to the sample entries below and follow them precisely. The first line of every entry is flush with the left margin; all other lines are indented one-half inch or five spaces, and all entries end with a period.

Journal Article, One Author

Greene, W. C. (1993, September). AIDS and the immune system. *Scientific American, 269,* 99–105.

- Since *Scientific American* is a monthly magazine, note where the month of publication is included: after the year of publication.
- Note the use of capitalization in the article title: first word and proper nouns only. The title is neither underlined nor placed in quotation marks.
- Note that the volume number is included here and is italicized.
- Note that the page numbers for a journal or magazine article are *not* preceded by "p." or "pp."
- Note that all the page numbers of the article are listed, not just the one or two you might have referred to for in-text documentation. This article begins on page 99 and runs through page 105.
- Pay attention to the placement of commas and periods.

Journal Article, Two Authors

Broadhead, R. S., & Heckathorn, D. D. (1994). AIDS prevention outreach among injection drug users: Agency problems and new approaches. *Social Problems, 41,* 473–495.

- Note the order of the names: last name first followed by initials. The names are separated by a comma and the second name is introduced by an ampersand.
- The year of publication comes next, noted parenthetically.
- Note that the "A" in "Agency" is capitalized because it is the first word in the subtitle.
- Note that the volume number follows the title of the journal; it is also italicized.

Journal Article, Three or More Authors

Laga, M., Alary, M., Nzila, N., Manoka, A. T., Tuliza, M., Behets, F., Goeman, J., St. Louis, M., & Piot, P. (1994). Condom promotion, sexually transmitted diseases treatment, and declining incidence of HIV-1 infection in female Zairian sex workers. *The Lancet, 344,* 246–248.

Steiner, S., Lemke, A., & Roffman, R. A. (1994). Risk behavior for HIV transmission among gay men surveyed in Seattle bars. *Public Health Reports, 109,* 563–566.

- When there are three to five authors, list all their names.
- Separate the names with commas and introduce the last name with an ampersand.

- When an article has more than five authors, list all of their names in your reference list citation, but in the body of your essay, document the source using only the first author's surname followed by "et al." and the year of publication: (Laga et al., 1994).

Journal Article from Periodical with Continuous Pagination

Many academic journals employ **continuous pagination:** they number the pages of each volume consecutively even if that volume is published in several issues. For example, many academic journals are published quarterly—a single volume of the journal is published in four "numbers" or "issues" over the course of a year: volume 100, issue 1; volume 100, issue 2; and so forth. Suppose volume 100, issue 1, is published in April and contains 200 pages: the first page would be numbered "1" and the last page "200." Suppose volume 100, issue 2, is published in July of the same year: with continuous pagination, its first page number would be "201."

In a reference list citation for a journal using continuous pagination, you do not need to include the source's issue number or the month it was published. You need to include only the volume and page numbers:

Broadhead, R. S., & Heckathorn, D. D. (1994). AIDS prevention outreach among injection drug users: Agency problems and new approaches. *Social Problems, 41,* 473–495.

- Note that the volume number and specific page number of the article follow the title of the journal. You do not include the issue number.

Journal Article from Periodical without Continuous Pagination

When a journal does not employ continuous pagination, every issue of the journal begins with page "1." When this is the case, your citation needs to include both volume and issue numbers. The issue number follows the volume number, is noted parenthetically, and is not italicized:

Philipson, T. J., Posner, R. A., & Wright, J. H. (1994). Why AIDS prevention programs don't work. *Issues in Science and Technology, 10* (3), 33–35.

- Note the order of information at the end of the citation and the punctuation: include the title of the journal and the volume number (both italicized), the issue number (noted parenthetically but not italicized), then the inclusive page numbers.

Article from a Monthly Periodical

Greene, W. C. (1993, September). AIDS and the immune system. *Scientific American, 269,* 99–105.

- For a monthly periodical, indicate the month of publication after the year, separating the two with a comma.
- Be sure to include the volume number as well, after the journal title.

Article from a Weekly Periodical

Cowley, G. (1993, March 22). The future of AIDS. *Newsweek, 121,* 46–52.

- Indicate the month and day of publication after the year, separating the year and month with a comma.
- Include the volume number after the journal title.

Newspaper Article

Walsh, P. M. (1995, February 7). AIDS epidemic becomes more diverse. *The Boston Globe,* p. 32.

- Note the placement of the date: year followed by month and day, with a comma separating the year and month.
- The title of the newspaper is capitalized and italicized.
- Precede the page number with "p." if the article is on one page and with "pp." if it runs longer than one page.

Newspaper Article, No Author

Volunteers take up slack in AIDS care. (1993, July 6). *Times-Picayune,* p. B4.

- When there is no author, begin the citation with the title.
- Note how the section is noted with the page number when the newspaper is divided into sections.

Book with One Author

Stine, G. J. (1993). *Acquired immune deficiency syndrome: Biological, medical, social and legal issues.* Englewood Cliffs, NJ: Prentice-Hall.

- Note that the order of information for citing a book parallels the order of information for citing an article.
- Book titles are italicized. The first word in the title is capitalized and so are all proper nouns and proper adjectives and the first word in the subtitle (the "B" in "Biological" above).
- Following the title, indicate the city of publication and the publisher.

Book with Two or More Authors

Douglas, P. H., & Pinsky, L. (1991). *The essential AIDS fact book.* New York: Pocket Books.

Rabkin, J., Remien, R., & Wilson, C. (1994). *Good doctors, good patients: Partners in HIV treatment.* New York: NCM Publishers.

- List multiple authors by their last names and initials, separating them with commas, and using an ampersand to introduce the final author.
- If a book has more than five authors, list all of their names in your reference citation, but in the body of your paper, when you cite them parenthetically for documentation, use only the first author's name followed by "et al." and the year of publication.

Two or More Works by the Same Person

Kübler-Ross, E. (1975). *Death: The final stage of growth.* Englewood Cliffs, NJ: Prentice-Hall.

Kübler-Ross, E. (1987). *AIDS: The ultimate challenge.* New York: Macmillan.

- Arrange the citations in chronological order, the earliest first.

Book, Corporate Author

National Gay and Lesbian Task Force. (1987). *Anti-gay violence: Victimization and defamation in 1986.* New York: Author.

- If the publisher is the same as the corporate author, simply write "Author" after the city where the work was published.

Book, Later Edition

DeVita, V. T., Jr., Hellman, S., & Rosenberg, S. A. (1996). *AIDS: Etiology, diagnosis, treatment and prevention* (4th ed.). Philadelphia: Lippincott.

- If you are using a later edition of a book, list the edition number parenthetically after the title.

Edited Book

Corinne, S. (Ed.). (1993). *Women and AIDS: Psychological perspectives.* London: Sage.

- If one person edited the book, place "(Ed.)" after his name. If more than one person edited the work, place "(Eds.)" after their names.
- Pay particular attention to the periods in this citation. It is easy to leave some of them out.

Book, No Author or Editor

AIDS and the third world (3rd ed.). (1988). London: Panos Institute.

- When the title page of a book lists no author, begin your citation with the title.
- Note that in this entry, the edition number precedes the year of publication.

Multivolume Book

Daintith, J., Mitchell, S., & Tootill, E. (Eds.). (1981). *A biographical encyclopedia of scientists* (Vols. 1–2). New York: Facts on File.

- Indicate for your reader how many volumes comprise the work. This information follows the title.

One Volume of a Multivolume Book

Daintith, J., Mitchell, S., & Tootill, E. (Eds.). (1981). *A biographical encyclopedia of scientists* (Vol. 1). New York: Facts on File.

- When you use just one volume of a multivolume work, indicate the volume number parenthetically after the title.

English Translation of a Book

Jager, H. (Ed.). (1988). *AIDS phobia: Disease pattern and possibilities of treatment* (J. Welch, Trans.). New York: Halsted Press.

- Open the citation with the name of the author or editor.
- Following the title, give the translator's name followed by "Trans."
- Note that in giving the translator's name, you begin with her initials, followed by the last name.
- Again, pay attention to all the periods included in this citation.

Article or Chapter from an Anthology

Many times in writing a source-based paper you will use a work contained in an anthology of readings. When this is the case, follow this format in your reference list:

Patton, C. (1993). With champagne and roses: Women at risk from/in AIDS discourse. In C. Squire (Ed.), *Women and AIDS* (pp. 165–187). London: Sage.

- Open your citation with the name of the author whose ideas or language you included in your paper. Your in-text documentation for this source would be "(Patton, 1993)."
- Next, give the title of the specific reading you referred to in the body of your essay.
- Next, give the name of the author or editor of the anthology and the larger work's title (the title of the book is italicized). Precede this information with the word "In" (note capitalization).
- Follow the title with the specific page numbers on which the article can be found. In this case, Patton's article can be found on pages 165–187 of Squire's book.
- Close the entry with the publishing information.

Article in a Reference Work

Acquired immune deficiency syndrome. (1990). In *The new encyclopaedia Britannica* (Vol. 1, p. 67). Chicago: Encyclopaedia Britannica.

Haseltine, W. A. (1992). AIDS. In *Encyclopedia Americana* (Vol. 1, pp. 365–366). Danbury, CT: Grolier.

- When the entry in the reference work is signed, begin the citation with the author's name; when it is not signed, begin the citation with the title of the entry.
- Include the year the reference work was published, the title of the work (italicized), the volume number and inclusive page numbers of the entry (noted parenthetically), followed by the publishing information.

Personal Interview

Under APA guidelines, all personal communications are to be cited in the text only. Include the name of the person you interviewed (first and middle initials, full last name), the words "personal communication," and the date of the interview (month, day, year), all separated by commas:

(F. Smith, personal communication, June 24, 1995)

Electronic Sources of Information

The standards for citing electronic sources of information are still in flux. You can find the most current version of the APA's standards online at www.apa.org/journals/webref.html.

Information on CD-ROM or Diskette

AIDS. (1995). *The 1995 Grolier multimedia encyclopedia.* [CD-ROM]. (Version 7.05). Danbury, CT: Grolier.

- List the name of the author or authors (if known), last name first followed by first and middle initials. Because this source text has no author, the entry begins with the title.
- List the date of publication in parentheses.
- Give the title of the chapter or entry you consulted for your paper.
- Give the title of the publication that contained the chapter or entry.
- Indicate the electronic medium (i.e., CD-ROM or diskette) in square brackets.
- Give the version or edition number of the complete work in parentheses.
- List the publication information.

Online Information Databank

AIDS. (1999). *Encyclopaedia Britannica online.* Retrieved July 22, 1999, from http://members.eb.com/bol/topic?eu=4225&sctn=1&pm=1

- Give the name of the author or authors (if known).
- Give the title of the entry or chapter you consulted when gathering information for your paper. If there is no author, begin the entry with the title of the entry or chapter.
- Give the date of publication.
- Give the title of the database, italicized.

- Give the date of access and the electronic address (or URL). The URL can be broken at a slash if need be to make it fit on a line in your reference list.
- Do not end the entry with a period.

Article from an Online Publication

This is the format to use if your source text exists only electronically. If the article does not also appear in print somewhere, use this form for your reference list entry:

Murphy, C. (1997, June 3). AIDS: Privacy vs. public health. *Atlantic Unbound*. Retrieved July 22, 1999, from http:// www.theatlantic.com/unbound/forum/aids/intro.html

- Give the name of the author or authors (if known), last name first followed by first and middle initials.
- Give the date of publication in parentheses.
- Give the title of the article.
- Give the title of the publication, italicized.
- Give the date of access followed by the electronic address.

Previously Published Article Found Online

Underwood, A. (1999, July 12). How the plague began. *Newsweek, 139*. Retrieved September 9, 1999, from http://www.newsweek.com/ nw-srv/printed/us/so/md0206_1.htm

- Give the name of the author or authors (if known).
- Give the date of publication.
- Give the title of the article.
- Give the title of the magazine or journal along with the volume number of the publication and the original page number or numbers (if known).
- Give the date of access and the electronic address.

Work from an Online Service

Stolberg, S. (1994, August 31). Cruel link: Hemophilia and AIDS. *Los Angeles Times*, p. A1+. Retrieved September 11, 1999, from *SIRS Researcher* database.

- Give the name of the author or authors (if known).
- Give the date of publication.
- Give the title of the article.
- Give the name of the original publication and any relevant issue or volume numbers.
- Give the original pagination.
- Give the date of retrieval and the name of the online service (italicized).

E-Mail

The fifth edition of APA's *Publication Manual* considers e-mail messages to be "personal communication," which should be cited in text only. In parentheses, include the name of the person who sent you the e-mail message (first and middle initials followed by the full last name), the words "personal communication," and the date of the communication (month, day, year):

(F. Smith, personal communication, December 1, 1998).

SAMPLE APA-STYLE REFERENCE LIST

List all of your references at the end of your paper, beginning the list on a new page. At the top of the page, center the word "References." After the heading, double-space and list your citations in alphabetical order according to the last name of the author or first key word in the title if there is no author. Indent the first line of every citation five spaces or one-half inch, and double-space all entries.

References

Acquired immune deficiency syndrome. (1990). In *The new*

encyclopaedia Britannica (Vol. 1, p. 67). Chicago: Encyclopaedia

Britannica.

AIDS. (1995). *The 1995 Grolier multimedia encyclopedia.* [CD-ROM].

(Version 7.05). Danbury, CT: Grolier.

AIDS. (1999). *Encyclopaedia Britannica online.* Retrieved July 22, 1999,

from http://members.eb.com/bol/topic?eu=4225&sctn=1&pm=1

AIDS and the third world (3rd ed.). (1988). London: Panos Institute.

Broadhead, R. S., & Heckathorn, D. D. (1994). AIDS prevention

outreach among injection drug users: Agency problems and new

approaches. *Social Problems, 41,* 473–495.

Corinne, S. (Ed.). (1993). *Women and AIDS: Psychological*

perspectives. London: Sage.

Cowley, G. (1993, March 22). The future of AIDS. *Newsweek, 121,* 46–52.

Daintith, J., Mitchell, S., & Tootill, E. (Eds.). (1981). *A biographical*

encyclopedia of scientists (Vol. 1). New York: Facts on File.

DeVita, V. T., Jr., Hellman, S., & Rosenberg, S. A. (1996). *AIDS:*

Etiology, diagnosis, treatment and prevention (4th ed.).

Philadelphia: Lippincott.

Douglas, P. H., & Pinsky, L. (1991). *The essential AIDS fact book.* New

York: Pocket Books.

Greene, W. C. (1993, September). AIDS and the immune system.

Scientific American, 269, 99–105.

Haseltine, W. A. (1992). AIDS. In *Encyclopedia Americana* (Vol. 1, pp. 365–366). Danbury, CT: Grolier.

Jager, H. (Ed.). (1988). *AIDS phobia: Disease pattern and possibilities of treatment* (J. Welch, Trans.). New York: Halsted Press.

Kübler-Ross, E. (1975). *Death: The final stage of growth*. Englewood Cliffs, NJ: Prentice-Hall.

Kübler-Ross, E. (1987). *AIDS: The ultimate challenge*. New York: Macmillan.

Laga, M., Alary, M., Nzila, N., Manoka, A. T., Tuliza, M., Behets, F., Goeman, J., St. Louis, M., & Piot, P. (1994). Condom promotion, sexually transmitted diseases treatment, and declining incidence of HIV-1 infection in female Zairian sex workers. *The Lancet, 344,* 246–248.

Murphy, C. (1997, June 3). AIDS: Privacy vs. public health. *Atlantic Unbound*. Retrieved July 22, 1999, from http://www.theatlantic.com/unbound/forum/aids/intro.html

National Gay and Lesbian Task Force. (1987). *Anti-gay violence: Victimization and defamation in 1986*. New York: Author.

Patton, C. (1993). With champagne and roses: Women at risk from/in AIDS discourse. In C. Squire (Ed.), *Women and AIDS* (pp. 165–187). London: Sage.

Philipson, T. J., Posner, R. A., & Wright, J. H. (1994). Why AIDS prevention programs don't work. *Issues in Science and Technology, 10* (3), 33–35.

Rabkin, J., Remien, R., & Wilson, C. (1994). *Good doctors, good*

patients: Partners in HIV treatment. New York: NCM Publishers.

Steiner, S., Lemke, A., & Roffman, R. A. (1994). Risk behavior for HIV

transmission among gay men surveyed in Seattle bars. *Public*

Health Reports, 109, 563–566.

Stine, G. J. (1993). *Acquired immune deficiency syndrome: Biological,*

medical, social and legal issues. Englewood Cliffs, NJ: Prentice-Hall.

Stolberg, S. (1994, August 31). Cruel link: Hemophilia and AIDS. *Los*

Angeles Times, p. A1+. Retrieved September 11, 1999, from *SIRS*

Researcher database.

Underwood, A. (1999, July 12). How the plague began. *Newsweek,*

139. Retrieved September 9, 1999, from http://

www.newsweek.com/nw-srv/printed/us/so/md0206_1.htm

Volunteers take up slack in AIDS care. (1993, July 6). *Times-Picayune,*

p. B4.

Walsh, P. M. (1995, February 7). AIDS epidemic becomes more diverse.

The Boston Globe, p. 32.

CBE FORMAT

SAMPLE REFERENCE LIST ENTRIES

The CBE style manual describes two different ways of citing material in papers—the citation-sequence system and the name-year system—and two corresponding types of reference list citations. The material contained in both types of citation is the same, but the order of the information and some of the punctuation are different. The CBE style manual also notes that individual scientific journals may require slightly different versions of these two basic types of citation. Therefore, as you examine the models offered below, keep in mind that you might see slight variations in the journals you consult while doing research. As always, if you have any question concerning proper form, consult your instructor or the style manual itself.

In general, CBE citations include the author's last name followed by first and middle initials, the title of the work, and publication information. The names of multiple authors are separated by commas. Article and book titles are not underlined, italicized, or placed in quotation marks, and only the first word and any proper nouns and proper adjectives are capitalized; do not automatically capitalize the first word of a subtitle. Journal names are not underlined or italicized, and those longer than one word are abbreviated following the *American National Standard for Bibliographic References* (you can get a copy of this work from your school's reference librarian). Do not use "p" or "pp" to indicate specific page numbers: simply list the page numbers at the appropriate place in the citation. For books, include the total number of pages in the work. All entries are single-spaced and end with a period.

If you are employing the citation-sequence system, the entries in the reference list at the end of your paper will be numbered and listed in the order they are cited in the text: source "1" will be the first work listed, source "2" the second one listed, and so on. If you are using the name-year system, the sources are listed in alphabetical order by the authors' last names on the reference page at the end of your paper. Under both systems, second and subsequent lines of an entry begin under the first letter of the first line. Some journals leave a blank line between entries; some do not. See the sample reference lists below for further explanations and examples.

Journal Article, One Author

Citation-Sequence System

[1] Greene WC. AIDS and the immune system. Sci Am 1993 Sep;269(3):99–105.

- Note the punctuation of the author's name: do not include a comma after the last name or periods between the initials.

- Note the capitalization in the article title: only the first word and any proper nouns and proper adjectives are capitalized.
- The article title is neither underlined nor placed in quotation marks.
- The journal title is abbreviated without periods and is followed by year and month of publication (because *Scientific American* is a monthly magazine), the volume number, the issue number (in parentheses), and inclusive page numbers.
- The date of publication is followed by a semicolon; the issue number is followed by a colon.
- Note the lack of spaces between the month of publication, volume number, issue number, and page numbers.

Name-Year System

Greene WC. 1993 Sep. AIDS and the immune system. Sci Am 269(3):99–105. or

Greene WC. 1993. AIDS and the immune system. Sci Am 269(3):99–105.

- Note that the year of publication follows the author's name.
- Again, note the lack of punctuation in the title and the lack of spaces between the volume number, issue number, and page numbers.

Journal Article, Two Authors

Citation-Sequence System

[2] Broadhead RS, Heckathorn DD. AIDS prevention outreach among injection drug users: agency problems and new approaches. Soc Prob 1994;41:473–95.

- Note how the authors' names are listed: last name followed by first and middle initials. There is no comma between the author's last name and his initials and no periods between the initials. The names of the authors are separated by commas.
- Note the placement of the year of publication and volume number.
- Because this journal employs continuous pagination, you do not need to list an issue number.

Name-Year System

Broadhead RS, Heckathorn DD. 1994. AIDS prevention outreach among injection drug users: agency problems and new approaches. Soc Prob 41:473–95.

- Note how to punctuate and separate the authors' names properly.
- The year of publication follows the authors' names.
- The volume number follows the title of the periodical.

Journal Article, Three to Ten Authors

Citation-Sequence System

[3] Carlson RG, Wang J, Siegal HA, Falck RS, Guo J. An ethnographic approach to targeted sampling: problems and solutions in AIDS prevention research among injection drug and crack-cocaine users. Hum Org 1994;53:279–86.

[4] Laga M, Alary M, Nzila N, Manoka AT, Tuliza M, Behets F, Goeman J, St. Louis M, Piot P. Condom promotion, sexually transmitted diseases treatment, and declining incidence of HIV-1 infection in female Zairian sex workers. Lancet 1994;344:246–8.

[5] Steiner S, Lemke A, Roffman RA. Risk behavior for HIV transmission among gay men surveyed in Seattle bars. Pub H Rep 1994;109:563–6.

- List all of the authors up to ten. If there are more than ten authors, list the names of the first ten authors, and then write "and others."

Name-Year System

Carlson RG, Wang J, Siegal HA, Falck RS, Guo J. 1994. An ethnographic approach to targeted sampling: problems and solutions in AIDS prevention research among injection drug and crack-cocaine users. Hum Org 53:279–86.

Laga M, Alary M, Nzila N, Manoka AT, Tuliza M, Behets F, Goeman J, St. Louis M, Piot P. 1994. Condom promotion, sexually transmitted diseases treatment, and declining incidence of HIV-1 infection in female Zairian sex workers. Lancet 344:246–8.

Steiner S, Lemke A, Roffman RA. 1994. Risk behavior for HIV transmission among gay men surveyed in Seattle bars. Pub H Rep 109:563–6.

- List all of the authors up to ten. If there are more than ten authors, list the names of the first ten authors, and then write "and others."

Journal Article from Periodical with Continuous Pagination

For a definition of "continuous pagination" see the APA example on page 220.

Citation-Sequence System

[2] Broadhead RS, Heckathorn DD. AIDS prevention outreach among injection drug users: agency problems and new approaches. Soc Prob 1994;41:473–95.

- Note how the authors' names are listed: last name followed by first and middle initials. There is no comma between the author's last name and her initials and no periods between the initials. The names of the authors are separated by commas.

- Note the placement of the year of publication and volume number.
- Because this journal employs continuous pagination, you do not need to list an issue number.

Name-Year System

Broadhead RS, Heckathorn DD. 1994. AIDS prevention outreach among injection drug users: agency problems and new approaches. Soc Prob 41:473–95.

- Note how to punctuate and separate the authors' names properly.
- When a journal employs continuous pagination, you do not need to include the issue number, only the volume number.
- Be sure to list all the page numbers for the article in your citation.

Journal Article from Periodical without Continuous Pagination

Citation-Sequence System

[6] Philipson TJ, Posner RA, Wright JH. Why AIDS prevention programs don't work. Issues Sci Tech 1994;10(3):33–5.

- When a journal does not use continuous pagination, indicate the issue number in parentheses following the volume number.
- Note the lack of spaces between the volume number, the issue number, and the page numbers.

Name-Year System

Philipson TJ, Posner RA, Wright JH. 1994. Why AIDS prevention programs don't work. Issues Sci Tech 10(3):33–5.

- Note the issue number parenthetically following the volume number.
- Note where the year of publication is placed.

Article from a Monthly Periodical

Citation-Sequence System

[1] Greene WC. AIDS and the immune system. Sci Am 1993 Sep;269(3):99–105.

- Indicate the month of publication after the year of publication.
- Be sure to include the volume number as well.

Name-Year System

Greene WC. 1993 Sep. AIDS and the immune system. Sci Am 269(3):99–105.

or

Greene WC. 1993. AIDS and the immune system. Sci Am 269(3):99–105.

- Note that the year of publication follows the author's name.
- Including the month of publication is optional.
- Again, note the lack of punctuation in the title and the lack of spaces between the volume number, issue number, and page numbers.

Article from a Weekly Periodical

Citation-Sequence System

[7] Cowley G. The future of AIDS. Newsweek 1993 Mar 22;121(12):46–52.

- Indicate the month and day of publication following the year.
- Note the lack of punctuation between the year, month, and day.

Name-Year System

Cowley G. 1993 Mar 22. The future of AIDS. Newsweek 121(12):46–52.

- Indicate the year, month, and day of publication after the author's name. Do not place commas between the year, month, and day.
- Note the issue number parenthetically after the volume number.

Newspaper Article

Citation-Sequence System

[8] Walsh PM. Growing AIDS epidemic becomes more diverse. Boston Globe 995 Feb 7;32(col 1).

- After indicating the author and title of the piece, give the title of the newspaper (note that the title is not underlined).
- Next, give the year, month, and day of publication followed by the section (if applicable) and page and column numbers where the article begins.

Name-Year System

Walsh PM. 1995 Feb 7. Growing AIDS epidemic becomes more diverse. Boston Globe;32(col 1).

- Note how the year, month, and day of publication follow the author's name.

Newspaper Article, No Author

Citation-Sequence System

[9] [Anonymous]. Volunteers take up slack in AIDS care. Times-Picayune 1993 Jul 6; Sect B:4(col 1).

- In place of the author's last name, write "Anonymous" in square brackets.

Name-Year System

[Anonymous]. 1993 Jul 6. Volunteers take up slack in AIDS care. Times-Picayune; Sect B:4(col 1).

- "Anonymous" in square brackets takes the place of the author's name.

Book with One Author

Citation-Sequence System

[10] Stine GJ. Acquired immune deficiency syndrome: biological, medical, social and legal issues. Englewood Cliffs, NJ: Prentice-Hall; 1993. 462 p.

- Note the way author's name is arranged, capitalized, and punctuated: last name first followed by initials. No comma between the last name and the initials, no periods between the initials.
- Note that book titles are not underlined or italicized.
- In book titles, only the first word and proper nouns and proper adjectives are capitalized.
- A semicolon precedes the date of publication and a period follows.
- At the end of the entry, give the total number of pages in the book.

Name-Year System

Stine GJ. 1993. Acquired immune deficiency syndrome: biological, medical, social and legal issues. Englewood Cliffs, NJ: Prentice-Hall. 462 p.

- Here, the year of publication follows the author's name.
- Be sure to include the total number of pages in the book.

Book with Two or More Authors

Citation-Sequence System

[11] Douglas PH, Pinsky L. The essential AIDS fact book. New York: Pocket Books; 1991. 108 p.

[12] Rabkin J, Remien R, Wilson C. Good doctors, good patients: partners in HIV treatment. New York: NCM; 1994. 201 p.

- If a book has multiple authors, list all of them, last name first followed by initials. Use commas to separate authors.

Name-Year System

Douglas PH, Pinsky L. 1991. The essential AIDS fact book. New York: Pocket Books. 108 p.

Rabkin J, Remien R, Wilson C. 1994. Good doctors, good patients: partners in HIV treatment. New York: NCM. 201 p.

- Note where to place the year of publication and how to separate the authors' names.

Two or More Works by the Same Person

Citation-Sequence System

[13] Kübler-Ross E. Death: the final stage of growth. Englewood Cliffs, NJ: Prentice-Hall; 1975. 181 p.

[14] Kübler-Ross E. AIDS: the ultimate challenge. New York: Macmillan; 1987. 329 p.

Name-Year System

Kübler-Ross E. 1975. Death: the final stage of growth. Englewood Cliffs, NJ: Prentice-Hall. 181 p.

Kübler-Ross E. 1987. AIDS: the ultimate challenge. New York: Macmillan. 329 p.

- Arrange the citations in chronological order, the earliest first.

Book, Corporate Author

Citation-Sequence System

[15] National Gay and Lesbian Task Force. Anti-gay violence: victimization and defamation in 1986. New York: National Gay and Lesbian Task Force; 1987. 113 p.

- List the corporate author first.
- Note that the first word of a subtitle is not capitalized.

Name-Year System

[NGLTF] National Gay and Lesbian Task Force. 1987. Anti-gay violence: victimization and defamation in 1986. New York: NGLTF. 113 p.

- With the name-year system, open the entry with an abbreviation of the corporation's name; you can use this abbreviation for in-text documentation, as well.

Book, Later Edition

Citation-Sequence System

[16] DeVita VT Jr, Hellman S, Rosenberg SA. AIDS: etiology, diagnosis, treatment and prevention. 4th ed. Philadelphia: Lippincott; 1996. 770 p.

- If you use a later edition of a book, list the edition number after the title.

Name-Year System

DeVita VT Jr, Hellman S, Rosenberg SA. 1996. AIDS: etiology, diagnosis, treatment and prevention. 4th ed. Philadelphia: Lippincott. 770 p.

• Again, the edition number follows the title of the book.

Edited Book

Citation-Sequence System

[17] Squire C, editor. Women and AIDS: psychological perspectives. London: Sage; 1993. 196 p.

• Write "editor" after the editor's name, "editors" if more than one person edited the work.
• Note that there is no period after the editor's initials.
• Note the semicolon between the publisher's name and the year of publication.

Name-Year System

Squire C, editor. 1993. Women and AIDS: psychological perspectives. London: Sage. 196 p.

• The year of publication follows the editor's name.

Book, No Author or Editor

Citation-Sequence System

[18] [Anonymous]. AIDS and the third world. 3rd ed. London: Panos Institute; 1988. 198 p.

• If there is no author, open the entry with "Anonymous" placed in square brackets.

Name-Year System

[Anonymous]. 1988. AIDS and the third world. 3rd ed. London: Panos Institute. 198 p.

Multivolume Book

Citation-Sequence System

[19] Daintith J, Mitchell S, Tootill E. A biographical encyclopedia of scientists. 2 volumes. New York: Facts on File; 1981. 935 p.

• For multivolume works, indicate the total number of volumes between the book title and city of publication.

Name-Year System

Daintith J, Mitchell S, Tootill E. 1981. A biographical encyclopedia of scientists. 2 volumes. New York: Facts on File. 935 p.

One Volume of a Multivolume Book

Citation-Sequence System

[20] Daintith J, Mitchell S, Tootill E. A biographical encyclopedia of scientists. Volume 1. New York: Facts on File; 1981. 458 p.

- If you use only one volume of a multivolume work, list that volume number after the title.
- If the volume has a separate title, give it after the volume number, preceded by a comma.

Name-Year System

Daintith J, Mitchell S, Tootill E. 1981. A biographical encyclopedia of scientists. Volume 1. New York: Facts on File. 458 p.

English Translation of a Book

Citation-Sequence System

[21] Jager H, editor. AIDS phobia: disease pattern and possibilities of treatment. Welch J, translator. New York: Halsted; 1988. 124 p. Translation of: AIDS-phobie.

- First, list the author or editor of the work, then the translated title.
- Next, give the name of the translator, last name first followed by "translator."
- Following the publication information, give the original title of the work.

Name-Year System

Jager H, editor. 1988. AIDS phobia: disease pattern and possibilities of treatment. Welch J, translator. New York: Halsted. 124 p. Translation of: AIDS-phobie.

Article or Chapter from an Anthology

Citation-Sequence System

[22] Patton C. With champagne and roses: women at risk from/in AIDS discourse. In: Squire C, editor. Women and AIDS. London: Sage; 1993. p 165–87.

- Begin with the name of the author who wrote the article you are using.

- Next, give the title of the piece you use in your paper.
- Next, give the name of the person who edited the longer work, last name first, preceded by "In" and a colon.
- Next, give the title of the longer piece that contains the material you are using.
- Close with the publication information and the inclusive page numbers of the article, preceded with "p" for an article of any length.

Name-Year System

Patton C. 1993. With champagne and roses: women at risk from/in AIDS discourse. In: Squire C, editor. Women and AIDS. London: Sage. p 165–87.

- Note where the year of publication is included.
- Note the period following the publisher.

Article in a Reference Work

The CBE style manual offers no specific instructions on how to cite entries from reference works. However, a survey of scientific journals shows that a common practice is to follow the form used for a work contained in a collection of essays (the preceding form).

Citation-Sequence System

[23] [Anonymous]. Acquired immune deficiency syndrome. In: The new encyclopaedia Britannica. Volume 1. Chicago: Encyclopaedia Britannica; 1990. p 67.

[24] Haseltine WA. AIDS. In: Encyclopedia Americana. Volume 1. Danbury, CT: Grolier; 1992. p 365–6.

- When the piece in the reference work is signed, begin your entry with the writer's name; when it is not, begin with "Anonymous" in square brackets.
- Include the title of the entry and volume number of the reference work.
- Include the page number or numbers of the entry.

Name-Year System

[Anonymous]. 1990. Acquired immune deficiency syndrome. In: The new encyclopaedia Britannica. Volume 1. Chicago: Encyclopaedia Britannica. p 67.

Haseltine WA. 1992. AIDS. In: Encyclopedia Americana. Volume 1. Danbury, CT: Grolier. p 365–6.

- Note where you place the year of publication.

Personal Interview

Personal communications are noted only in text, not in reference lists. After the material, place in parentheses the words "personal communication."

Electronic Sources of Information

The sixth edition of the CBE style manual offers little guidance on constructing reference list entries for electronic sources of information. The sample entries offered below are based on current practice.

Information on CD-ROM or Diskette

Citation-Sequence System

25 [Anonymous]. AIDS. In: The 1995 Grolier multimedia encyclopedia. [CD-ROM]. Version 7.05. Danbury, CT: Grolier; 1995.

- Give the name of the author or authors. If none is listed, put "Anonymous" in square brackets followed by a period.
- Give the title of the chapter or entry you referred to in the body of your paper.
- Give the complete title of the work, preceded by "In" and a colon.
- Indicate the electronic medium (i.e., CD-ROM or diskette) in square brackets.
- Give the version or edition number.
- Supply the publication information: city of publication, publisher, and date of publication.
- Titles of entries or chapters are not placed in quotation marks, and titles of complete works are not underlined.
- Note which words are capitalized in the title of the complete work.

Name-Year System

[Anonymous]. 1995. AIDS. In: The 1995 Grolier multimedia encyclopedia. [CD-ROM]. Version 7.05. Danbury, CT: Grolier.

- Give the name of the author or authors. If none is listed, put "Anonymous" in square brackets followed by a period.
- Give the date of publication.
- Give the title of the chapter or entry you referred to in the body of your paper.
- Give the complete title of the work, preceded by "In" and a colon.
- Indicate the electronic medium (i.e., CD-ROM or diskette) in square brackets.
- Give the version or edition number.
- Supply the remaining publication information: city of publication and publisher.

Online Information Databank

Citation-Sequence System

[26] [Anonymous]. AIDS. In: Encyclopaedia Britannica online. 1999. Available via the Internet; http://www.eb.com. Accessed 1999 July 22.

- Give the name of the author or authors. If none is listed, put "Anonymous" in square brackets followed by a period.
- Give the title of the chapter or entry that supplied the information you used in your paper.
- Give the title of the database you consulted.
- Give the date the database was published or last updated.
- Give the URL of the database.
- Give the date you accessed the information.

Name-Year System

[Anonymous]. 1999. AIDS. In: Encyclopaedia Britannica online. Available via the Internet; http://www.eb.com. Accessed 1999 July 22.

- Give the name of the author or authors. If none is listed, put "Anonymous" in square brackets followed by a period.
- Give the date of publication.
- Give the title of the chapter or entry that supplied the information you used in your paper.
- Give the title of the database you consulted.
- Give the electronic address of the database.
- Give the date you accessed the information.

Article from an Online Publication

Citation-Sequence System

[27] Murphy C. AIDS: privacy vs. public health. Atlantic Unbound [serial online] 1997 June 3. Available from: Academic Universe via the Internet; http://www.theatlantic.com/unbound/forum/aids/intro.html. Accessed 1999 July 22.

- Give the name of the author or authors (last name first followed by initials).
- Give the title of the article.
- Give the title of the online publication.
- Give the type of medium (e.g., online monograph or online serial) in square brackets.
- Give the date of publication.
- Give the availability information (the search engine used to locate the source text).
- Give the date you accessed the information.

Name-Year System

Murphy C. 1997 June 3. AIDS: privacy vs. public health. Atlantic Unbound [serial online]. Available from: Academic Universe via the Internet; http://www.theatlantic.com/unbound/forum/aids/intro.html. Accessed 1999 July 22.

- Give the name of the author or authors (last name first followed by initials).
- Give the date of publication.
- Give the title of the article.
- Give the title of the online publication.
- Give the type of medium (e.g., online monograph or online serial) in square brackets.
- Give the availability information (the search engine used to locate the source text).
- Give the date you accessed the information.

Previously Published Article Found Online

Citation-Sequence System

[28] Underwood A. How the plague began. Newsweek [online] 1999 Feb. 8;134(2):32. Available from: Academic Universe via the Internet; http://www.newsweek.com/nw-srv/printed/us/so/md0206_1.htm. Accessed 1999 Sept. 9.

- Give the name of the author or authors.
- Give the title of the article.
- Give the title of the magazine or journal.
- Indicate, in square brackets, the electronic medium.
- Give the publication information of the magazine or journal article. (Because *Newsweek* is a weekly publication, list the day, month, and year of publication along with the volume and issue numbers.)
- Indicate the search engine that was used to find the article.
- Give the date of access.

Name-Year System

Underwood A. 1999 Feb. 8. How the plague began. Newsweek [online]; 134(2):32. Available from: Academic Universe via the Internet; http://www.newsweek.com/nw-srv/printed/us/so/md0206_1.htm. Accessed 1999 Sept. 9.

- Give the name of the author or authors.
- Give the date of publication.

- Give the title of the article.
- Give the title of the magazine or journal.
- Indicate, in square brackets, the electronic medium.
- Give the volume number, issue number, and pagination for the magazine or journal article.
- Indicate the search engine that was used to find the article.
- Give the date of access.

E-Mail

Personal communications are noted only in the text, not in reference lists. After the material, place in parentheses the words "e-mail communication" or "personal communication."

SAMPLE CBE-STYLE REFERENCE LISTS

Begin your reference list on a new page at the end of your paper under the heading "References" or "Cited References" centered at the top of the page. Double-space after the heading and begin your citations.

If you are using the citation-sequence system in your paper, the reference entries will be numbered and listed in the order they are cited in the text. Source "1" will be the first work listed, source "2" the second one listed, and so on. If you list your sources on the reference page using superscript numerals, align the second and subsequent lines of an entry under the first letter of the first line. If, instead, you list your sources with standard numerals, follow the number with a period, and then indent five spaces. Align the second and subsequent lines of an entry under the first letter of the first line. Here are two examples:

[1] Greene WC. AIDS and the immune system. Sci Am 1993 Sep;269(3):99–105.

[2] Broadhead RS, Heckathorn DD. AIDS prevention outreach among injection drug users: agency problems and new approaches. Soc Prob 1994;41:473–95.

1.   Greene WC. AIDS and the immune system. Sci Am 1993 Sep;269(3):99–105.

2.   Broadhead RS, Heckathorn DD. AIDS prevention outreach among injection drug users: agency problems and new approaches. Soc Prob 1994;41:473–95.

If you are using the name-year system, the entries are listed in alphabetical order by the authors' last names. Begin every line of these entries on the left margin. Some journals leave a blank line between entries; some do not. See the sample reference lists below for examples.

Citation-Sequence Format

References

[1] Greene WC. AIDS and the immune system. Sci Am 1993 Sep;269(3):99–105.

[2] Broadhead RS, Heckathorn DD. AIDS prevention outreach among injection drug users: agency problems and new approaches. Soc Prob 1994;41:473–95.

[3] Carlson RG, Wang J, Siegal HA, Falck RS, Guo J. An ethnographic approach to targeted sampling: problems and solutions in AIDS prevention research among injection drug and crack-cocaine users. Hum Org 1994;53:279–86.

[4] Laga M, Alary M, Nzila N, Manoka AT, Tuliza M, Behets F, Goeman J, St. Louis M, Piot P. Condom promotion, sexually transmitted diseases treatment, and declining incidence of HIV-1 infection in female Zairian sex workers. Lancet 1994;344:246–8.

[5] Steiner S, Lemke A, Roffman RA. Risk behavior for HIV transmission among gay men surveyed in Seattle bars. Pub H Rep 994;109:563–6.

[6] Philipson TJ, Posner RA, Wright JH. Why AIDS prevention programs don't work. Issues Sci Tech 1994;10(3):33–5.

[7] Cowley G. The future of AIDS. Newsweek 1993 Mar 22; 121(12):46–52.

[8] Walsh PM. Growing AIDS epidemic becomes more diverse. Boston Globe 1995 Feb 7;32(col 1).

[9] [Anonymous]. Volunteers take up slack in AIDS care. Times-Picayune 1993 Jul 6;Sect B:4(col 1).

[10] Stine GJ. Acquired immune deficiency syndrome: biological, medical, social and legal issues. Englewood Cliffs, NJ: Prentice-Hall; 1993. 462 p.

[11] Douglas PH, Pinsky L. The essential AIDS fact book. New York: Pocket Books; 1991. 108 p.

[12] Rabkin J, Remien R, Wilson C. Good doctors, good patients: partners in HIV treatment. New York: NCM; 1994. 201 p.

[13] National Gay and Lesbian Task Force. Anti-gay violence: victimization and defamation in 1986. New York: National Gay and Lesbian Task Force; 1987. 113 p.

[14] DeVita VT Jr, Hellman S, Rosenberg SA. AIDS: etiology, diagnosis, treatment and prevention. 4th ed. Philadelphia: Lippincott; 1996. 770 p.

[15] Squire C, editor. Women and AIDS: psychological perspectives. London: Sage; 1993. 196 p.

[16] Daintith J, Mitchell S, Tootill E. A biographical encyclopedia of scientists. Volume 1. New York: Facts on File; 1981. 458 p.

[17] Jager H, editor. AIDS phobia: disease pattern and possibilities of treatment. Welch J, translator. New York: Halsted; 1988. 124 p. Translation of: AIDS-phobie.

[18] Patton C. With champagne and roses: women at risk from/in AIDS discourse. In: Squire C, editor. Women and AIDS. London: Sage; 1993. p 165–87.

Name-Year Format

References

[Anonymous]. 1993 Jul 6. Volunteers take up slack in AIDS care. Times-Picayune; Sect B:4(col 1).

[Anonymous]. 1995. AIDS. In: The 1995 Grolier multimedia encyclopedia. [CD-ROM]. Version 7.05. Danbury, CT: Grolier.

[Anonymous]. 1999. AIDS. In: Encyclopaedia Britannica online. Available via the Internet; http://www.eb.com. Accessed 1999 July 22.

Broadhead RS, Heckathorn DD. 1994. AIDS prevention outreach among injection drug users: agency problems and new approaches. Soc Prob 41:473–95.

Carlson RG, Wang J, Siegal HA, Falck RS, Guo J. 1994. An ethnographic approach to targeted sampling: problems and solutions in AIDS prevention research among injection drug and crack-cocaine users. Hum Org 53:279–86.

Cowley G. 1993 Mar 22. The future of AIDS. Newsweek 121(12):46–52.

Daintith J, Mitchell S, Tootill E. 1981. A biographical encyclopedia of scientists. Volume 1. New York: Facts on File. 458 p.

DeVita VT Jr, Hellman S, Rosenberg SA. 1996. AIDS: etiology, diagnosis, treatment and prevention. 4th ed. Philadelphia: Lippincott. 770 p.

Douglas PH, Pinsky L. 1991. The essential AIDS fact book. New York: Pocket Books. 108 p.

Greene WC. 1993 Sep. AIDS and the immune system. Sci Am 269(3):99–105.

Jager H, editor. 1988. AIDS phobia: disease pattern and possibilities of treatment. Welch J, translator. New York: Halsted. 124 p. Translation of: AIDS-phobie.

Laga M, Alary M, Nzila N, Manoka AT, Tuliza M, Behets F, Goeman J, St. Louis M, Piot P. 1994. Condom promotion, sexually transmitted diseases treatment, and declining incidence of HIV-1 infection in female Zairian sex workers. Lancet 344:246–48.

Murphy C. 1997 June 3. AIDS: privacy vs. public health. Atlantic Unbound [serial online]. Available from: Academic Universe via the Internet; http://www.theatlantic.com/unbound/forum/aids/intro.html. Accessed 1999 July 22.

[NGLTF] National Gay and Lesbian Task Force. 1987. Anti-gay violence: victimization and defamation in 1986. New York: NGLTF. 113 p.

Patton C. 1993. With champagne and roses: women at risk from/in AIDS discourse. In: Squire C, editor. Women and AIDS. London: Sage. p 165–87.

Philipson TJ, Posner RA, Wright JH. 1994. Why AIDS prevention programs don't work. Issues Sci Tech 10(3):33–5.

Rabkin J, Remien R, Wilson C. 1994. Good doctors, good patients: partners in HIV treatment. New York: NCM. 201 p.

Squire C, editor. 1993. Women and AIDS: psychological perspectives. London: Sage. 196 p.

Steiner S, Lemke A, Roffman RA. 1994. Risk behavior for HIV transmission among gay men surveyed in Seattle bars. Pub H Rep 109:563–6.

Stine GJ. 1993. Acquired immune deficiency syndrome: biological, medical, social and legal issues. Englewood Cliffs, NJ: Prentice-Hall. 462 p.

Underwood A. 1999 Feb. 8. How the plague began. Newsweek [online]; 134(2):32. Available from: Academic Universe via the Internet; http://www.newsweek.com/nw-srv/printed/us/so/md0206_1.htm. Accessed 1999 Sept. 9.

Walsh PM. 1995 Feb 7. Growing AIDS epidemic becomes more diverse. Boston Globe;32(col 1).

MLA FORMAT

SAMPLE WORKS CITED ENTRIES

In a works cited list following MLA style, include the name of the author and full title of the works you cited in the body of your essay, along with relevant publication information. When listing the authors, include their full names, last name first. Titles of articles are placed in quotation marks; titles of books are underlined. In titles, the first and last words are capitalized along with any key words, proper nouns, and proper adjectives in between. Journal titles are underlined, and you should list all the pages you read in the source text. Do not precede page numbers with "p." or "pg."; simply list inclusive page numbers. Finally, MLA style employs reversed indentation: begin the first line of each entry at the left margin and indent all subsequent lines one-half inch or five spaces.

Journal Article, One Author

Greene, Warner C. "AIDS and the Immune System." <u>Scientific American</u> Sept. 1993: 99–105.

- Give the full name of the author as it is printed with the article, last name first. Place a period after the name.
- The title of the article is placed in quotation marks. Note how the first and last word of the title are capitalized as are all key words in between. Also note that the period at the end of the article title goes inside the closing quotation mark.
- The title of the journal is underlined. Because *Scientific American* is a monthly publication, provide the month of the issue containing the information you used.
- Indicate the inclusive page numbers of the article.

Journal Article, Two or Three Authors

Broadhead, Robert S., and Douglas D. Heckathorn. "AIDS Prevention Outreach among Injection Drug Users: Agency Problems and New Approaches." <u>Social Problems</u> 41 (1994): 473–95.

Steiner, Sue, Audie Lemke, and Roger A. Roffman. "Risk Behavior for HIV Transmission among Gay Men Surveyed in Seattle Bars." <u>Public Health Reports</u> 109 (1994): 563–66.

- When there are two or three authors, list all of them in the order they appear in the article. Give the first author's last name, then his first name. Give the other authors' names first name first. Separate the names with commas and introduce the last name with "and."

Journal Article, More Than Three Authors

Carlson, Robert G., et al. "An Ethnographic Approach to Targeted
Sampling: Problems and Solutions in AIDS Prevention Research
among Injection Drug and Crack-Cocaine Users." Human
Organization 53 (1994): 279–86.

- When there are more than three authors, list only the first author, last
name first. Follow that name with the expression "et al." (which means
"and others").

Journal Article from Periodical with Continuous Pagination

For a definition of "continuous pagination," see page 220.

Broadhead, Robert S., and Douglas D. Heckathorn. "AIDS Prevention
Outreach among Injection Drug Users: Agency Problems and New
Approaches." Social Problems 41 (1994): 473–95.

- When a journal numbers its pages continuously, you need include only the
volume and page numbers.
- The volume number follows the title. The year of publication is noted parenthetically, then the inclusive page numbers for the piece.
- Note the spacing and punctuation. There are blank spaces before and after
the volume number.

Journal Article from Periodical without Continuous Pagination

Philipson, Thomas J., Richard A. Posner, and John H. Wright. "Why AIDS
Prevention Programs Don't Work." Issues in Science and Technology
10.3 (1994): 33–35.

- If a journal begins each issue with page 1, you need to indicate the issue
number of the source you are using. First list the volume number, add a
period, and then indicate the issue number. Follow this information with
the year of publication and inclusive page numbers.

Article from a Monthly Periodical

Greene, Warner C. "AIDS and the Immune System." Scientific American
Sept. 1993: 99–105.

- Note the month of publication after the title. Months can be abbreviated.
- Note that there is *no* comma between the month and year.
- Note that you do *not* include the volume number of the work, only the
month and year.

Article from a Weekly Periodical

Cowley, Geoffrey. "The Future of AIDS." Newsweek 22 Mar. 1993: 46–52.
- After giving the title of the piece, list the day, month, and year of its publication in that order, without any punctuation between them.

Newspaper Article

Walsh, Pamela M. "Growing AIDS Epidemic Becomes More Diverse."
Boston Globe 7 Feb. 1995: 32.

- If the newspaper article is signed, give the writer's name, last name first.
- After the title of the piece, give the name of the newspaper, underlined.
- Next, give the date of publication: day, month, then year without any intervening punctuation.
- Give the page number, indicating the section number or letter when applicable.

Newspaper Article, No Author

"Volunteers Take Up Slack in AIDS Care." Times-Picayune 6 July 1993: B4+.

- If the article is unsigned, begin the entry with the title.
- Use a plus sign (+) to indicate interrupted pagination.

Book with One Author

Stine, Gerald J. Acquired Immune Deficiency Syndrome: Biological, Medical,
Social and Legal Issues. Englewood Cliffs, NJ: Prentice-Hall, 1993.

- If you think your reader will not recognize the city of publication, add the state abbreviation.
- Again, note how the entry begins with the author's last name.
- Note how the title is underlined and how the first, last, and key words are capitalized.

Book with Multiple Authors

Douglas, Paul Harding, and Laura Pinsky. The Essential AIDS Fact Book.
New York: Pocket Books, 1991.

Rabkin, Judith, Robert Remien, and Christopher Wilson. Good Doctors,
Good Patients: Partners in HIV Treatment. New York: NCM, 1994.

- When a book has two or three authors, list all their names. Begin with the last name of the first author; the names of the other authors are listed first name first. Separate the names with commas and use "and" before the last name.
- If there are more than three authors, list only the first author and follow it with "et al." (Smith, John, et al.)

Two or More Books by the Same Person

Kübler-Ross, Elisabeth. AIDS: The Ultimate Challenge. New York:
Macmillan, 1987.

---. Death: The Final Stage of Growth. Englewood Cliffs, NJ: Prentice-Hall,
1975.

- When you have two or more books by the same author or authors, list them on your works cited list in alphabetical order by the first key word in the title.
- For the first work by the author, give her full name, last name first. For subsequent entries by the author, instead of repeating the name, type three hyphens followed by a period. Then list the title of the work and the relevant publishing information.

Book, Corporate Author

National Gay and Lesbian Task Force. <u>Anti-Gay Violence: Victimization and Defamation in 1986</u>. New York: National Gay and Lesbian Task Force, 1987.

- Treat a corporate author just as you would an individual author.

Book, Later Edition

DeVita, Vincent T., Jr., Samuel Hellman, and Steven A. Rosenberg. <u>AIDS: Etiology, Diagnosis, Treatment and Prevention</u>. 4th ed. Philadelphia: Lippincott, 1996.

- Indicate the edition number after the title.

Edited Book

Squire, Corinne, ed. <u>Women and AIDS: Psychological Perspectives</u>. London: Sage, 1993.

- If one person edited the work, place "ed." after his name. If there is more than one editor, use "eds."

Book, No Author or Editor

<u>AIDS and the Third World</u>. 3rd ed. London: Panos Institute, 1988.

- When there is no author, begin the entry with the title.

Multivolume Book

Daintith, John, Sarah Mitchell, and Elizabeth Tootill, eds. <u>A Biographical Encyclopedia of Scientists</u>. 2 vols. New York: Facts on File, 1981.

- Indicate the number of volumes in a multivolume work after the title.

One Volume of a Multivolume Book

Daintith, John, Sarah Mitchell, and Elizabeth Tootill, eds. <u>A Biographical Encyclopedia of Scientists</u>. Vol. 1. New York: Facts on File, 1981.

- If you use only one volume of a multivolume work, indicate the volume number after the title.

English Translation of a Book

Jager, Hans, ed. AIDS Phobia: Disease Pattern and Possibilities of
Treatment. Trans. Jacquie Welch. New York: Halsted Press, 1988.

- Begin the entry with the name of the author or editor whose work has
  been translated, followed by the title of the work.
- Next, write "Trans." followed by the name of the translator, first name
  first.

Article or Chapter from an Anthology

Patton, Cindy. "'With Champagne and Roses': Women at Risk from/in
AIDS Discourse." Women and AIDS. Ed. Corinne Squire. London:
Sage, 1993. 165–87.

- First, list the name of the author whose article or chapter you are using.
- Next, give the title, in quotation marks. If the title of an entry already contains quotation marks (as this one does), the original quotation marks are
  shifted to single quotation marks in the citation.
- Next, give the title of the work that contained the article and the name of
  the editor or editors, preceded by either "Ed." if one person edited the
  work or "Eds." if more than one editor was involved.
- Finally, list the publication information and the page numbers in the
  larger work where the article or chapter can be found.
- Pay attention to the use of periods at the end of the citation.

Article in a Reference Work

"Acquired Immune Deficiency Syndrome." Encyclopaedia Britannica:
Micropaedia. 1990 ed.

Haseltine, William A. "AIDS." Encyclopedia Americana. 1992 ed.

- If the author of the entry in the reference work is listed, begin with that.
  If it is not, begin with the heading of the entry, in quotation marks.
- After indicating the heading of the entry, list the name of the reference
  work and the edition.

Personal Interview

Alexander, Jane. Telephone interview. 16 June 1995.

Smith, John. Personal interview. 16 June 1995.

- List the name of the person interviewed, the nature of the interview
  (whether done in person, over the telephone, etc.), and the date of the
  interview: day, month, and year.

ELECTRONIC SOURCES OF INFORMATION

The most up-to-date information on MLA formats for citing electronic sources of information is available at www.mla.org/set_stl.htm.

Information on CD-ROM or Diskette

"AIDS." The 1995 Grolier Multimedia Encyclopedia. CD-ROM. Version 7.05. Danbury, CT: Grolier, 1995.

- Give the name of the author (if known), last name first.
- Give the title of the chapter or entry from which you drew the information (in quotation marks).
- Give the title of the publication.
- Indicate the publication medium (i.e., CD-ROM or diskette).
- List the edition, version, or release number.
- Indicate the place of publication, the publisher, and the date of publication.
- Note where periods are placed in the entry.
- If in your paper you make use of the entire source text, begin the entry with the title of the publication.

Online Information Databank

"AIDS." Encyclopaedia Britannica Online. 1999. Encyclopaedia Britannica. 22 July 1999 <http://www.eb.com>.

- Give the author's name (if known), last name first.
- Give the title of the article or entry. This particular source text is unsigned, so the entry begins with the title.
- Give the title of the complete work. Note that the title of the entry is placed in quotation marks and the title of the complete work is underlined.
- Give the name of the editor (if known).
- Give the version or edition number of the databank (if known).
- Give the date of publication for the databank (if known).
- Give the name of the databank's sponsoring institution or organization.
- List the date of access. Note how it is listed and punctuated.
- Indicate the databank's electronic address. Place the electronic address inside angle brackets. The electronic address (or URL) can be broken at a slash if need be to make it fit on a line in your works cited entry.

Article from an Online Publication

This is the format to use if your source text exists only electronically. If the article does not also appear in print somewhere, use this form for your works cited entry:

Murphy, Cullen. "AIDS: Privacy vs. Public Health." Atlantic Unbound 3 June 1997. 22 July 1999 <http://www.theatlantic.com/unbound/forum/aids/intro.html>.

- Give the author's name, last name first.

- Indicate the title of the work, in quotation marks.
- Give the name of the periodical, underlined. Because this periodical is not an academic journal, volume and issue numbers are not needed; otherwise they would be.
- Indicate the date of publication.
- Give the total number of pages (if the pages are numbered in the source text, e.g., 12 pp.) or the total number of paragraphs (if the paragraphs are numbered in the source text, e.g., 12 pars.).
- Indicate the date of access.
- Give the electronic address.
- Note how the dates are listed and punctuated.
- Be sure to end the entry with a period.

Previously Published Article Found Online

Employ this form when the source text you are using also appears in print. If you refer to the electronic version of the article rather than to the print version, use this form for your works cited entry.

Underwood, Anne. "How the Plague Began." Newsweek 8 Feb. 1999. 9
    Sept. 1999 <http://www.newsweek.com/nw-srv/printed/us/so/
    md0206_1.htm>.

- Give the name of the author or authors.
- Give the title of the article in quotation marks.
- Give the title of the publication, underlined.
- Give the date of publication: day, month, and year for popular press magazines; volume and issue numbers and year for academic journals.
- List the inclusive page numbers of the article (if known).
- Indicate the date of access: day, month, year.
- Give the electronic address of the source text.

Work from an Online Service

Use this form if you used a library's online service, such as SIRS Researcher or Academic Universe (Lexis/Nexis), to locate information for your paper.

Stolberg, Sheryl. "Cruel Link: Hemophilia and AIDS." Los Angeles Times
    31 Aug. 1944: A1+. SIRS Researcher. University of Dayton Roesch
    Lib. 11 Sept. 1999 <http://researcher.sirs.com>.

- Give the name of the author, last name first.
- Give the title of the article in quotation marks.
- Give the name of the publication where the material originally appeared.
- Give the original date of publication and pagination (if known).
- Give the name of the online service you used, underlined.
- Indicate the name of the subscribing library you visited.
- Give the date of access.
- Give the electronic address of the service's homepage.

E-Mail

Give the name of the writer (last name first), the title of the message (taken from the "subject" line), an indication of who received the message (for example, "E-mail to author" or "E-mail to Jane Smith"), and the date of the message.

Edwards, John. "Re: AIDS Sources." E-mail to author. 31 July 1999.
Francis, Heather. E-mail to Karen Wilhoit. 24 June 1999.

- If the subject line of the message is blank, leave out that part of the entry.
- Note how the date of the message is listed: day, month, year.

SAMPLE MLA-STYLE WORKS CITED LIST

Begin the works cited list on a separate sheet of paper at the end of your essay. Centered at the top, write "Works Cited" and then double-space before you begin listing your entries. Entries are alphabetized by the author's last name or by the first key word in the title if there is no author. The first line of each entry begins on the left margin, and all subsequent lines of each entry are indented one-half inch or five spaces. The entire list is double-spaced.

Works Cited

"Acquired Immune Deficiency Syndrome." Encyclopaedia Britannica: Micropaedia. 1990 ed.

"AIDS." Encyclopaedia Britannica Online. 1999. Encyclopaedia Britannica. 22 July 1999 <http://www.eb.com>.

"AIDS." The 1995 Grolier Multimedia Encyclopedia. CD-ROM. Version 7.05. Danbury, CT: Grolier, 1995.

AIDS and the Third World. 3rd ed. London: Panos Institute, 1988.

Alexander, Jane. Telephone interview. 24 June 1995.

Broadhead, Robert S., and Douglas D. Heckathorn. "AIDS Prevention Outreach among Injection Drug Users: Agency Problems and New Approaches." Social Problems 41 (1994): 473–95.

Carlson, Robert G., et al. "An Ethnographic Approach to Targeted Sampling: Problems and Solutions in AIDS Prevention Research among Injection Drug and Crack-Cocaine Users." Human Organization 53 (1994): 279–86.

Cowley, Geoffrey. "The Future of AIDS." Newsweek 22 Mar. 1993: 46–52.

Daintith, John, Sarah Mitchell, and Elizabeth Tootill, eds. A Biographical Encyclopedia of Scientists. Vol. 1. New York: Facts on File, 1981.

DeVita, Vincent T., Jr., Samuel Hellman, and Steven A. Rosenberg. AIDS: Etiology, Diagnosis, Treatment and Prevention. 4th ed. Philadelphia: Lippincott, 1996.

Douglas, Paul Harding, and Laura Pinsky. The Essential AIDS Fact

   Book. New York: Pocket Books, 1991.

Edwards, John. "Re: AIDS Sources." E-mail to author. 31 July 1999.

Francis, Heather. E-mail to Karen Wilhoit. 24 June 1999.

Greene, Warner C. "AIDS and the Immune System." Scientific American

   Sept. 1993: 99-105.

Haseltine, William A. "AIDS." Encyclopedia Americana. 1992 ed.

Jager, Hans, ed. AIDS Phobia: Disease Pattern and Possibilities of

   Treatment. Trans. Jacquie Welch. New York: Halsted Press, 1988.

Kübler-Ross, Elisabeth. AIDS: The Ultimate Challenge. New York:

   Macmillan, 1987.

---. Death: The Final Stage of Growth. Englewood Cliffs, NJ: Prentice-

   Hall, 1975.

Murphy, Cullen. "AIDS: Privacy vs. Public Health." Atlantic Unbound 3

   June 1997. 22 July 1999 <http://www.theatlantic.com/unbound/

   forum/aids/intro.html>.

National Gay and Lesbian Task Force. Anti-Gay Violence: Victimization

   and Defamation in 1986. New York: National Gay and Lesbian

   Task Force, 1987.

Patton, Cindy. "'With Champagne and Roses': Women at Risk from/in

   AIDS Discourse." Women and AIDS. Ed. Corinne Squire. London:

   Sage, 1993. 165–87.

Philipson, Thomas J., Richard A. Posner, and John H. Wright. "Why

   AIDS Prevention Programs Don't Work." Issues in Science and

   Technology 10.3 (1994): 33–35.

Rabkin, Judith, Robert Remien, and Christopher Wilson. Good Doctors,

Good Patients: Partners in HIV Treatment. New York: NCM, 1994.

Smith, John. Personal interview. 24 June 1995.

Squire, Corinne, ed. Women and AIDS: Psychological Perspectives.

London: Sage, 1993.

Steiner, Sue, Audie Lemke, and Roger A. Roffman. "Risk Behavior for

HIV Transmission among Gay Men Surveyed in Seattle Bars."

Public Health Reports 109 (1994): 563–66.

Stine, Gerald J. Acquired Immune Deficiency Syndrome: Biological,

Medical, Social and Legal Issues. Englewood Cliffs, NJ: Prentice-

Hall, 1993.

Stolberg, Sheryl. "Cruel Link: Hemophilia and AIDS." Los Angeles

Times 31 Aug. 1944: A1+. SIRS Researcher. University of Dayton

Roesch Library. 11 Sept. 1999 <http://researcher.sirs.com>.

Underwood, Anne. "How the Plague Began." Newsweek 8 Feb. 1999. 9

Sept. 1999 <http:// www.newsweek.com/nw-srv/printed/us/so/

md0206_1.htm>.

"Volunteers Take Up Slack in AIDS Care." Times-Picayune 6 July 1993:

B4+.

Walsh, Pamela M. "Growing AIDS Epidemic Becomes More Diverse."

Boston Globe 7 Feb. 1995: 32.

Chapter 12

TIMED WRITING ASSIGNMENTS

DEFINITION

Regardless of your major, in college you will write a number of timed, in-class essays. Teachers who assign these papers usually expect you to compose a complete, fully developed essay or test answer in one class period. When the allotted time is up, you have to turn in your work for evaluation—whether you are finished or not.

Timed writing assignments are so common in college because they serve a number of purposes. Some teachers use them to determine how well you understand the material covered in class, asking you to summarize course material in your essay. Other teachers use timed essays to determine whether you can critique the course material. Their assignments require you to analyze, evaluate, or synthesize class readings, lectures, demonstrations, or presentations. Still other teachers ask you to apply in new ways material you covered in class. You might be asked, for example, to explain how certain theories you studied could explain a hypothetical case or solve a problem you are seeing for the first time. Finally, some teachers use timed, in-class writing assignments to determine how well you can write essays without assistance. You can get help writing papers outside of class, but under controlled, timed conditions, you are on your own. In fact, teachers often require students to complete both out-of-class and in-class assignments for this very reason, to assess their ability to write both with and without assistance.

Writing a timed essay is stressful for any writer. However, understanding the purpose of the assignment and approaching the task in a systematic way can help you write with confidence.

A RANGE OF TIMED WRITING ASSIGNMENTS, PURPOSES, AND CONDITIONS

Among the most common timed writing assignments are essay test questions, comprehensive finals, and take-home examinations. The writing conditions for these assignments can vary. Sometimes teachers give you the actual assignment or a list of possible writing tasks prior to the test so you can plan your answer; other times, they do not. Sometimes you can consult your notes and source texts as you compose your answer; other times, you may not. Each type of timed writing assignment and each set of test conditions call for a different type of preparation and a different set of test-taking skills.

COMMON TIMED WRITING TASKS

When teachers assign *essay test questions*, they usually expect fully developed, clear, organized responses that directly answer the question being asked and reveal your understanding of the course material. Assignments may ask you to summarize readings or lectures, critique the course material, draw connections among the authors studied in class, explore the relationship between the course material and your own experience, apply course material to new situations, or argue for or against positions or theories presented in the course. Most teachers expect essay test answers to have a solid beginning, middle, and end; to be clearly written; and to make appropriate references to material studied in the course. Being able to write strong responses to essay test questions is an especially important skill for college writers. A number of studies of writing requirements across the curriculum reveal that answering essay test questions is the most common writing task for students regardless of their major.

Given at the end of a course, *comprehensive finals* ask you to work with information presented over the entire term. You typically have more time in class to write these responses than you do when writing essay test answers, so you must plan your essays more carefully. Teachers typically expect you to make multiple references to course material in a comprehensive final; to present fairly sophisticated critiques of the readings, lectures, or laboratory exercises; to synthesize information in new and interesting ways; and to develop your own positions on issues covered in class.

Unlike the other types of timed writing tasks, you can complete *take-home examinations* outside of class. Take-home examinations can consist of a series of essay test questions or a single, comprehensive writing task. Teachers will typically tell you how much time they expect you to spend writing your response and trust you to keep to those guidelines. Sometimes they will require you to type your answer; other times, they will want you to turn in handwritten responses, perhaps in examination booklets they distribute in class. Teachers who ask you to write take-home examinations typically expect your answers to be more comprehensive, more organized, and more formally correct than responses written in class. They typically do not, however, expect the prose to be as polished as it would be in a formal essay. Remember to discuss the grading criteria with your teacher if you have any questions. Because most timed writing assignments in college are not completed outside of class, the rest of this chapter focuses on in-class essays.

RHETORICAL AIMS

In-class, timed writing assignments usually have one of three rhetorical goals: exposition, argument, or personal expression. Understanding the rhetorical goal of the assignment—whether you are being asked to convey information, argue a point, or share your own responses to course material—is the most important aspect of composing a successful timed essay. If you write an expository essay when the teacher expects an argument, you will be missing the entire point of the assignment.

Expository assignments ask you to inform your reader about a topic. Some expository assignments ask you to recapitulate information covered in class ("What were the major judicial reforms instituted by Henry V?"). Others require you to compare and contrast various source texts ("What are the theories of childhood language acquisition offered by Piaget and Vygotsky?"). These assignments do not ask you to assert and defend a position of your own; instead, your grade is largely based on how clearly you convey information.

Argumentative assignments, in contrast, ask you to explain and support a position of your own on a topic ("How successful were the judicial reforms instituted by Henry V?" or "In presenting his theory of language acquisition, who is more convincing, Piaget or Vygotsky?"). Your thesis asserts a position that you then explain and defend in the body of your essay. When evaluating argumentative timed writing assignments, teachers tend to focus on the clarity and accuracy of your position, the quality of textual support you supply, and the sophistication of your reasoning skills. Writing successful timed arguments is difficult, requiring you to employ a wide range of reading, writing, and reasoning skills. As discussed later in this chapter, dividing this task into manageable subtasks and preparing yourself thoroughly before you begin to write can help you complete the assignment successfully.

Responsive timed assignments ask you to convey your subjective reactions to course material ("What do you think about the judicial reforms instituted by Henry V?" or "Based on your own experience, whose theories of language acquisition make more sense, Piaget's or Vygotsky's?"). Here the teacher wants to know your reaction to the information covered in class, what you liked or did not like, understood or did not understand, found useful or did not find useful. More important, the teacher also wants to know the basis of your response—you need to explain why you responded in a particular way. When evaluating these assignments, teachers typically look for clarity and comprehensiveness—whether they fully understand your response to the material and the basis for your reaction.

ACCESS TO SOURCE MATERIAL

In most cases, when writing your timed essay, you will not be able to consult the material you studied in class. Nevertheless, your teachers will expect you to refer to this material in your essay, citing specific and relevant authors, studies, findings, dates, or criticism. While they may not expect direct quotations of this material, they will certainly expect you to summarize and paraphrase information and data accurately and appropriately.

Sometimes teachers will assign open-note tests, allowing you to consult readings, class notes, or other source material as you compose your response. Having access to this course material can be both a blessing and a curse. Being able to consult the material means you have less to memorize; as you write, you can look up information you need. You are also in a better position to quote material in your answer since you can copy it directly from your readings or notes. However, since you have access to the material when you write, your teachers are likely to expect your answers to be more thorough and precise, criteria they will employ when evaluating your response. Open-note tests also require you to manage your time more carefully than do closed-note tests. Many students fail to finish their essays in the allotted time because they spend too much time flipping through their textbooks to find information they need or copying long quotations into their answers. You ought to prepare yourself equally well for both open- and closed-note tasks so that you spend most of your time responding to the question or questions being asked.

ACCESS TO POSSIBLE ASSIGNMENTS

College teachers differ in letting students know prior to the test day what the assignment will be. Some teachers distribute the assignment days or weeks in advance, answer any questions you have about the task, and even encourage students to discuss the assignment with each other outside of class. Other teachers may distribute several possible questions or assignments ahead of time but not tell you before the day scheduled for the timed writing which assignment they want you to complete. Still other teachers never let their students know prior to the test day what the assignment will be. When the students come to class, they see the question for the first time.

QUALITIES OF A GOOD TIMED ESSAY

Timed essays can assume many forms. Successful responses, however, have several features in common. They are appropriate, concise, supported, organized, and clear and correct.

- *Appropriate*—the response addresses the question being asked.
- *Concise*—the response is direct and to the point.
- *Supported*—the response correctly and effectively refers to course material to explain or defend statements or assertions.
- *Organized*—the response is built around an introduction, body, and conclusion united by a thesis statement, topic sentences, and transitions.
- *Clear and correct*—the response avoids sentence-level errors and word choice errors that inhibit understanding.

APPROPRIATE

The most common—and most costly—error students make when completing timed writing assignments is failing to answer the question being asked. They may write an interesting essay, but—given the assigned task—their response is inappropriate. Students write inappropriate responses when they misunderstand or disregard the wording of the assignment, develop an idea that does not relate clearly to the rest of their essay, panic and write anything to fill the page, or compose an essay that tries to achieve the wrong rhetorical aim—for example, composing an expository essay when the assignment calls for an argumentative response. Preparing yourself to write prior to the test day, carefully analyzing the wording of the assignment, and asking the right questions as you compose and revise your work can help ensure that your responses are appropriate.

CONCISE

Because you are writing under timed conditions, your prose has to be direct, focused, and precise. Your response should focus on the question being asked, so avoid the temptation to follow tangents that take you too far afield. In addition, make your sentences as precise and economical as possible. With timed writing, if you can say something in two words rather than three, say it in two; if you can adequately develop an idea in one paragraph rather than two, develop it in one. Remember, the time you take to work on one section of your response leaves less time to work on other sections.

SUPPORTED

Almost all of the timed essays you write in school will ask you to work with the material you covered in class. When appropriate, your response to the assignment should refer to this material—the more specific you can be, the better. Generally, in academic writing—even in timed essays—supported assertions carry more weight and are more convincing than unsupported assertions. In open-note tests, try to quote source material in your response. In closed-note tests, you are more likely to summarize and paraphrase information. Integrating course material into your answer will help you produce effective, convincing timed essays.

ORGANIZED

Timed essays require careful planning and organization. Like any formal writing assignment, a timed essay ought to have an effective opening paragraph, a clear thesis that guides and controls the body of the essay, topic sentences that direct the paragraphs, and transitions throughout that help unite the piece and lead readers through the essay. Perhaps more than any other type of assignment, timed writing tasks test your ability to plan responses quickly, apply the organizational skills you have learned in school, and solve problems as they arise.

CLEAR AND CORRECT

When evaluating timed writing assignments, most instructors are less strict about sentence-level errors than they might be with more formal assignments. They know correct punctuation, spelling, and grammar are important, but they understand that writing under time constraints may prevent students from adequately revising and proofreading their work. Not every instructor, however, is so forgiving. It is a good idea, therefore, to talk to your instructor about her evaluation criteria. Of course, your essay will not succeed if errors make it too difficult to read the piece. If nearly every sentence contains a mistake, if sentence boundaries are confused, if the language is incomprehensible, you are much less likely to get a passing grade. As discussed in more detail later in this chapter, part of learning how to write timed essays successfully is understanding, locating, and correcting the errors that most seriously affect a reader's ability to understand your essay and the errors that you, as a writer, most commonly make.

WRITING TIMED ASSIGNMENTS

Adopting a process approach to composing timed writing assignments will help you complete them more easily and successfully. As with any other assignment, your best approach to composing a timed essay is to divide the task into a series of manageable steps: carefully analyze the assignment, engage in some planning, draft a response, and then reread and revise what you have written until you feel you have produced your best work. The trick with timed assignments is to complete the process before time runs out. Below are several steps you should consider following as you prepare for and draft timed writing assignments. Modify these suggestions to suit your individual composing style.

PREPARE FOR THE ASSIGNMENT OUTSIDE OF CLASS

Success at timed writing assignments depends on preparation well before you sit down to write the first word of the essay. Because timed writing assignments test not only your writing skills but also your study skills, engaging in a series of steps prior to test day can help you write a strong essay.

First, be sure you *review the course material* before you sit down to write your essay. Besides reviewing the assigned readings and your class notes, discuss the material with your classmates. Together, try to identify the most important information, findings, or theories covered in class. Even if you will be able to consult your notes or readings as you write your essay, studying the material and discussing it with others before the test will still be helpful: you will form a better understanding of the information, you will likely gain insights from others, and you will commit more information to memory, saving yourself time later as you write your response.

Second, if your instructor does not distribute the assignment prior to the test, *try to anticipate what he might ask.* Trying to imagine what the teacher is likely to ask will help you sort through the course material, identifying what is truly important. Instead of distributing test questions or timed writing assignments prior to the test day, some teachers, especially in the natural sciences, place copies of old examinations or assignments on a web page or on reserve at the library or department office. If your teacher does this, be sure to consult these old assignments as you study. Again, working with others to anticipate assignments or test questions can be very productive. Anticipating test answers can be dangerous, however, if you convince yourself that you have psyched out the teacher and know what the assignment will be or if you decide what you want to write even if it is not what the teacher ends up assigning. In either case, you will likely compose an inappropriate response. If you accurately predict the assignment, then you are that much more prepared on the day you write your essay. If you do not accurately predict it, you need to plan your essay in response to the task at hand.

Finally, as you study for the test, *work out possible responses or answers.* If the teacher distributes the assignment before the test, give yourself plenty of time to plan your answer. If you have to guess what the assignment might be, you should still determine how you would answer each possible question. When planning these responses, work closely with the course's source texts. Decide which readings or parts of readings would help you write particular responses, and select the quotes or examples you think would be good to incorporate into your essay. Even if you do not end up using this material in your response, simply working through it prior to the assignment will help you master the material.

Working with others to develop possible answers or responses can be quite helpful. As a group, you can brainstorm possible responses and critique ideas. However, such collaboration should only supplement your individual efforts to prepare for the timed writing assignment. Even when you work with others, you should still develop your own response to the assignment. Students composing nearly identical in-class essays will likely be suspected of plagiarism. The purpose of group work prior to writing a timed essay is to gain a better understanding of the course material, to work out a range of possible responses, and to establish the relative strengths and weaknesses of those responses, not to develop a single, shared "group" response.

READ AND ANALYZE THE ASSIGNMENT OR TEST QUESTION

Carefully analyzing the language of the assignment is crucial when you are writing timed essays. As you read the assignment, you need to make a series of decisions concerning the instructor's intention. First, you may need to identify the actual assignment itself. Sometimes teachers will ask a series of questions to get you thinking about the topic before they ask the test question or state the assignment. In such a case, it is easy to confuse the actual assignment and the accompanying questions. Consider, for example, the following assignment used in a course on Native American history. Assume you are a student seeing it for the first time and have only fifty minutes to write your response:

> Consider the relationship between the Hopewell and Fort Ancient cultures. Are they truly distinct? Do they represent separate cultures, or is it more accurate to claim they represent different stages of development of only one culture? How might researchers answer this question?

What, exactly, is the test question in this example? Should your answer address similarities and differences between the Hopewell and Fort Ancient cultures, or should it focus on research methodologies more generally, using ancient Native American cultures as examples? Should it do both? Making the wrong decision would lead to an inappropriate response. If you have trouble understanding the assignment, be sure to ask your teacher for clarification.

Second, pay particular attention to the verbs the teacher uses in the assignment. The verbs often will tell you what to write and indicate how you might organize your response. Below are some verbs you are likely to find in timed writing assignments, along with an explanation of their common meanings:

Verb	*Writing Task*
analyze	divide something into parts
compare	show similarities
contrast	show differences
define	explain the meaning of something
discuss	examine multiple sides of an issue, being as comprehensive as possible
explain	clarify what others think is confusing
illustrate	give examples of something
prove	defend a position with evidence that others will find convincing
summarize	briefly recount the main points of something

PLAN YOUR ESSAY OR ANSWER

Once you have a clear idea of what the teacher is asking you to do in your response, you need to plan your answer. A common mistake students make when writing timed essays is beginning their responses before adequately planning their answers. Without adequate planning, responses are usually unfocused and underdeveloped. Taking time to plan your answer may be nerve-racking—you may feel pressured to begin composing your response immediately. However, the three to five minutes you spend planning your response will actually make it easier for you to write your essay and will likely result in a better paper.

At a minimum, before you begin to draft your response, you need to develop your thesis and outline your essay. In most cases, your thesis should be a one-sentence answer to the question being asked. You will develop and support this thesis in the body of your essay. Write out and revise your thesis on scrap paper or even on the assignment sheet itself until you are satisfied with its wording. Next, outline your response on the same sheet of paper. This outline does not need to be formal or elaborate. It can be simply a list of the main points you want to make, preferably in the order you plan to present them. Make sure the order of ideas presented in your outline matches the order in which the ideas are presented in your thesis. Finally, you might want to indicate on your outline where you can insert source material into your response— which authors you can cite, which examples you can use, which quotations you can employ. The time you spend at this stage of the writing process will help you draft an effective answer, for you will continually refer to this outline as you write your essay.

DRAFT YOUR ESSAY OR ANSWER

Once you have taken a few minutes to draft your thesis and plan your response, you will be able to compose your response section by section. First, *write an effective opening*, one that introduces the topic of your essay, states your thesis, and captures your reader's interest through a provocative question, an interesting observation, a significant quotation, or some other device that will help your essay stand out from others completed in class. This opening section should remain brief—only a paragraph or two.

Once you have completed your introduction, *compose your response paragraph by paragraph using your outline as a guide*. Try to begin each new section of your essay with a clearly stated topic sentence that both introduces the idea you will develop and refers back to the language of your thesis. As you compose each paragraph, look for opportunities to make references to the material covered in class—quoting or paraphrasing readings or lectures, supplying documentation when necessary.

The actual process of writing your response may lead you to form some new ideas about the assignment, ideas you want to include in your essay. When this happens, do not trust your insight to memory—you already have too much on your mind in a timed writing situation. Instead, go back to your outline and quickly jot down the new idea where you think you might want to include it in your essay. If you need to insert this material in a section of the essay you have already written, you can do so: write out the passage, bracket it, and then indicate with marginal arrows, lines, or notes where you would like it to go. Most teachers will honor your intention and read the paragraphs in the order you indicate.

Finally, *be sure to write a concluding paragraph.* Many students forget to include a conclusion when they write timed essays, letting their responses end with the last point they make. Writing a conclusion gives you the opportunity to reemphasize important assertions, to bring your essay to a logical end, and to echo the strategy you employed to capture your reader's interest in the opening paragraph, giving your essay symmetry and your reader a sense of closure.

REVISE YOUR ESSAY OR ANSWER

Just as you should set aside time to plan your response before you begin to write, you need to reserve time at the end of the process to revise your work before you turn it in. Since you will have only a limited amount of time to revise, you need to work toward a limited set of revision goals.

First, as you reread your work, *make sure your response is appropriate.* Review the assignment, then your response, checking to see that you have met all of the assignment's requirements. Cut material that is not relevant, and add any examples, explanations, or elaborations you think you need. Delete material by drawing a single line through it. Add material by placing a caret below the place where you want it to go and write the material in the space above the line. As you revise your work at this point, you want to be sure you have met the demands of the assignment and have been true to your own intentions as well.

Second, *check each paragraph for adequate development.* Do you need to add another illustrative example? Can you make another reference to a source text? Does a particular assertion need further elaboration? Now is the time to add any needed support.

Next, *check for any problems with organization.* As you revise, add any transition words or phrases that might make your essay easier to read. If you need to insert a paragraph break, now is the time to indicate with a paragraph marker (¶) where you would like it to go. If you need to eliminate a paragraph break, in the margin of your paper write "no paragraph." If you failed to include an introductory or concluding paragraph, now is the time to add one.

Finally, *check for clear word choice.* Have you used any terms that might confuse your reader? Is your language as precise and economical as it can be? Make any needed changes.

PROOFREAD YOUR ESSAY OR ANSWER

Because you have very little time to proofread your work in a timed writing situation, first *proofread for the types of errors that seriously interfere with a reader's ability to understand your essay,* especially errors involving sentence boundaries. For example, try to correct any problems with sentence fragments, run-on sentences, comma splices, and missing end punctuation. Second, keeping in mind your known weaknesses as a writer, *proofread for the errors you are most likely to make.* If you know you typically forget to include apostrophes in possessive case constructions, proofread for that. If you know you misspell certain words, check them in your essay. If you have problems with capitalization, correct any such errors you find. Use standard proofreading symbols to indicate any corrections you make.

FINAL THOUGHTS

Writing in-class essays tests not only your ability to think, plan, and write under pressure, but also your ability to manage time. Here are a few tips to help you write successfully against the clock. First, *prepare, prepare, prepare.* The more time you spend preparing yourself for a timed writing assignment, the easier it will be for you to complete the task once the clock is running. Second, *adopt a process approach to completing the assignment.* When you get the assignment, do not dive right into writing. Instead, carefully analyze the assignment and reserve time to plan, revise, and proofread your work. As a general guideline, if you have fifty minutes to write your essay, take five minutes to plan your response, forty minutes to draft and revise your answer, and five minutes to proofread the final draft. Finally, *watch the clock as you write.* Many students become so focused on completing the assignment that they forget to monitor how quickly time is passing. If possible, bring a watch to class on the day you write your essay. If that is not possible, ask the teacher to keep track of time for you on the blackboard.

Summary Chart

HOW TO WRITE TIMED ESSAYS

1. **Prepare for the assignment outside of class.**

   - *Decide how to order your ideas, arguments, or findings.*

   - *Review the course material.*

   - *Analyze the assignment or test questions if the teacher distributes them prior to the test day.*

   - *Anticipate possible assignments or test questions if the teacher does not distribute them early.*

   - *Imagine possible responses to the assignments or test questions.*

   - *Discuss possible or actual assignments, test questions, and responses with classmates.*

2. **Read and analyze the assignment or test question.**

   - *Identify the assignment or test question.*

   - *Analyze the verbs to determine the nature of your response.*

   - *Clarify the rhetorical goal of the assignment or test question.*

3. **Plan your essay or answer.**

   - *Develop your thesis.*

   - *Outline your response, formally or informally.*

   - *Note on your outline where you might effectively incorporate source material.*

4. **Draft your essay or answer.**

   - *Write an opening paragraph that, at a minimum, introduces the topic of your response, indicates your thesis, and captures your reader's interest.*

   - *Construct your response paragraph by paragraph, following the outline you already designed.*

   - *When new ideas come to you as you compose your response, note them appropriately on your outline and include them in your essay.*

   - *Be sure to write a concluding paragraph.*

5. **Revise your essay or answer.**

- *First, check to see that your response is appropriate, that it properly addresses the assignment or test question.*

- *Check each paragraph for adequate development.*

- *Check for problems with organization, especially the use of effective topic sentences and transitions.*

- *Check for clear word choice.*

6. **Proofread your essay or answer.**

- *Find and correct errors that might interfere with a reader's ability to understand your essay.*

- *Find and correct the types of errors you most commonly make when writing.*

- *Correct any spelling or grammatical errors you find.*

Appendix

REVISION CHECKLISTS

QUOTATION CHECKLIST

	Yes	No
1. Did you check your quoted passages against the original to make sure the wording is accurate?	_____	_____
2. Is the capitalization of words in the quotation proper and accurate?	_____	_____
3. Is the punctuation in the quotation proper and accurate?	_____	_____
4. Do you need to add italics, underline certain words, or use single quotation marks in the quotation?	_____	_____
5. Did you check the punctuation you employed to introduce the quotation?	_____	_____
6. Did you check the format of your block quotations?	_____	_____
7. If you added words to or deleted words from the source passage, did you confirm that you have not misrepresented the author?	_____	_____
8. Is the format of your documentation at the end of the quotation in the correct style?	_____	_____
9. Did you list the right page number or numbers in your documentation?	_____	_____

PARAPHRASE CHECKLIST

	Yes	No
1. Have you provided the full title of the source and identified its author?	_____	_____
2. Have you employed a variety of methods to paraphrase the material?	_____	_____
3. Have you checked to be sure your paraphrase accurately captures the author's ideas?	_____	_____
4. Have you remained as objective as possible in choosing language for your paraphrase?	_____	_____
5. Have you avoided offering your opinions on the topic of the reading or on the writer's style?	_____	_____
6. Have you checked your language to make sure each word you have chosen means what you think it means, has the connotation you want it to have, and fits the general tone of your paraphrase?	_____	_____
7. Have you reviewed your sentence structure for clarity and variety?	_____	_____
8. Have you provided appropriate transitions between the ideas you paraphrase?	_____	_____
9. Have you provided proper and accurate documentation?	_____	_____
10. Have you properly punctuated your documentation?	_____	_____

SUMMARY CHECKLIST

	Yes	No
1. In the opening section of your summary have you		
• introduced the topic of the essay?	_____	_____
• given the full title of the source text?	_____	_____
• given the full name of the author?	_____	_____
• included *your* thesis?	_____	_____
2. In the body of your essay do you summarize only one point at a time?	_____	_____
3. Have you accurately and fairly put into your own words all of the author's important findings, arguments, or ideas?	_____	_____
4. Have you identified the primary means of support the author provides for each finding, argument, or idea?	_____	_____
5. By cutting material or words, have you tried to make your summary as brief as possible while still being comprehensive?	_____	_____
6. To be neutral, have you avoided comments on the		
• topic of the piece?	_____	_____
• author's ideas?	_____	_____
• author's style?	_____	_____
7. To help ensure that your summary will make sense to someone who has not read the original work, have you		
• defined any unusual or technical terms?	_____	_____
• identified any people you refer to in your work?	_____	_____
• provided a sufficient context for understanding the author's assertions or findings?	_____	_____
8. Do you have adequate paragraph breaks and transitions?	_____	_____
9. Have you supplied proper documentation?	_____	_____

RESPONSE ESSAY CHECKLIST

	Yes	No

1. In the introductory section of your essay, have you
   - introduced the topic of the reading? _____ _____
   - included the full and exact title of the reading? _____ _____
   - included the full name of the author? _____ _____
2. Have you included a thesis statement that captures your overall response to the reading, a response you develop in the body of your essay? _____ _____
3. Have you considered the accuracy and honesty of the responses you include in your essay? _____ _____
4. Have you clearly stated each of these responses? _____ _____
5. Have you explained the terms you used to characterize each of your responses? _____ _____
6. Have you tied each of your responses to some aspect of the source that gave rise to it? _____ _____
7. Have you explained how the material in the source text gave rise to your response? _____ _____
8. Have you developed only one response at a time in each section of your essay? _____ _____
9. Have you used language that helps your reader understand when you are moving from your discussion of one response to the next? _____ _____
10. Have you explained the connection between each response you explore and your overall thesis? _____ _____
11. Have you reviewed the language you use to make sure your word choice is clear and accurate? _____ _____

CRITIQUE CHECKLIST

	Yes	No

1. Have you included the title of the reading and the author's name in your introduction? _____ _____
2. Does your thesis make clear your overall assessment of the reading? _____ _____
3. Toward the beginning of your critique, have you provided a brief summary of the reading? _____ _____
4. In the body of your critique, do you examine only one element of the reading at a time? _____ _____
5. Do you clearly state a judgment concerning each element of the reading you explore? _____ _____
6. Do you provide examples from the reading to support and illustrate your judgment of each element you examine? _____ _____
7. Do you clearly and thoroughly explain your judgments concerning each example you provide from the reading? _____ _____
8. Have you employed proper evaluative criteria and standards? _____ _____
9. Have you provided clear transitions between the major sections of your paper? _____ _____
10. Is there a clear relationship between each section of your paper and your thesis? _____ _____
11. Have you provided proper documentation for all quoted, paraphrased, and summarized material? _____ _____
12. Have you revised your paper for accuracy? In other words, does the final draft reflect your honest appraisal of the reading? _____ _____
13. Have you reviewed the language in your paper to make sure your words adequately capture and communicate your judgments? _____ _____
14. As you review your work, do your judgments still stand? Do you need to change your thesis or any part of your paper? _____ _____

SYNTHESIS CHECKLIST

	Yes	No

1. Have you checked your assignment to be sure you have written the proper kind of synthesis—informative or argumentative?   _____ _____
2. In your introduction do you
   - introduce the topic of the paper?   _____ _____
   - try to capture your readers' interest?   _____ _____
   - offer your thesis?   _____ _____
3. Check the wording of your thesis. Does it clearly indicate the type of synthesis you are writing and the stand you will assume?   _____ _____
4. Review the structure of your paper. Do you explore only one point or only one author's work at a time?   _____ _____
5. Look at your transitions. Have you provided adequate signals to guide your reader through your paper?   _____ _____
6. Check each section in the body of your paper. Do you
   - provide examples from one or more readings to support your contentions?   _____ _____
   - explain the relationship between the examples you offer and the assertion you are making?   _____ _____
   - explain the relationship between the examples you employ, the assertions you make, and your thesis?   _____ _____
7. The first time you refer to an author's work, do you give the full title of the piece and the author's full name?   _____ _____
8. Have you properly documented all quoted, summarized, and paraphrased material?   _____ _____
9. Have you reviewed your quotations for accuracy and variety?   _____ _____
10. Have you reviewed your word choice for clarity and accuracy?   _____ _____

PLAGIARISM CHECKLIST

	Yes	No
1. Are all of your quotations properly documented?	_____	_____
2. Does your thesis make clear your overall assessment of the reading?	_____	_____
3. Is all paraphrased material properly documented?	_____	_____
4. Have you acknowledged or documented the help you have received in writing your paper?	_____	_____
5. If this is a group project, have you checked the original assignment to be sure your work conforms to the teacher's guidelines?	_____	_____
6. Does the paper truly represent your own work and effort?	_____	_____

INDEX

CREDITS

Ansen, David. "Forrest Gump," *Newsweek,* June 11, 1994. From *Newsweek,* June 11, 1994. Copyright ©1994 Newsweek, Inc. All rights reserved. Reprinted by permission.

Beck, Joan. "Clear Message to Teens: 'It's OK to Have Sex,'" *Chicago Tribune,* September 10, 1989. Reprinted by permission of Tribune Media Services.

Clark, Margaret Pruitt. "Condom Availability Promotes Health, Saves Lives," *The School Administrator,* September 1992. Reprinted with permission from the September 1992 issue of *The School Administrator.*

Connerly, Ward. "Q: Does Diversity in Higher Education Justify Racial Preferences? No: Diversity of viewpoint, not racial set-asides based on stereotypes, should guide the admissions," *Insight,* May 14, 2001. Reprinted with permission of *Insight.* Copyright 2002 News World Communications, Inc. All rights reserved.

Delattre, Edwin J. "Apply Peer Pressure, Not Latex, against Casual Sex," *The School Administrator,* September 1992. Reprinted with permission from the September 1992 issue of *The School Administrator.*

Johnson, Brian D. "The Fool on the Hill," *Macleans,* July 11, 1994. Reprinted by permission of *Maclean's Magazine,* Maclean Hunter Publishing Limited, July 11, 1994.

Kenny, Shirley Strum. "Q: Does Diversity in Higher Education Justify Racial Preferences? Yes: We must open college education to students of all economic and racial backgrounds," *Insight,* May 14, 2001. Reprinted with permission of *Insight.* Copyright 2002 News World Communications, Inc. All rights reserved.